Victorian England

Other Books in the Turning Points Series:

Turning|Points

IN WORLD HISTORY

Victorian England

Clarice Swisher, *Book Editor*

David L. Bender, *Publisher*
Bruno Leone, *Executive Editor*
Bonnie Szumski, *Editorial Director*
David M. Haugen, *Managing Editor*

Greenhaven Press, Inc., San Diego, California

Library of Congress Cataloging-in-Publication Data

Victorian England / Clarice Swisher, book editor.
    p.   cm. — (Turning points in world history)
    Includes bibliographical references and index.
    ISBN 0-7377-0221-4 (lib. : alk. paper). —
ISBN 0-7377-0220-6 (pbk.)
    1. Great Britain—History—Victoria, 1837–1901. I. Swisher,
Clarice, 1933–   . II. Series: Turning points in world history
(Greenhaven Press)
DA550.V535 2000
941.081—dc21   99-12771
                                                                  CIP

Cover photo: Archive Photos/Popperfoto

©2000 by Greenhaven Press, Inc.
P.O. Box 289009, San Diego, CA 92198-9009

Printed in the U.S.A.

Contents

communicate with fellow prisoners and nurtured insects and mice in the absence of human interaction.

Chapter 4: Ideas That Changed Values, Views, and Events

Chapter 5: Social and Cultural Changes

over the purposes they should fulfill. By 1900 poor workers had been taught to read, and women could attend universities.

Foreword

Certain past events stand out as pivotal, as having effects and outcomes that change the course of history. These events are often referred to as turning points. Historian Louis L. Snyder provides this useful definition:

> A turning point in history is an event, happening, or stage which thrusts the course of historical development into a different direction. By definition a turning point is a great event, but it is even more—a great event with the explosive impact of altering the trend of man's life on the planet.

History's turning points have taken many forms. Some were single, brief, and shattering events with immediate and obvious impact. The invasion of Britain by William the Conqueror in 1066, for example, swiftly transformed that land's political and social institutions and paved the way for the rise of the modern English nation. By contrast, other single events were deemed of minor significance when they occurred, only later recognized as turning points. The assassination of a little-known European nobleman, Archduke Franz Ferdinand, on June 28, 1914, in the Bosnian town of Sarajevo was such an event; only after it touched off a chain reaction of political-military crises that escalated into the global conflict known as World War I did the murder's true significance become evident.

Other crucial turning points occurred not in terms of a few hours, days, months, or even years, but instead as evolutionary developments spanning decades or even centuries. One of the most pivotal turning points in human history, for instance—the development of agriculture, which replaced nomadic hunter-gatherer societies with more permanent settlements—occurred over the course of many generations. Still other great turning points were neither events nor developments, but rather revolutionary new inventions and innovations that significantly altered social customs and ideas, military tactics, home life, the spread of knowledge, and the human condition in general. The developments of writing, gunpowder, the printing press, antibiotics, the electric light, atomic energy, television, and the computer, the last two of which have recently ushered in the world-altering information age, represent only some of these innovative turning points.

Each anthology in the Greenhaven Turning Points in World History series presents a group of essays chosen for their accessibility. The anthology's structure also enhances this accessibility. First, an introductory essay provides a general overview of the principal events and figures involved, placing the topic in its historical context. The essays that follow explore various aspects in more detail, some targeting political trends and consequences, others social, literary, cultural, and/or technological ramifications, and still others pivotal leaders and other influential figures. To aid the reader in choosing the material of immediate interest or need, each essay is introduced by a concise summary of the contributing writer's main themes and insights.

In addition, each volume contains extensive research tools, including a collection of excerpts from primary source documents pertaining to the historical events and figures under discussion. In the anthology on the French Revolution, for example, readers can examine the works of Rousseau, Voltaire, and other writers and thinkers whose championing of human rights helped fuel the French people's growing desire for liberty; the French *Declaration of the Rights of Man and Citizen*, presented to King Louis XVI by the French National Assembly on October 2, 1789; and eyewitness accounts of the attack on the royal palace and the horrors of the Reign of Terror. To guide students interested in pursuing further research on the subject, each volume features an extensive bibliography, which for easy access has been divided into separate sections by topic. Finally, a comprehensive index allows readers to scan and locate content efficiently. Each of the anthologies in the Greenhaven Turning Points in World History series provides students with a complete, detailed, and enlightening examination of a crucial historical watershed.

Introduction: Victorian England

In the strictest sense, the Victorian period in England corresponds to the reign of Queen Victoria, beginning in June 1837 and ending with her death in January 1901. In the broadest sense, the Victorian period is associated with the growth of the British Empire and the Industrial Revolution. As historian Anthony Wood says, "Victorianism, in some ways, preceded Victoria,"[1] and its influence lasted long after. To the outside world in the early nineteenth century, England was a leader, rapidly and peacefully developing its resources and growing in wealth. To the people who lived in England, the predominant experience in their lives was change. The Victorian period was a jigsaw puzzle of change—economic, political, social, cultural, intellectual, and spiritual, but unlike a jigsaw puzzle, the pieces fitted together loosely, overlapping and interconnecting.

When Victoria came to the throne, England already had an empire, which included India, Canada, Australia, New Zealand, and South Africa. During her reign the empire expanded to cover one-fourth of the earth's land and include one-fourth of the world's population, and England became the dominant power in international shipping and communications. England added possessions like Hong Kong to acquire shipping ports, islands to provide coaling stations for naval and merchant ships, and territories to protect the safety of shipping routes such as the Suez. Colonies provided raw materials for British industry and markets for manufactured goods. England succeeded in the territories of the empire because it sent men and capital into them, creating deepwater ports, building railroads and bridges, and setting up a network of telegraph lines and underwater cables. Pride in the new empire climaxed with Queen Victoria's Diamond Jubilee in 1897 when Britons celebrated the nation's commercial strength and world position.

When Victoria came to the throne, the Industrial Revolution, like imperialism, was already underway. The invention of steam power had made it possible to run machinery in factories to manufacture goods on a large scale. Steam power also ran the trains that transported raw materials to factories and manufactured goods to local markets and seaports. The coal and iron mining industries grew, as did the number of factories and rail lines, because iron was needed to build engines and coal to run them. New inventions made it possible for the textile and iron industries to be the first industries to convert to the factory system. The factory, the heart of the Industrial Revolution, centralized production under one roof by making goods in large quantities with labor-saving machinery and regimented labor. The efficiency of the factory system lowered prices of goods and, in turn, made improved standards of living possible. By 1850 most British industries operated under the factory system, giving England the reputation as "the Workshop of the World."[2]

With the development of mining and manufacturing came changes in demographics. During the nineteenth century, the population of England more than tripled, growing from 11 to 37 million. Moreover, because factories drew workers from the country and immigrants from Ireland and Scotland to the cities, England became the first modern urbanized society. In 1801 a fifth of the people lived in cities; in 1851 almost half lived in cities; and by 1901 three-quarters of the people were urban dwellers. Cities that were transportation and factory centers grew the fastest. London grew from 4 percent of the population to 14 percent in a century; the Manchester population quadrupled in a half century; and Liverpool, Birmingham, Leeds, and Sheffield became large cities soon after Victoria became queen. Following the development of the commuter trains and the subway, or underground train which began in 1863, the suburbs grew rapidly.

The economic changes caused by industrialization and urbanization led to changes in the class system, breaking down the rigid class divisions and bringing greater freedom to move between classes. Before the Industrial Revolution, England had become an agrarian society controlled by the aristocracy, or gentry, the small population who owned the land. Tenant farmers rented tracts of land of about a hundred acres or more from the large landowners, and the majority of men, women, and children worked as agricultural laborers, farm servants, and shepherds. As the factory system grew and the agricultural economy declined, large numbers of workers flocked to the cities seeking better wages; those workers who remained in the country became the poorest class and were the last to gain political power as the century wore on. In the cities, a new middle class—factory owners, merchants, shopkeepers, and professionals—was gaining economic and social power, challenging the power and status of the aristocracy. City factory workers, however, were still almost as poor and powerless as their country counterparts. Bitter class tensions arose as groups struggled either to gain power and wealth or to hold on to them.

Tensions were particularly high in the early 1830s. Because of overproduction, factory owners had laid off workers who subsequently lacked the means to provide food for themselves and their families. In 1830 workers rioted in Hampshire, Wiltshire, and Berkshire, and middle-class radicals, discontent because the middle class had neither representation in Parliament nor the right to vote, joined the workers. In October 1831 England came close to violent revolution. Afraid of widespread disorder, the aristocratic leaders in Parliament introduced a bill to bring more equitable representation in Parliament. The First Reform Bill became law in June 1832. The number of members in the House of Commons remained the same, but some representation was given to the middle class, and 814,000 middle-class voters had been added to the electorate. In no way did the First Reform Bill of 1832 bring democracy to England, but, as Wood says, it "had opened a door, and through that door there was to come a whole mass of social and administrative reform, which was to bring in its wake the succeeding Parliamentary Reform Acts of the nineteenth century."[3]

Conditions in Factory and Mining Cities

Besides the problems of poverty and periodic unemployment, the working class endured difficult working conditions in the mines and factories, and no laws existed before the 1840s to protect them. Low wages meant that entire families worked to survive. Miners hewed ore in underground seams so small that they crawled on their knees or walked bent over. They worked twelve-hour shifts in near darkness—their lamps gave off less light than that of a candle—in seams filled with dust, bad air, and sometimes water and rats. Women and older children worked as putters, crawling on all fours dragging trucks of coal, and children from five to eight years old carried coal in baskets in the narrowest seams or worked as trappers, the first ones into the pits to open and close doors that controlled ventilation and the last to leave their posts, often fourteen hours later. Factory work was little better. In the textile factories workers sat at steam-powered looms performing the same monotonous job for twelve-hour shifts. Children as young as six cleaned up around the machines until they were old enough to perform the simple machine tasks. In pottery factories children from six to ten years old carried moulds from the potters to the stoves for twelve hours a day in rooms with temperatures up to 120 degrees. In match factories women and children suffered from phosphorous contamination, which deteriorated their jaws and teeth. Workers had barely enough time off to eat and lost that benefit if they were caught dozing on the job. Machines were dangerous, and tired workers had accidents causing injuries that went unattended.

Living conditions in factory and mining cities were as dismal as the working conditions. Owners provided housing on land around the factories and mines, buildings crowded together with an inadequate water supply and without any sewer system or lighting. Waste filled the streets, and large piles of refuse from mines and coal-burning furnaces built up around the homes; coal-burning machines belched smoke that covered everything with gray soot. In his novel *Hard Times*, Charles Dickens describes Coketown, an imaginary factory town that resembled its real-life counterparts:

> It was a town of red brick, or of brick that would have been red if the smoke and ashes had allowed it; but as matters stood it was a town of unnatural red and black like the

painted face of a savage. It was a town of machinery and tall chimneys, out of which interminable serpents of smoke trailed themselves forever and ever, and never got uncoiled. It had a black canal in it, and a river that ran purple with ill-smelling dye, and vast piles of buildings full of windows where there was a rattling and trembling all day long, and where the piston of the steam-engine worked monotonously up and down like the head of an elephant in a state of melancholy madness. It contained several large streets all very like one another, and many small streets still more like one another, inhabited by people equally like one another, who all went in and out at the same hours, with the same sound upon the same pavements, to do the same work, and to whom every day was the same as yesterday and tomorrow, and every year the counterpart of the last and the next.[4]

Not all factory owners, however, exploited their workers. In the 1850s in Yorkshire, for example, mill owner Sir Titus Salt moved his large mill to open country and laid out the town of Saltshire around it. He built houses each with a parlor, a kitchen, two or three bedrooms, and a backyard. He provided a school, a church, and a park on the riverbank. Other owners provided housing with some degree of convenience, but, according to historian W.J. Reader, most cared not "how to promote the health and comfort of the occupants, but how many cottages could be built upon the smallest space of ground and at the least possible cost."[5]

Conditions in Nonfactory Cities

Little difference existed for workers living in factory cities and those living in nonfactory cities such as London and Bath; they all endured poverty and similar squalid conditions. Workers in London, for example, tried to find jobs in service, such as chimney sweeping, in a trade working for a bricklayer, or as a day laborer on the docks. Journalist and sociologist Henry Mayhew investigated the working class in the 1840s and called them "all that large class who live by either selling, showing, or doing something through the country . . . street-folk—street-sellers, street-buyers, street-finders, street-performers, street-artisans or working pedlars and street-labourers."[6] Their common quality was poverty.

The working poor in London lived in old houses abandoned by middle-class families, houses now rented by the room. One room with one bed served as living quarters for an entire family. Historians Hilary and Mary Evans report that in a large room in one tenement "four families—eighteen persons in all—lived with one bed per family, with no partitions or privacy of any sort."[7] One makeshift privy was shared by many families, and for the homeless who slept in hallways or on streets, there were no toilets. Streets were never cleaned nor garbage collected. The sanitation problems were compounded by the lack of water, which had to be carried by hand from tanks or from a standing pipe. Reader reports, "A man living in Bath about 1840 could get no good water nearer than a quarter of a mile. 'It is as valuable as strong beer,' he said. 'We can't use it for cooking, or anything of that sort, but only for drinking and tea.'"[8] The family cooked their meager food in muddy and stinking river water. A Lancaster miner reported that he only washed his neck, face, and ears, never his body; he let his shirt rub the dirt off.

Bad Conditions Lead to Protests

Poverty, overcrowding, and a lack of clean water and sanitation caused poor health and diseases among the poor. Malnutrition caused stunted growth and rickets, a bone distortion usually found in children who lack calcium and vitamin D. Typhoid, an intestinal disease spread by infected water or milk; typhus, a blood disease carried by lice; tuberculosis, a lung disease; diphtheria, a respiratory disease; and other infectious diseases spread regularly among the poor and caused epidemics. Cholera, transmitted through water and food contaminated by feces, causes rapid dehydration and death. Four cholera epidemics in Britain—1831–1832, 1848–1849, 1853–1854, and 1866—killed a total of 140,000 people, primarily in the poor districts. Because doctors disagreed about the causes of diseases until the germ theory was discovered later in the century, progress toward tackling epidemics was slow. Results of an investigation into the causes of diseases were published in 1842 in Edwin Chadwick's *Report on the Sanitary Condition of the Labouring Population*, which became a best seller, and it horrified all right-thinking people. It was a factual document well illustrated and included a map of Leeds which unequivocally showed that the great cholera epidemic of 1831–3 had been largely confined to the poorest quarters. The report made it quite clear that good sanitation meant good health.[9]

A number of factors coalesced to prolong the plight of the working poor. The rising middle class did nothing to help them politically because a large population of powerless workers supplied a large pool of cheap labor for their factories and mines. People who held the moral view that God rewards virtue and punishes vice blamed the poor for their own misfortunes; they argued that if the poor practiced sobriety, worked hard, and were devoted to their masters' wishes, they would not be poor. Another hindrance was the prevalence of the laissez-faire philosophy, the belief that the state has no right to interfere between employer and worker or to tax one section of society to benefit another. Finally, Reader says, "the good Bible-reading Christian was inclined to take a rather fatalistic view of the whole affair. Had it not been said, on the highest authority, 'the poor ye have always with you'?"[10]

Tensions between classes rose again in the late 1830s when the workers began to organize and hold meetings protesting economic and social injustices. Workers were disappointed because the First Reform Bill of 1832, for which they had agitated, had not given them representation or the right to vote. Moreover, they were angry that the factory act passed by Parliament reduced work hours only for children, leaving intact long twelve-hour shifts for adults. Workers also bitterly resented the 1834 Poor Law, a law based on the belief that work is virtuous; the unemployed were sent to workhouses, where they were "given a chance" to work in exchange for wages that amounted to less than the wages of those who held jobs. In the eyes of the poor, this law brought humiliation and loss of freedom.

Working-class discontent led to a variety of protest movements in the late 1830s and 1840s that were collectively called Chartism, which was a political movement demanding reform to eliminate injustices. Chartists received their name because they formulated their demands for reform in a petition, which, they hoped, would become law. In 1838 participants drew up the People's Charter, making six demands: universal suffrage, secret voting, no property qualifications for MPs (members of Parliament), salary for MPs so that poor people could seek election, annual elections to Parliament, and equal electoral districts. The government passed acts fulfilling these demands, but then simply ignored them, and the Chartist movement died by 1848 from lack of organization and leadership. Slowly, however, within the next one hundred years, all of the Chartists' demands were passed and observed as law except annual elections to Parliament.

The Rising Middle Class

While the working class remained poor and powerless for much of the nineteenth century, the middle class had become wealthy and influential before the 1850s. Two factors especially propelled them to success: opportunity and attitude. Historian Elizabeth Burton explains that middle-class entrepreneurs took advantage of "new costly machinery, new factories and mills, booming trade and a labor force of underpaid men, women and children . . . [in] an age of production, of export, of enormous prosperity."[11] Shopkeepers, merchants, and bankers thrived from the prosperity of manufacturing. In addition, many opportunities arose in the professions: Engineers built railways and designed machinery for factories, lawyers offered professional advice to businessmen, and accountants managed finances for growing enterprises. This growing society needed doctors and chemists and teachers. When schools did not exist to educate middle-class children, they started them, focusing on practical knowledge that led directly to employment and, in turn, increased their wealth and status.

Members of the middle class worked with urgency and determination because they believed that, with discipline and competition, they could acquire the things formerly available only to those born into the upper class: wealth, property, and social position. In his book *Self Help*, political and social reformer Samuel Smiles expresses the central tenets of the middle class: "Individual effort, backed by austerity of life, would propel any man, no matter what his origins, to success in this world."[12] And many did succeed; the industrial world was run by the middle class, which gradually developed subclasses of differing levels of wealth. Burton explains:

> Many employers when they made money, moved away from the sources of their fortunes, bought country estates, which gave them the privileges only land could confer, and hoped to become landed gentry. Sometimes they succeeded. Their managers ringed the industrial towns with handsome new villas and created new and prosperous suburbs. Skilled workmen lived in or at the edge of the town in new houses built in new streets.[13]

At the peak of middle class prominence around 1850, the newly rich were proud materialists and relished every opportunity to display their success. They built houses with decorative external designs; inside, they filled the rooms with heavy, carved furniture, covered the walls with elaborately designed paper, and placed decorative objects and knick-knacks in all available spaces. Rich gentlemen wore suits and high-top hats. Women wore hats and were corseted into long dresses covering them from chin to toe, full-skirted dresses displaying ruffles, bows, and embroidered braid. They promenaded on the fashionable streets; they took carriage rides in Hyde Park, where they could be seen and admired. Attending picnics, sporting events, and drawing-room dinners offered opportunities to display finery. The middle class had become social trendsetters.

Middle-Class Morality and Respectability

Middle-class influence extended beyond materialism and also set standards for morality and respectability. Victorian middle classes were shocked at drunkenness, and many worked actively in temperance organizations, urging others to sign pledges of abstinence. Radical teetotalers envisioned a temperance reformation reshaping society; but, as historian David M. Fahey explains, when they "demanded unfermented wine in the eucharist, traditionalists denounced

them as troublemakers."[14] As an expression of the importance of the family, Victorian middle classes espoused strict
standards regarding sexual morality. Sexual experiences, especially for women, were confined to marriage, and sexual
pleasure was considered a sin; a sexual scandal, even a rumor
of one, could destroy a woman's reputation. Volunteer
women's organizations fought against prostitution, which
was a supplement to the income of many working-class girls.

The middle class identified proper roles for men and
women to fit their materialistic and moral values. Because
work was now done outside of the home more extensively
than it had been in the past, men worked and women cared
for children and home. A husband was supposed to be
strong, active, and intellectual, and a wife was supposed to be
fragile, passive, and emotional, obviously so in ways that best
showed her husband's prowess as a wise and knowledgeable
protector. The proper middle-class woman lounged idly because that image indicated that she had married a husband
who could afford the servants to free her from work; middle-
class women in their newfound wealth, however, lacked skills
to manage the servants their husbands could afford to hire.
Those were the ideals which, no doubt, varied considerably
in actual day-to-day life of middle-class Victorians.

Criticism and the Climate of Reform

Not everyone in the middle class subscribed to the same
goals or held the same values. The majority of writers and
intellectuals attacked the politics and practices of middle-
class industry and business. Essayist Thomas Carlyle, for example, was shocked at materialism, money worship, and the
appalling conditions of the working class. Philanthropist and
religious writer Francis Cobbe wrote about the stress of
rushing that he associated with the demands of earning
money, "that constant sense of being driven—not precisely
like 'dumb' cattle, but cattle who must read, write, and talk
more in twenty-four hours than twenty-four hours will permit."[15] Essayist John Ruskin hated the ugliness of industry
and thought utilitarianism and the industrial society depleted the human soul. Novelist William Makepeace Thack-

eray "took upon himself to expose the shallowness, cruelty, hypocrisy, and greed of the socially privileged."[16] Novelist Charles Dickens attacked some social evil in almost every one of his books by painting vivid pictures of what life was like for ordinary working people. In a coincidental way, the critical voices of writers overlapped with the reform actions taken by Parliament. Whether the writers' exposé of society's wrongs directly affected politicians is debatable, but politicians did pass reforms correcting many of the conditions that writers had attacked.

Through most of Victoria's reign, Parliament was controlled by the aristocracy, but the members of Parliament who won elections and served as prime ministers were liberal minded and wanted reform. At the beginning of the nineteenth century, the Whig Party called for moderate reforms, as historian Angus Hawkins explains, in order to "preserve the respect, gratitude and loyalty of the lower social ranks for the propertied and the aristocracy."[17] A change in attitude—from the notion that the lower "ranks" existed for the upper classes to the notion that middle and working classes exist with their own rights—was apparent as Victoria came to the throne; politician Robert Peel issued a manifesto that unified Parliament and initiated reforms. Peel proclaimed "his support for moderate reforms 'undertaken in a friendly temper, combining, with the firm maintenance of established rights, the correction of proven abuses and the redress of real grievances.'"[18] While there was certainly an element of good will and a sense of justice among MPs, they also acted because they wanted to maintain order and avoid violence and revolution.

Economic, Social, and Political Reforms

During Victoria's reign some of the parliamentary reforms improved the standard of living for the working and middle classes. Permanent repeal of the Corn Laws in 1849 benefited both classes (in England the word *corn* means all grains, such as wheat and barley). The Corn Laws were tariffs placed on imported grain in 1815 to keep cheap grain products out of the country for the benefit of British landowners, who could then charge high prices for the grain they grew. In the 1830s the unemployed workers could not afford bread made from grain priced artificially high. As tariffs were removed, bread prices decreased, benefiting the workers. Repeal of the Corn Laws brought with it the reduction of tariffs on other goods used by middle-class factory owners, a savings in the cost of manufacturing, and thus an increase in profits.

Other reforms improved working and living conditions for the poor in cities. A series of factory acts improved safety, reduced hours, and provided benefits for mine and factory workers. The Public Health Act of 1848 required a sewer system and available clean water in working-class neighborhoods. Public baths and washhouses made cleanliness easier, and housing schemes alleviated overcrowding and filth. Historian Paul H. Friesen says that reform happened slowly and was often met with resistance, as MP Lord Shaftesbury discovered:

> Shaftesbury's social interests extended beyond those of most Victorian reformers. He brought before the government—and a startled public—the pitiful condition of women and children in the mines (1840), the plight of the chimney sweeps (1840), the terrible conditions of urban boarding houses (1851), and the urgent need for urban sanitation reform (1846–1851), to name but a few. In each case he worked enthusiastically to change the conditions, often against considerable initial opposition.[19]

Trade unions had been working since the 1830s for better conditions, but their proposals for reform had also met with opposition. Trade unions formed around workmen in various industries, such as engineers or shoemakers, to negotiate wages, improve working conditions, fund sickness benefits and strike pay, and to press for reforms. Because middle-class factory owners wanted to prevent workers from gaining power, they devised methods to restrict meetings and threatened the jobs of leaders and participants. Finally in 1871 the Trade Union Act granted legal status to unions, giving workers the right to organize, meet, and press for reforms.

By midcentury the aristocracy willingly collaborated with

the working classes because the wealthy and influential middle class was threatening the power of the upper classes. Consequently, Parliament passed numerous reforms after 1850. The Reform Bill of 1867 added more than a million voters, enfranchising artisans and workers who lived in the city but not agricultural workers. Following the passage of this bill, other measures cleaned up the electoral system and instituted the secret ballot, important for assuring that workers would not be intimidated into voting in the way an authority dictated. The Reform Bill of 1884 enfranchised all male voters throughout the United Kingdom, finally including agricultural workers, and added an additional 2.5 million voters. Yet 40 percent of males were not registered to vote, women were entirely excluded, representative districts lacked uniformity, and corruption still existed. Historian Bruce L. Kinzer says, "Nevertheless, the reforms of the nineteenth century had set Britain firmly and irrevocably on the path toward electoral democracy."[20] And equally important, Great Britain had the most stable government in Europe.

Educational Reforms

Much needed education reform lagged far behind social and political reform. In Shakespeare's day England had a national elementary and grammar school system with a rigorous curriculum taught by qualified teachers; during the first half of Victoria's reign, public elementary and grammar schools hardly existed, and a boy could become an adult without having received any formal education. Industry required a literate work force trained in arithmetic. Likewise, humanitarians believed that education should be a birthright. Politicians, meanwhile, squabbled over government control, curriculum, teaching methods, and the place of religion in school. In the absence of public schools, elementary education was available in most villages only in schools run by charities or by religious groups, and secondary education was available in proprietary schools, which were boarding schools run for profit and notorious for poor food and flogging. The upper classes hired tutors for young children and sent older boys to high-cost academies like Eton and Rugby, which prepared them for the university. By 1860, when the middle class pressured Parliament for secondary education, a commission recommended a three-tier system to prepare students for the university, business and industry, or skilled work.

In 1870 Parliament finally passed the Elementary Education Act, sponsored by W.E. Forster, establishing national elementary schools available to all children in England and Wales, and by 1880 attendance was compulsory to the age of ten. Historian David Hopkinson reports on the growing urgency for education: "There was by 1890 a widespread conviction that a democratic political system in a modern industrial and trading society must by backed by a much better-educated people."[21] Within a decade Parliament created the Board of Education with a president who was the national minister for all education up to the university. In 1899 school was made compulsory to age twelve, and three years later secondary school was universally accessible.

The changing society also required reforms in postsecondary education, but the changes came late. Traditionally, higher education meant Cambridge and Oxford, universities that were available to upper-class boys belonging to the Church of England and educated in preparatory schools. During the Victorian period the universities first opened up to boys from other religions and then to women, but new institutions were needed. The University of London was the first to be established, emphasizing an education in science and modern languages. Between 1870 and 1890 at least six colleges opened for women, and Cambridge and Oxford University men taught extension classes in London emphasizing science and engineering. For those interested in a career in medicine, new teaching hospitals were opened with extensive course work followed by an apprenticeship. For the sons of middle-class industrialists, mechanics institutes provided education in the scientific principles involved in manufacturing, and in 1883 the Finsbury Technical Institute opened to train laborers in technological studies. Historian Alan Rauch says that by the Paris Exhibition of 1867, it was apparent that British industry was lagging behind industry on the continent. By 1902 "the lack of a systematic education program and the misunderstanding of technical education's role had resulted in a serious decline in British industry and technology."[22]

The Role of Theoretical Science

The numerous additions of science and science-related curricula to British education underscore the importance of science in Victorian England. While science education in general may have been tardy, important scientific activity in both theory and application nonetheless took place from the beginning of Victoria's reign. The word *science*, as we think of it today with its scientific method and experimentation, acquired its present meaning during the Victorian period; previously those who studied nature were called "natural philosophers." Much of the debate during the period centered on the value of pure, or theoretical, science studied in universities as opposed to the study of its practical application. Historian Richard R. Yeo explains:

> Accordingly, boundaries were drawn between technology, with its artisan and commercial connotations, and the concept of "pure" science as a pursuit fitted, like Latin and Greek, to train the minds of gentlemen. Scientists of different generations, such as astronomer John Herschel and the physicist James Clerk Maxwell, agreed that science was a facet of human speculation, which should not be curtailed by pragmatic criteria.[23]

Discoveries by Victorian scientists in theoretical physics, chemistry, geology, and biology became the underpinnings of extensive research by later scientists and of many technological advancements.

Publications by two scientists, Charles Lyell and Charles Darwin, instigated greater controversy than any other scientific study during the Victorian period. In 1830 Charles Lyell published *Principles of Geology*; in it he reported that layers of rock formations spanned long periods of time and showed that the earth was likely formed around 1 billion years ago. For Christians who believed in the notion of a static universe created by God on October 23, 4004 B.C., this discovery meant confusion and loss. Many believers accommodated this new information by reasoning that God, after all, might have created the universe in long stages rather than all at once. Charles Darwin's publication of *Origin of Species* in 1859 dealt an even harsher blow to the traditional religious order. Darwin's evidence found that species changed by a process of natural selection, that only the strongest individuals survive to form new species, and those unequal to the struggle die out—a theory that is still being investigated at the end of the twentieth century. Nonetheless, the mass of evidence compiled by Darwin presented a persuasive case that all forms of life had in one way or another evolved from a single primordial form and had continued to evolve by natural selection. The editors of *British Literature* imagine the effect this information had on Victorian believers:

> One can vaguely imagine the explosion which this theory set off. In one terrible blow it seemed to destroy the traditional conceptions of man, of nature, and of the origin of religion and morality; and to substitute for each an interpretation that was deeply distressing. Man was reduced to an animal, the descendant of apes. Nature, which had been the witness of a divine and beneficent God and a source of moral elevation, became a battlefield in which individuals and species alike fought for their lives, and the victor was the best, not morally but physically, the toughest and the roughest.[24]

The public response to these reports, widely publicized and discussed in the newspapers and periodicals, varied. The working classes, lacking enough education to grasp the significance, easily shrugged off the news but enjoyed the cartoonists who satirized Darwin. The middle class diverted their attention with their hard work. It was the Christian clergy and the intellectuals who struggled trying to reconcile the scientists' findings with their traditional Christian beliefs.

The Roles of Medical and Applied Science

Besides important discoveries in theoretical science, Victorians made significant breakthroughs in medical science. At the beginning of the Victorian period, doctors could do little but keep a patient comfortable and let nature cure. During the middle years, 1840 to 1860, three advancements in medical science occurred. First, the bacterial theory of disease was confirmed; that is, bacteria cause disease, and cleanliness to prevent or remove bacteria promotes better health. As a result of this theory, doctors began using antiseptics in surgery, for example, to prevent infections. Second, anesthetics were developed to alleviate pain. Because Queen Victoria was given anesthetics during the birth of her last two children, the procedure became popular, but she also drew criticism from those who believed that anesthetics were dangerous and unnatural. Third, during the Victorian period medicine became a science based on experimentation, and the use of animals for research began with the availability of anesthetics. Implementation of these advancements met with resistance from those dedicated to the traditional belief in the miasma theory of disease. According to this theory, bad odors cause disease in people who are susceptible because they are morally or physically weak. Ironically, followers of this theory improved health in the slums by cleaning up the stinking filth, but they increased cholera when they dumped the filth into the river that supplied drinking water, unaware of or disbelieving the germ theory. By 1870 traditional practices of harsh drugs and bloodletting and the miasma theory began to break down, but it took until 1890 before the new science of medicine was secure.

A third phase of science was essential to industrial development; invention and technology lay at the heart of the factory system. The Victorian ethic of self-help was, as historian R.A. Buchanan says,

> a stimulus to hard work and persistence in trying out new ideas, because success in such ventures guaranteed both wealth and social approval. The great inventors like James Watt became household models of successful self-help, so that young people in Victorian Britain were brought up in an environment that provided a positive spur to invention.[25]

Successful invention rests on both theoretical science and on technology. In the first half of the nineteenth century the educational system was inadequate to bring the two branches together, but as inventions became more complex, scientists and technologists saw the necessity of reconciling the two. For example, knowledge of the physics of thermodynamics is necessary for building high-pressure steam engines; knowledge of chemistry is needed for the invention of artificial dyes, synthetic textiles, plastics, and high explosives. Besides invention of products, scientists developed new processes to produce cheaper products. For example, the application of the new electrical science led to the telephone and the radio and to the electrolytic process, making it cheaper to extract aluminum from ore.

Even when British industry began to decline, the Victorians' enthusiasm for their age did not dampen. Scientists and engineers continued to produce new inventions. Electricity, the internal combustion engine, and steel were the basic elements of the new technological age. These gave Victorians lighted streets, the motor car, and the underground electric train. Victorians got their first telephones and could send messages by wireless communication across the channel to the continent. Chemists invented new soaps and new drugs. Engineers changed the nature of work in offices when they designed typewriters and adding machines. Faster ships and refrigeration brought fresh produce and new foods from around the world. As Anthony Wood sums up, "The list is endless, and one invention following upon another only confirmed the average Victorian in his belief that all was for the best in this unprecedented age of progress."[26]

Reevaluating Victorianism

As successful and proud as Victorians were, they did not escape harsh criticism either at home or abroad. In reevaluating the period, historian Richard Altick points out that if Victorians had been the fools that some critics have accused them of being, so grossly incompetent in personal and public matters, their society would have collapsed into chaos. If, on the other hand, their leaders had been as wise as some of their contemporaries thought them to be, "they would not have left the twentieth century quite so daunting a heritage of unsolved problems."[27] Altick laments the problems fostered by Victorian materialism, conformity, sexual inhibitions, hypocrisy, excessive pragmatism, and bad taste. Historians have been overwhelmed by the sheer volume of records left by Victorian reformers, writers, artists, inventors, businessmen, and soldiers, making responsible and intelligent assessment of the Victorian jigsaw puzzle difficult. Lytton Strachey, a biographer of the time, commented wryly that the history of the Victorian age shall never be written because too much is known about it.

Notes

1. Anthony Wood, *Nineteenth Century Britain, 1815–1914*. New York: David McKay, 1960, p. 96.

2. Sally Mitchell, ed., *Victorian Britain: An Encyclopedia*. New York: Garland, 1998, p. 280.

3. Wood, pp. 87–88.

4. Charles Dickens, *Hard Times*. 1854. Reprint, New York: New American Library, 1961, pp. 30–31.

5. W.J. Reader, *Victorian England*. New York: G.P. Putnam's Sons, 1973, p. 105.

6. Quoted in Reader, p. 99.

7. Hilary and Mary Evans, *The Victorians: At Home at at Work*. New York: Arco, 1973, p. 31.

8. Reader, p. 107.

9. Elizabeth Burton, *The Pageant of Early Victorian England, 1837–1861*. New York: Charles Scribner's Sons, 1972, pp. 203–204.

10. Reader, p. 98.

11. Burton, p. 10.

12. Quoted in Reader, p. 146.

13. Burton, p. 11

14. Quoted in Mitchell, p. 789.

15. Quoted in Hazelton Spencer et al., *British Literature: 1800 to the Present*, vol. 2, 3rd ed. Lexington, MA: D.C. Heath, 1974, p. 407.

16. Bernard D. Grebanier et al., *English Literature and Its Backgrounds*, vol. 2, *From the Forerunners of Romanticism to the Present*, rev. ed. New York: Dryden, 1949, p. 444.

17. Quoted in Mitchell, p. 856.

18. Mitchell, p. 586.

19. Quoted in Mitchell, p. 713.

20. Quoted in Mitchell, p. 255.

21. Quoted in Mitchell, p. 247.

22. Quoted in Mitchell, p. 248.

23. Quoted in Mitchell, p. 695–96.

24. Spencer, p. 419.

25. Quoted in Mitchell, p. 785.

26. Wood, p. 334.

27. Richard D. Altick, *Victorian People and Ideas*. New York: W.W. Norton, 1973, p. 309.

Chapter 1

Queen Victoria and the Victorian Period

The Reign of Queen Victoria

Asa Briggs

Asa Briggs describes the influence Queen Victoria and her husband, Prince Albert, had on the era identified by the queen's name. Crowned at eighteen, from the start she insisted on moral and dignified behavior. Her husband, though less popular, promoted intellectual endeavors and causes that helped common people. Asa Briggs, a lecturer at the University of Oxford and the University of Leeds in England, was a member of the Institute for Advanced Study in Princeton, New Jersey. He is the author of *History of Birmingham, Victorian People,* and *Friends of the People.*

When Victoria came to the throne in 1837 at the age of 18 the monarchy was at a low ebb. There was little republican sentiment and much talk of 'altar, throne and cottage', but William IV's early popularity had withered away. Victoria's initial advantages were threefold—her youth, her sex, and her already clearly formed sense of duty. When George IV and William IV[1] ascended the throne they had a past behind them; Victoria, whose succession to the throne had been far from certain, had only a future. Her sex, which might in different circumstances have been a handicap, enabled her to make a special appeal not only to the public but to her prime minister, Melbourne.[2] He was fascinated by the 'girl-Queen' and she by him, and the first phase of their 'partnership' between 1837 and 1839 was stimulating and happy for both of them. Moreover, from the start the Queen displayed great strength of character and responsibility. She wrote in her journal on the day of her accession that she would do her utmost to fulfil her

1. Kings of Great Britain and Ireland; George IV 1820–1830; William IV 1830–1837 2. Lord Melbourne, a British politician, served as prime minister 1834 and 1835–1841.

Excerpted from Asa Briggs, *The Age of Improvement* (London: Longmans, 1959). Reprinted by permission of Pearson Education Limited. (Footnotes in the original have been omitted in this reprint.)

duty to her country, and despite her youth and lack of experience she immediately took it for granted that others would obey her. Her first triumph of character was over the experienced and worldly-wise Melbourne, whose occupations and habits she revolutionized. 'I have no doubt he is passionately fond of her as he might be of his daughter if he had one', Greville[3] wrote, 'and the more because he is a man with capacity for loving without having anything in the world to love. It has become his province to educate, to instruct, and to form the most interesting mind and character in the world.' He watched his language—usually 'interlarded with damns'—sat bolt upright rather than lounged in his chair, and greatly restricted the range of his anecdotes.

The Young Queen Sets Her Tone

Victoria's childish resolves 'to be good' were in harmony with a new spirit in society, and Melbourne was responding to pressures which even at the time were applied not only by the Queen but by 'respectable' opinion. He enjoyed the one form of pressure but hated the second. 'All the young people are growing mad about religion', he once lamented. As it was, he could scarcely protest when the etiquette of the Court was tightened up and the Queen revealed herself as a stern and self-determined moralist, on one occasion at least exposing herself to great unpopularity by wrongly 'suspecting the worst' of a member of her Court. Admission to the Court was made to depend on good character, and 'rakishness' which Melbourne thought 'refreshing' the Queen considered at best 'melancholy' and at worst 'bad'. Manners as well as morals changed. The relatively easy informality of 'drawing room' and 'levées', during which the King might talk frankly or even rudely to people he knew, gave way to far more restrained and dignified ceremonial. Victoria's own sense of dignity was prominently displayed in 1839 when after Melbourne's defeat in the House of Commons she quarrelled with Peel[4] about the party affiliations of the

3. Charles Cavendish Fulke Greville, author of *The Greville Memoirs*   4. Sir Robert Peel, a British politician, served as prime minister 1834–1835 and 1841–1846

Ladies of the Bedchamber and prevented him from forming a new government. 'The Queen maintains *all* her ladies', she wrote to Melbourne (her dignity had been the surface defence of her warm affection for her old prime minister) 'and thinks her Prime Minister will cut a sorry figure indeed if he resigns on this'. Melbourne was back in office again for two more years and Peel, condemned simply because he did not share Melbourne's delightful qualities, was left with the cares of 'responsible opposition'.

Victoria, the Hope of England

The British newspaper the Observer *printed this tribute to Queen Victoria on July 7, 1838, a year after her coronation.*

[Queen Victoria] is indeed the Hope of England, and up to the present moment all that she has done and all that she has said appear to justify that hope, and to promise its most happy realisation. One of our contemporaries has designated her 'an institution', and accounts for the enthusiasm with which she was received by that designation. . . .

Her sex awoke the gallantry—her manners, her disposition as manifested in her behaviour, have won the affection—of her subjects. They confide in her, because in every thing she has done up to the present they have seen a noble feeling; a regard for liberty—a sympathy with everything humane, marking her out as one by nature and education fit to be trusted with a nation's destinies; and they love her because they confide in her.

The little incident which occurred in the Abbey of her sympathetically springing from her seat on the Throne to assist an aged nobleman who had stumbled and fallen in approaching to perform the ceremony of the homage, will endear her to all. It showed that even in the midst of regal state and formality she was keenly alive to the kindly feelings of our nature. She does not because she is a Queen forget that she is a woman.

Marion Miliband, ed., *The Observer of the Nineteenth Century: 1791–1901.* London: Longmans, Green, 1966.

The Queen Marries Prince Albert

The position was altered, however, as a result of the Queen's marriage in February 1840, and after the influence of her husband had established itself—almost at once—Melbourne was inevitably pushed more and more into the background. It had long been the ambition of King Leopold of the Belgians, the Queen's uncle and one of her earliest *confidants*, to marry his niece to her cousin, Prince Albert of Saxe Coburg Gotha, and there had been much gossip about the match from 1837 onwards. Fortunately for Victoria, the marriage which had been planned was also a marriage of love. Albert, in her own words, 'completely won my heart', and the wedding, celebrated quietly in St. James's Palace, with no signs of enthusiasm in the country, began the happiest period of her life. Her husband was still six months under the age of 21 in 1840 and he was a far from popular figure with the aristocracy, the crowds, or the House of Commons—by a majority of 104 votes the annuity of £50,000 the government proposed to pay him was reduced to £30,000—but he was just as resolved as Victoria to take the task of government seriously and willing in so doing to sink 'his own *individual existence* in that of his wife'. Stiff and conservative, his first efforts were devoted to reinforcing the Queen's own desire to set an example of strict propriety at Court.

The difference between old ways and new was well brought out in an early clash of ideas with Melbourne about the nature of social morality. 'Character', Melbourne maintained, 'can be attended to when people are of no consequence, but it will not do when people are of high rank'. Albert cared far less about rank than industry and integrity, and besides being willing to work long hours with a Germanic thoroughness that Smiles could not have excelled, he displayed all those 'Victorian' virtues of character which Melbourne regarded as unnecessary in a man of his station. His 'seriousness' of purpose is witnessed by the causes to which he gave his full support. His first public speech was at a meeting on behalf of the abolition of slavery; he was a vigorous advocate of scientific research and education, of official patronage of art, and of reformed universities; he took an active interest in the work of the Society for Improving the Condition of the Labouring Classes, founded in 1844, and when criticized by Lord John Russell[5] for attending one of its meetings replied firmly that he conceived 'one has a *Duty* to perform towards the great mass of the working classes (and particularly at this moment) which will not allow one's yielding to the fear for some possible inconvenience'; he helped to design and plan the building of a block of houses known as Prince Albert's 'model houses for families'; and last, but perhaps most important of all, he played such an important part in organizing the Great Exhibition of 1851[6] that if it had not been for his efforts, it is doubtful whether the Exhibition would have been held. In all these efforts Albert met with resistance and opposition, much of it centred in the country houses and the universities, places where old prejudices were strong and suspicions difficult to break down.

Albert had perforce to follow the dictates of self-help as much as Stephenson or Paxton,[7] and on many doors which were open to them he had to knock loudly. Two years after the Queen had written in 1853 that the nation appreciated him and fully acknowledged what he had done 'daily and hourly for the country', he was being lampooned in the popular press and attacked in the clubs more than ever before. If there was any truth in the Queen's claim that he eventually succeeded in raising monarchy to 'the *highest* pinnacle of respect' and rendering it 'popular beyond what it *ever* was in this country', it was entirely as a result of his own exertions and courage. He had no deficiency of spirit. When times were blackest for him on the eve of the Crimean War, he could still write that he looked upon his troubles as 'a fiery ordeal that will serve to purge away impurities'.

Friendship with Peel was as important to Albert as friendship with Melbourne had been to Victoria, and it helped in

5. British politician, served as prime minister 1846–1852 and 1865–1866   6. international exhibition of industry, science, and commerce held at Hyde Park, London, in the Crystal Palace; the exhibit was viewed by 6 million people   7. George Stephenson invented the railway and opened lines in 1825 and 1830; Joseph Paxton designed the Crystal Palace in Hyde Park that housed the Great Exhibition of 1851.

itself to set the tone of mid-Victorian England. Between 1841 and 1846 the Queen and her husband came to put their full trust in their great prime minister and the causes for which he stood—sound administration, strong government, and free trade. As early as 1843 the Queen wrote to the King of the Belgians praising Peel as 'a great statesman, a man who thinks but little of party and never of himself'; after Peel's death she wrote that Albert felt the loss *'dreadfully'*. He feels 'he has lost a second father'.

The Prince Consort's Unpopularity

There was something in common, indeed, between Peel and Albert, not only in their dislike of the noisy clamour of party but in their desire for practical improvement and their resentment of unthinking aristocracies. During the Crimean War Albert complained of the 'hostility or bitterness towards me' not only of the radicals but 'of the old High Tory or Protectionist Party on account of my friendship with the late Sir Robert Peel and of my success with the Exhibition', and the bitterness certainly went deep. If in the case of Peel the main taunt was one of betrayal of the landed interest, in the case of Albert it was one of never having belonged to it, of being un-English, of working by slow deliberation, not by instinct, of paying attention to the wrong things in the wrong way. In such a context of criticism even Albert's virtues could appear as vices. He was ridiculed in *Punch* for trying to act twenty different character parts; he was criticized in army messes for his zealous interference; he was attacked in Cambridge University for trying to do too much as Chancellor, not too little. He had won a hotly contested election for the Chancellorship in 1847, and it is easy to guess the reaction of Cambridge dons to his earnest desire to look at 'schemes of tuition' and examination papers on subjects in which he was particularly interested. His collection of information on every conceivable issue of public policy, his investigation of statistics, his preparation of memoranda, and his considerable European correspondence were all activities calculated to alienate aristocratic holders of power. So too was his stern insistence on the morality of the Court.

There was an interesting incident in 1852 when the new prime minister, Lord Derby,[8] submitted his list of names for household appointments and Albert noted with horror that 'the greater part were the Dandies and Roués of London and the Turf'. The Prince cared little for aristocratic company or aristocratic pursuits—in 1861, the year of his death, for instance, he described Ascot[9] as rendered 'much more tedious than usual by incessant rain'—and he did not attempt to hide his preference for the company of authors, scientists, social reformers, and pioneers of education. 'Culture superseded blood, and South Kensington became the hub of the universe'. The result was that the Court stood aloof from the rest of the London world, and had 'but slender relations with the more amusing part of it'.

The Queen's Popularity

Victoria did not share all Albert's enthusiasms or even understand them. She cared little for the company of scientists, showed no interest in royal patronage of art, and in only few of her letters referred to literature. She delighted, however, in the Exhibition of 1851 and thrilled to the bravery of British troops in the Crimea.[10] On thirty occasions she visited the Crystal Palace, noting in her *Journal* that she never remembered anything before that everyone was so pleased with as the Exhibition; during the war she wrote that 'the conduct of our *dear noble* Troops is *beyond praise*', said that she felt as if 'they were *my own children*', and objected to those critics of the military system who detracted from British victories by 'croaking'. Just because she genuinely shared such English sentiments and was not tempted, as Albert was, to seek for forms of intellectual expression, she was far more popular than he. She was not, of course, in any sense a democratic monarch responding to mass pressures or gaining publicity through the influence of mass communications, but she won loyalty and respect from the majority of the population, including the middle classes, many of whose qualities

8. Edward George Stanley Derby, prime minister of Great Britain and Ireland 1852, 1858–1859 and 1866–1868   9. the Royal Ascot horse races, held annually on Ascot Heath   10. Crimean war, 1854–1856

and limitations she shared. Perhaps the most vivid impression of her impact on English society can be gained from a perusal of newspaper reports of her visits to the provinces in the 1850s. In 1858 she visited both Birmingham and Leeds. Everywhere there were great crowds 'who behaved as well in the streets as could any assemblage of the aristocracy at a Queen's drawing room'. The local newspapers, while praising the interest of the Prince Consort in science and industry, reserved their loudest praise for a queen who 'is as it were partner with the great and multitudinous people who do gladly obey her, joins with them in legislation, shares with them in government, and makes them to a great extent their own rulers'. They extolled her combination of 'feminine grace and royal dignity' and her lofty eminence above all party faction, but above all they argued that 'what consummates the whole is, that she is a wife and a mother of so lofty a purity and discharging her duties so well that she forms the brightest exemplar to the matrons of England'. . . .

Not the least of the achievements of Victoria and Albert was to provide for the country a pattern of obviously happy domestic life which contrasted sharply with the pattern provided by all the Queen's recent predecessors. At her marriage ceremony the 'royal family' was a collection of aged and for the most part discredited minor personalities, better known for their defects than for their merits. By 1861, there were nine royal children, the eldest of whom, the Princess Royal, had already produced a grandchild for the Queen, the future Emperor William II of Germany. On more than one state occasion in the '40s and '50s the royal children accompanied the Queen. In 1849, for instance, on the occasion of her first visit to Ireland (she went there again in 1853 and 1861) she took her four children with her. They were objects of universal attention and admiration. 'Oh, Queen, dear', screamed a stout old lady, 'make one of them Prince Patrick, and all Ireland will die for you.'

Victoria Mourns and Withdraws

The death of the Prince Consort from typhoid fever in 1861 was a tragic blow to the Queen from which she never fully recovered. 'The loss of her husband', wrote Lady Lewis to her brother, Lord Clarendon, 'has changed her from a powerful sovereign (which she was with the knowledge and judgement of her husband to guide her opinions and strengthen her will) into a weak and desolate woman with the weight of duties she has not the moral and physical power to support'. Conventional condolences meant nothing to her, and only those who could find the right words to demonstrate their understanding of the extent of her loss were likely to touch any chord in her heart. Strangely enough, it was Palmerston,[11] with whom both she and the Prince had had so many differences and had fought such hectic battles, who found the correct phrase and wrote to her of the Prince as 'that perfect Being'.

Victoria Resists Pressure to Be More Public

From 1861 to the end of the [nineteenth century] the Queen was in the deepest retirement, resolved irrevocably that Albert's 'wishes—his plans—about everything are to be my law'. Although she found some consolation in the affairs of her family and its network of associations with other European courts, and although she spent many peaceful days at Balmoral, her favourite home, she wore mourning, shrank from large crowds, and feared formal social gatherings. She hated the thought of appearing in public as a 'poor, broken-hearted widow' and declared that she 'would as soon clasp the hand of the poorest widow in the land if she had truly loved her husband and felt for me, as I would a Queen, or any other in high position'. It was natural, though hard for her to bear, that the public could not appreciate the reason for her social abdication. In 1865 *Punch* printed a famous cartoon in which Paulina (Britannia) unveiled the covered statue and addressed Hermione (Victoria) with the words 'Tis time! descend; be stone no more!' Two years later the Queen was still lost in an unfinished winter's tale and Bagehot[12] could dismiss her and the Prince of Wales in the ters-

11. Henry John Temple Palmerston, British politician, served as prime minister 1855–1858 and 1859–1865.   12. Walter Bagehot, a political theorist and editor of the *Economist*

est of phrases as 'a retired widow and an unemployed youth'.

In time the Queen's age and experience were to produce new waves of loyalty and admiration, but the comment of Bagehot is the epitaph on the mid-Victorian period. What would have happened had the Prince Consort lived is a speculative puzzle which has fascinated many specialists in historical 'ifs'.

An Age of Transition

Walter E. Houghton

Walter E. Houghton characterizes the Victorian period as an age of transition, especially significant because philosophers, writers, and ordinary citizens alike were aware that it was a time of great change. Houghton identifies longstanding medieval beliefs and practices that were eroding and new industries and political philosophies that were emerging. Walter E. Houghton taught English at Wellesley College in Massachusetts. He is the author of *The Art of Newman's* Apologia.

In 1858 a Victorian critic, [Sir Henry Holland in the *Edinburgh Review*] searching for an epithet to describe "the remarkable period in which our own lot is cast," did not call it the age of democracy or industry or science, nor of earnestness or optimism. The one distinguishing fact about the time was "that we are living in *an age of transition*." This is the basic and almost universal conception of the period. And it is peculiarly Victorian. For although all ages are ages of transition, never before had men thought of their own time as an era of change *from* the past *to* the future. Indeed, in England that idea and the Victorian period began together. When [philosopher and author] John Stuart Mill in 1831 found transition to be the leading characteristic of the time—"mankind have outgrown old institutions and old doctrines, and have not yet acquired new ones"—he noted that this had been recognized by the more discerning only "a few years ago," and that now "it forces itself upon the most inobservant."

To Mill and the Victorians the past which they had outgrown was not the Romantic period and not even the eighteenth century. It was the Middle Ages. They recognized, of

Excerpted from Walter E. Houghton, *The Victorian Frame of Mind, 1830–1870.* Copyright ©1957, Yale University Press. Reprinted by permission of Yale University Press. (Footnotes in the original have been omitted in this reprint.)

course, that there were differences between themselves and their immediate predecessors, but from their perspective it was the medieval tradition from which they had irrevocably broken—Christian orthodoxy under the rule of the church and civil government under the rule of king and nobility; the social structure of fixed classes, each with its recognized rights and duties; and the economic organization of village agriculture and town guilds. That was "the old European system of dominant ideas and facts" which [poet and critic Matthew] Arnold saw dissolving in the nineteenth century. But the process had begun much earlier, starting with the Renaissance and the Reformation, gaining momentum, quietly but steadily, through the next two centuries of philosophic rationalism and expanding business, until it finally broke into the open when the French Revolution of 1789 proclaimed the democratic Rights of Man and the atheistical worship of the Goddess of Reason. That was the first overt manifestation, in Mill's opinion, that Europe was in a state of transition. But it was not realized at the time, not in England. There it was not until the rising agitation for a reform bill (finally successful in 1832), the passage of Catholic Emancipation, the attack on the Church by Whig Liberals and Benthamite[1] agnostics, together with the outbreak of the 1830 revolutions abroad, that men suddenly realized they were living in an age of radical change. Then they began to say that "old opinions, feelings—ancestral customs and institutions are crumbling away, and both the spiritual and temporal worlds are darkened by the shadow of change."

For "old" and "ancestral" we may read "medieval" or "feudal." When Arnold observed that many people thought it possible to keep a good deal of "the past," his next sentence defined the term: the extremists, indeed, hoped "to retain or restore the whole system of the Middle Ages." "Until quite recently," wrote Baldwin Brown in his important lectures of 1869–70, *The Revolution of the Last Quarter of a Century*, ". . . our modes of thought and speech, our habits of ac-

---

1. based on the political theories of Jeremy Bentham, whose thesis was "It is the greatest happiness of the greatest number that is the measure of right and wrong."

tion, our forms of procedure in things social and political, were still feudal." To Carlyle and Ruskin and Thomas Arnold, the period is one of decaying or dying feudalism. This was not an abstract idea. Victorians like Thackeray[2] who had grown up in the 1820's felt they had lived in two distinct worlds:

> It was only yesterday; but what a gulf between now and then! *Then* was the old world. Stage-coaches, more or less swift, riding-horses, pack-horses, highway-men, knights in armour, Norman invaders, Roman legions, Druids, Ancient Britons painted blue, and so forth—all these belong to the old period. I will concede a halt in the midst of it, and allow that gunpowder and printing tended to modernise the world. But your railroad starts the new era, and we of a certain age belong to the new time and the old one. We are of the time of chivalry as well as the Black Prince of Sir Walter Manny. We are of the age of steam.

From a mere glance at the title page of Carlyle's *Past and Present*, any Victorian might have guessed that the book was a comparison of the Middle Ages with the nineteenth century.

Transition Is Both Destruction and Reconstruction

By definition an age of transition in which change is revolutionary has a dual aspect: destruction and reconstruction. As the old order of doctrines and institutions is being attacked or modified or discarded, at one point and then another, a new order is being proposed or inaugurated. Both tendencies were apparent by 1830. After his description of the breakup of timeworn landmarks, [novelist] Bulwer Lytton continued: "The age then is one of *destruction!* . . . Miserable would be our lot were it not also an age of preparation for reconstructing." Twenty years later at the center of the Victorian period, what new construction had emerged? Or rather—for this is the important question for getting at the temper of the age—what did men think distinguished their

---

2. essayists Thomas Carlyle and John Ruskin, educator Thomas Arnold, and novelist William Thackeray

time most significantly from the past? What did they think was peculiarly Victorian about "the state of society and of the human mind?"

By the late nineteenth century it was clear that the feudal and agrarian order of the past had been replaced by a democratic and industrial society. The emergence of democracy meant not only the transference of political power from the aristocracy to the people, mainly by the successive Reform Bills of 1832, 1867, and 1884, but also the arrival of what is often called a democratic society. The latter, indeed, was so striking that Mill once called the distinguishing feature of modern institutions and of modern life itself the fact "that human beings are no longer born to their place in life . . . but are free to employ their faculties, and such favourable chances as offer, to achieve the lot which may appear to them most desirable." This breakdown of the old conception of status owed something to democratic ideas about the rights of man, but its primary cause was economic. The development of commerce, drawing men off from the land and opening new and independent careers to talent, had been the main instrument in dissolving the feudal nexus of society. In politics, too, the Industrial Revolution underlay the democratic revolution. What Thomas Arnold had in mind when he remarked, on seeing the first train pass through the Rugby countryside, that "feudality is gone for ever," is made explicit by a passage in [Thomas Carlyle's] *Sartor Resartus*, written on the eve of the Reform Bill of 1832: "Cannot the dullest hear Steam-Engines clanking around him? Has he not seen the Scottish Brassmith's[3] IDEA (and this but a mechanical one) travelling on fire-wings round the Cape, and across two Oceans; and stronger than any other Enchanter's Familiar, on all hands unweariedly fetching and carrying: at home, not only weaving Cloth; but rapidly enough overturning the whole old system of Society; and, for Feudalism and Preservation of the Game, preparing us, by indirect but sure methods, Industrialism and the Government of the Wisest?"

3. the Scottish Brassmith is James Watt, inventor of the modern steam engine

The Impact of the Industrial Revolution

Whether wisest or not, the bankers and manufacturers who rose to political power through the revolutionary legislation of 1828–1835—the repeal of the Test and Corporation Acts, the Municipal Reform Act, and above all, the Reform Bill— owed their victory to the financial and psychological power they acquired from the Industrial Revolution. Both factors are seen in Disraeli's[4] analysis of the capitalist mind in *Coningsby*. Mr. Millbank is discussing the English peerage:[5] "I have yet to learn they are richer than we are, better informed, wiser, or more distinguished for public or private virtue. Is it not monstrous, then, that a small number of men, several of whom take the titles of Duke and Earl from towns in this very neighbourhood, towns which they never saw, which never heard of them, which they did not form, or build, or establish,—I say, is it not monstrous that individuals so circumstanced should be invested with the highest of conceivable privileges, the privilege of making laws?" Those are the social forces, wealth and outraged pride, which demanded the Reform Bill. And once the middle class attained political as well as financial eminence, their social influence became decisive. The Victorian frame of mind is largely composed of their characteristic modes of thought and feeling.

But far more striking at the time than democracy was the tremendous industrial development that came with the use of new machines for manufacturing and communication. The great inventions date from the later eighteenth century; and in the early decades of the nineteenth the introduction of more canals, macadam roads, railways, and steamboats hastened the growth of large-scale production by making possible a vast expansion of commerce. This development revolutionized the economic life of England. The old system of fixed regulations, which paralleled that in fixed social relations, was abandoned for the new principle of laissez-faire,[6] on which the manufacturer bought his materials in the

4. Benjamin Disraeli was a politician, a political novelist, and prime minister 1868 and 1874–1880.   5. men of the upper class, of the aristocracy who have titles; members of the House of Lords   6. an economic doctrine that opposes governmental regulation of or interference in commerce

cheapest market and sold them in the highest, and hired his labor wherever he liked, for as long as he pleased, at the lowest wages he could pay. In [poet and essayist Robert] Southey's *Colloquies on the Progress and Prospects of Society* (1829) and [essayist and historian Thomas] Macaulay's fighting review of it (1830), the world of big business and unlimited competition was debated by the old conservatism and the new liberalism.

The Pressure of Work

To live in this dynamic, free-wheeling society was to feel the enormous pressure of work, far beyond anything known before. When new and more distant sources of supply and demand were constantly being opened up by the railroad and the steamship, the battle for new markets became intense. To neglect them could mean ruin. So could failure to take advantage of the latest invention or adapt one's business methods to the most recent developments. Disraeli's Coningsby is startled to learn from Mr. Head, who is building a new mill at Staleybridge, that Manchester is already gone by. "If you want to see life," he says, "go to Staley-bridge or Bolton. There's high-pressure." Only the Manchester Bank has kept up with the times: "That's a noble institution, full of commercial enterprise; understands the age, sir; high-pressure to the backbone." The masters had to work almost as long hours as their hands—the Messrs. Carson, for example, who did not become acquainted with their agreeable daughters until their mill was burned down: "There were happy family evenings now that the men of business had time for domestic enjoyments." The same pressure was felt in the professions. "The eminent lawyer, the physician in full practice, the minister, and the politician who aspires to be a minister—even the literary workman, or the eager man of science—are one and all condemned to an amount and continued severity of exertion of which our grandfathers knew little." That was due as much to the social system as to business conditions. When class lines broke down and it became possible as never before to rise in the world by one's own strenuous efforts, the struggle for success was comple-

mented by the struggle for rank. Even apart from personal
ambitions, the very existence of hundreds of objects, once
unknown or within the reach of few, now made widely available and therefore desirable, increased the size of one's ex-
penses and the load of his work.[7] Moreover, the growing
wealth of the wealthy advanced the style of living in the middle and upper classes to a point where the Victorian had to
struggle for things his father had been able to ignore. [Nov-
elist] George Eliot remarked that £3,000 a year had seemed
wealth to provincial families in 1830, "innocent of future
gold-fields, and of that gorgeous plutocracy which has so
nobly exalted the necessities of genteel life."

The Pressure of Speed

Not only the tempo of work but the tempo of living had increased with striking impact, so much so that one observer
thought that "the most salient characteristic of life in this
latter portion of the 19th century is its SPEED." Until the
Victorian period the rate of locomotion and communication
had remained almost what it had been for centuries. The
horse and the sailing vessel were still the fastest things on
earth. But within a few years the speed of travel by land increased from twelve to fifty miles an hour on the new railroads (over 400 per cent) and the new steamships were doing
fifteen knots "with wonderful regularity, in spite of wind and
tide." But it was less the mechanical speed of the new inventions than the speed of living they produced which impressed the Victorians. Faster locomotion, of goods and letters and people, simply increased the number of things one
crowded into a day, and the rush from one to another. Once
upon a time [said philosopher Frederic Harrison] "people
did not run about the town or the land as we do." They trav-
eled less often, did not hurry to catch trains, wrote one letter a morning instead of ten. Now "we are whirled about,
and hooted around, and rung up as if we were all parcels,
booking clerks, or office boys." It seems far more modern

7. Mark Pattison [wrote in the] *Fortnightly Review*: "To live at all is a struggle; to keep
within reach of the material advantages which it is the boast of our century to have
provided is a competition in which only the strong can succeed—the many fail."

than Victorian. But if the speed of life has increased in the twentieth century, the sense of speed has declined, for what has become commonplace today was then a startling novelty. Our great-grandfathers may have had more leisure than we do but it seemed less. Even more than ourselves they felt they were living "without leisure and without pause—a life of *haste*—above all a life of excitement, such as haste inevitably involves—a life filled so full . . . that we have no time to reflect where we have been and whither we intend to go . . . still less what is the value, and the purpose, and *the price* of what we have seen, and done, and visited," [according to essayist W.R. Greg].

This sense of faster and more crowded living had its intellectual as well as its mechanical basis. The spread of education coupled with the enormous expansion of knowledge and the corresponding increase of publication, books and periodicals and newspapers, gave "every man . . . a hundred means of rational occupation and amusement which were closed to his grandfather," and led George Eliot, in a threnody[8] on the death of leisure ("gone where the spinning-wheels are gone, and the pack-horses, and the slow wagons, and the pedlers, who brought bargains to the door on sunny afternoons") to say that "even idleness is eager now,—eager for amusement; prone to excursion-trains, art-museums, periodical literature, and exciting novels; prone even to scientific theorizing, and cursory peeps through microscopes." By the sixties [writer and philanthropist] Frances Cobbe was comparing her own generation with that of 1800–30 in words which sound exactly like someone today comparing the generation of 1950 with that of 1850: "That constant sense of being driven—not precisely like 'dumb' cattle, but cattle who must read, write, and talk more in twenty-four hours than twenty-four hours will permit, can never have been known to them."

8. a poem or song of mourning or lamentation

The Rise of a Strong Middle Class

Hilary Evans and Mary Evans

Hilary and Mary Evans describe change in the social classes during the Victorian period: The formerly privileged aristocracy lost power, the middle class gained power, and the working class remained powerless and poor. Regardless of class, all Victorians approached life with confidence and an enthusiasm for new experiences and new ideas. Hilary Evans has been a writer, social historian, and librarian. He is the author of *Land of Lost Control* and *Beyond the Gaslight: Science in Popular Fiction*. Mary Evans has been a lecturer in sociology and women's studies at the University of Kent in Canterbury. She is the author of *Lucien Goldmann: An Introduction*, *Jane Austen and the State*, and *Battle for Britain*.

In the early Victorian period the aristocracy and the rich were largely the same people. They were often unimaginably rich. When we hear of an aristocrat like the first Earl of Durham saying he considered £40,000 per annum 'a moderate income—such a one as a man might jog along with'— and when we translate that sum into a real buying-power of at least £200,000 (and virtually tax-free into the bargain), we are liable to be indignant if not positively disgusted. But the majority of Victorians were still ready to acquiesce in such inequality. The aristocrat himself inherited without question the values of his forefathers along with their estates, genuinely believing that he was in some way superior to the great majority of his fellow-countrymen; and only a small minority of those fellow-countrymen questioned this belief.

Even if he felt conscience-bound to justify his own existence (in the sight of God, that is—to the opinion of his fellow-countrymen he was generally indifferent) by some service to the community, he nevertheless expected the community to repay his services by continuing to maintain him in a quite disproportionate degree of comfort.

Such a man would ride out from his elegant country seat or town house on a weekday morning, without troubling his mind that at the same moment thousands of his ill-fed ill-housed ill-dressed ill-educated fellow-creatures were sweating in mine and mill, and would do so for sixteen hours a day, six days a week, earning him the money to maintain his stables and the rest of his establishment. For every Shaftesbury[1] who forced his Factory Act on an unwilling Parliament, or Coke[2] who devoted his energies to revolutionising farming, there were thousands who contributed infinitely less to the community than they took out of it, and whose lives were geared to an artificial annual cycle of full-time leisure where the seasons were the shooting season, the hunting season and—to placate his wife and daughters—the London season (at a time of year when there was nothing to hunt or shoot in any case).

[Essayist Matthew] Arnold called them 'Barbarians' because, for all their fine breeding and gentlemanly tastes, they had learned nothing about their proper role in the community, were aware of their privileges but not of their responsibilities. And ultimately it was this failure to collaborate in the national effort which destroyed them. At the beginning of Victoria's reign they ruled the nation: at the end of it, their power was hardly more significant than that of the monarch herself. . . .

Achievements of the Middle Classes

The middle classes were the great success story of the Victorian age. At their worst they were small-minded, dull, hyp-

---

1. Anthony Ashley Cooper Shaftesbury fought for reforms for factory workers and miners and for better housing for the poor.   2. Thomas Coke of Norfolk, one of the "improving landlords," transformed his estate and made farming profitable for all classes.

ocritical, smug, tasteless, insular, bigoted, blinkered from all considerations except that of business; everything, in fact, that we most dislike about the period. But at their best, it was they who made the age what it was. They may not have been numerically the majority, but it was their strength which gave the Victorian community its backbone. It was they who demanded the right to elect the nation's leaders— and they who told the leaders what to do. They created the conventions of the age—and followed them. They forged its values—and lived by them.

They caused the railways and the bridges, the tarred roads and the canals to be constructed. They discovered natural selection and the geological foundations of prehistory. They traced the source of the Nile and unearthed the stones of Nineveh. They built the factories and the stores, the town halls and the art galleries. And because they were the heirs of [Lord Protector Oliver] Cromwell's puritan common- wealth, they inherited a puritan conscience which spurred them to legislate for better working and living conditions for all the community—and even for strangers outside it— against their own immediate personal interests. (It was cal- culated, for example, that the abolition of slavery cost British businessmen £20,000,000—equivalent to at least five times that sum today.) They found a nation where the only safe- guards of life and liberty were the personal inclinations of autocratic lords and despotic factory-owners; they left a na- tion where those safeguards were written into the law of the land. In real terms, they achieved more than Magna Carta.

They did not manage to do everything. The British social structure when Victoria died was still an ill-balanced, un- wieldy, convention-ridden edifice, hardly more than a pro- totype for the truly just society. But despite the changes and stresses which assailed it, it survived and functioned tolera- bly well—better, in any case, than that of most other nations. And so it became the exemplar not only for our own society today, but also for others throughout the world.

All this the Victorian middle classes achieved, but not without loss. Their victories were won only by neglecting many of the civilised elements in life. It is not without reason that we think of them as bigoted, hypocritical, blinkered; not for nothing that the French sneered at them as sacrificing everything to business and living by the motto 'Time is money'; not without cause that Matthew Arnold, middle class himself, labelled them 'Philistines'.

The Problems of the Working Class

Today we can speak of 'the working class' with some degree of meaningfulness—there is a body of people, possessing a measure of cohesion, about whom the term can usefully be employed. In Victorian times this was hardly so. The populace was an amorphous mass, unaware of its identity, which had to be told by others that it existed at all.

If the rise of the middle class was the great success story of the age, its great failure was its inability to prevent the formation of a working class which considered that its interests were directly opposed to those of the other classes. The change in the social order which wrested the power from the aristocracy should have bound the other strata of society together in a common purpose; but this did not happen, and the age as a whole endorsed what was merely a new version of the old feudal baron/serf relationship, but with a new resentment built into it because the superior status of the middle-class employer was so very evidently *not* of divine origin. The very fact that the label 'working' was reserved for the lower class of workers is symptomatic of the tragic misunderstanding—the cleavage between 'them' and 'us' which was to grow wider as the age wore on, wider still in the age which followed.

Nevertheless, uneasy partnership as it was, it accomplished much. The British workman made real the vision of the middle-class entrepreneur. He sliced his canals and railway cuttings through the British landscape. He spanned the rivers with bridges and pierced the hills with tunnels. He drove the locomotives and sailed the ships, he delivered Rowland Hill's[3] Penny Post and patrolled the streets in Peel's[4] blue uniform,

3. Rowland Hill invented the penny post and postage stamps.   4. Sir Robert Peel established the metropolitan police in 1829.

he farmed the land and marketed its produce, he served his superiors in home and office, and above all he and his wife and children operated the machines which in factory and mill up and down the country created the wealth which was the foundation of his country's greatness.

In return his country treated him appallingly. If he worked the land, he lived in a rural slum: if he worked in mill or mine, he lived in an urban slum. When Engels[5] studied life in the factory towns of England in 1844, he concluded that this race 'must really have reached the lowest stage of humanity'. Who, reading the ghastly facts, could disagree?

That the working class survived at all was due not to its own efforts, but to those of a minority of its 'betters', assisted by the reluctant consciences of the rest. At the beginning of Victoria's reign it was believed that enlightened self-interest could be relied on to maintain the just equilibrium of society, but the stresses inflicted on the social structure by the industrial revolution proved such theories inadequate. Reluctantly, Britain had to realise that man-made laws, not the spontaneous operations of divinely constituted Nature, could alone ensure that everyone in society got his deserts. And so, Act by creaking Act, the working man was provided with some degree of protection against the growing pains of a society striving towards adulthood. . . .

Common Values of the Victorians

Such a diversity of creatures might seem to defy generalisation. And yet there were values which they shared in common, which gave them a unity deeper than all their differences.

Confidence—in themselves, in their country, in their way of life—was a quality shared by Victorians of all walks of life. They believed in themselves, they were willing to gamble on their own efforts. There were many more self-employed than today, far fewer who worked for others. And though this individualism was frequently inefficient, and eventually

5. German scholar Friedrich Engels collaborated with Karl Marx on *The Communist Manifesto* in 1848.

failed to withstand the tougher economic pressures of the 20th century, it stimulated qualities in the individual which were generally admirable if not always attractive.

We can see this exemplified in the popular attitude to the Queen. Towards the close of her reign she was loved and lauded, but during the earlier decades she was lampooned and ridiculed far more virulently than our sovereigns today—first because she was widely thought of as German, a feeling not helped by her marriage to a prince from Saxe-Coburg-Gotha, and secondly when, after Albert's early death, it was felt she was shirking her responsibilities. Because the Victorian expected a lot from himself, he expected a lot from others. He never forgot that he had put his monarch on her throne and he could take her off again: he expected a fair day's work from her as from any other paid employee.

The least attractive side of his self-confidence was his self-satisfaction. The Victorian could see that his country was successful where other nations were not. He watched the revolutions of 1848 throughout Europe, the civil wars of Italy and Spain, France and Portugal, Belgium and America, the neighbourly wars of Germany and Denmark and Austria and France; how could he help pitying, and so despising, even these so-called civilised countries, to say nothing of savage lands farther afield?

When his own country went to war which he believed she did only in the best of causes—she invariably won. When she confined her efforts to commerce, she was even more spectacularly successful—in 1870 Britain's external trade was greater than that of France, Germany and Italy *together*, and three times that of the United States.

In almost every field of activity, from the building of railways to the mounting of exhibitions, from the opening up of unknown regions to the spreading of the Word of God, his country took the lead. That there might be faults and deficiencies in the structure of the machine, he was not so conceited as to doubt—but why tamper with a machine which was demonstrably working better than any other on show? Time enough to do that if the machine broke down, or someone else invented a better one.

It is easy enough, in retrospect, to sneer. The faults are so much plainer to see today. But let us not forget the physical limitations of the age. We blame the Victorians, for example, for their ruthless colonialism, and with reason; but we must not forget that many of the operations we condemn were carried out thousands of miles from the responsible leadership back home, and that news of them took weeks, not seconds, to travel. Under such circumstances, what is more to be wondered at is the fact that, in the face of a lack of communication which we today can hardly conceive, many Victorians *did* challenge the morality of their imperialism, *did* question the actions of their emissaries in far-off lands.

For above all, for good or ill, the Victorians were sincere. If they made mistakes, it was seldom with evil intent. They believed that it is better to be a success than a failure, better to be rich than poor; but they also believed that it is better to be kind than harsh, better to be honest than dishonest, better to be just than unjust. . . .

For they really were remarkable. Remarkable because they were genuinely a society of people working for themselves, not to instructions from a few superiors. Remarkable because their efforts were directed into all spheres of activity, not just one here and one there. Remarkable because they combined—they *had* to combine—the art of reconstructing the social fabric along with the business of changing its component parts, like rebuilding a railway locomotive while it is travelling. Because the Victorians were faced with so vast and so complex a problem, they deserve our sympathy; because they succeeded in solving it as well as they did, they earn our admiration.

Chapter 2

Inventions, Technology, and Medicine

Turning|Points

IN WORLD HISTORY

New Technologies Fostered the Industrial Revolution

T. Walter Wallbank and Alastair M. Taylor

T. Walter Wallbank and Alastair M. Taylor describe new power sources and inventions that led to the development of railroads and steamships. These inventions in turn led to canal building and improved steel production. The authors also explain that the development of new and faster methods of communication, coinciding with advances in transportation, allowed industrialists to move their goods faster and cheaper. T. Walter Wallbank taught at the University of Southern California in Los Angeles, and Alastair M. Taylor taught geography and political studies at the University of Edinburgh, Scotland, and Queen's University, Kingston, Ontario. They are coauthors of *The World in Turmoil, Promise and Perils*, and *Western Perspectives: A Concise History of Civilization*.

The economic history of early modern times showed the eventual commercial supremacy of England. Likewise, the new industrialism which was to transform economic life matured first in England. Why is this so? The changes that occurred in the industrial era took place first in England for several reasons. England possessed a strongly centralized and stable government which catered to the interests of the commercial classes. The revolution of 1688 had put an end to royal interference and unjust taxation, and Parliament now guaranteed property rights. The foreign situation also favored England's economic evolution. The royal navy protected the country from invasion and, at the same time, kept open the trade routes and ensured the supremacy of England's mercantile fleet. The military situation on the continent from 1793 to 1815 stimulated English industry especially. The European nations involved in the Napoleonic wars were not able to devote time to expanding home industry but had to rely heavily on English goods. So effective was this industrial aid to Napoleon's enemies that [historian] James T. Shotwell could say, "the wars against Napoleon were not won at Leipzig or Waterloo, but rather in the cotton factories of Manchester and iron mills of Birmingham."

The commercial prosperity of England had created a large supply of surplus capital which could be invested in the new industrial enterprises. England also possessed an abundance of labor, particularly unskilled labor. The enclosure system[1] in agriculture had thrown great numbers of peasants off their holdings, and they wandered to the cities to furnish cheap labor. The country was blessed with rich deposits of coal and iron, both vital to the new industrial order, while the quality of its wool was unsurpassed. England specialized particularly in staple goods, and these were readily adaptable to mass production in factories, whereas France manufactured luxury and high quality goods which demanded individual technique. Finally, the numerous scientific discoveries made in England during the eighteenth and nineteenth centuries were adapted to the needs of English manufacturing. . . .

Newly Developed Sources of Power

In the nineteenth century the lines of development plotted by England continued to mark out the course of industrial advance. New inventions continued to modify production methods, new sources of power were developed to run machines, new methods of using metals were discovered, and the railroad and steamship burgeoned forth as the dominant means of transportation. In addition, means of communication were revolutionized. Though by the nineteenth century technological advances were no longer the monopoly of English genius, England had set the pace and remained for

1. the conversion of arable land into pasture for raising sheep, a practice resulting from the growing demand for wool; because sheep raising demanded fewer hands than farming, many farm laborers were left without work

some time far ahead of the rest of the world in the degree of her industrialization.

Following up the invention of the steam engine by [James] Watt and its use in manufacturing, railroads, and

The Layout of the Railway System

By 1846 the railway system linked the chief industrial centers in the northeast—Lancashire, Yorkshire, and the Midlands—with one another and linked all of these areas with London. Only the southwest and Wales lacked a rail network in 1846.

steamships, a further development took place in steam with the invention of the steam turbine in the latter half of the nineteenth century. This new device made use not of the piston but of a series of blades that revolved inside a closed cylinder. The turbine does not lose energy through the constant reversal of motion which takes place with the piston. "The development of the large turbines has thus resulted in fuel economies roughly proportionate to the economies realized by Watt's engines in comparison with the Newcomen engine."[2] The turbine has a smooth pull which makes it of particular value in propelling steamships.

While the steam engine was being developed as a source of power, various scientists, including Benjamin Franklin, [Italian scientists Luigi] Galvani and [Alessandro] Volta, were experimenting with electricity. But it was not until the nineteenth century that electricity was produced mechanically on a large scale and came into practical use. In 1831 [English scientist] Michael Faraday came upon the principle of the dynamo and demonstrated how mechanical power could be converted into electrical power. Not until 1873, however, was a really practical dynamo available when "at the Vienna exhibition . . . it was accidentally discovered that [a certain] dynamo was, in fact, a reversible engine and could be used as a motor." From this time on, electrical engineering made rapid progress. The steam turbine proved of great value in propelling dynamos, while France and Italy took advantage of the waterfalls in the Alps to harness their waterpower.

The development of the internal-combustion engine has also revolutionized modern life. The power in the gasoline engine is created through the explosion of vaporized gas by an electric spark within the cylinder. But because gasoline is expensive, [German engineer] Rudolf Diesel in 1897 invented a machine making use of a cheaper and heavier oil which is sprayed into the cylinders. "The efficiency of this engine excited the greatest interest. Three tons thirteen hundred weight of oil costing twelve dollars delivered more power through a Diesel engine than twelve tons fifteen hun-

2. an early version of the steam engine devised by Thomas Newcomen in 1705–1706

dred weight of coal costing fifty dollars burned under a steam boiler," [according to historian Friedrich C. Dietz]. . . .

Important Developments in Metallurgy

The nineteenth century saw important developments in metallurgy following upon the making of wrought iron by the puddling process.[3] Of greatest importance to the new metallurgic age was the development of steel. Steel is an alloy of iron possessing less than one per cent of carbon and is both stronger and more elastic than other forms of iron. To obtain steel, a process had to be devised which could extract more carbon than the puddling process was able to extract. In 1856 in England, the son of a French refugee, Sir Henry Bessemer, hit upon a scheme. He poured molten iron into a large egg-shaped container (converter) in the bottom of which were numerous holes. Through these holes air was sent into the liquid iron; the oxygen combined with the carbon and silicon and the impurities were automatically burned out. To the pure iron was then added the right quantity of carbon and manganese needed to make steel. The Bessemer converter allowed steel to be manufactured quickly and cheaply; in fact, between 1856 and 1870 British steel fell to one half the price formerly charged for the best grades of iron, while production increased sixfold.

New Modes of Transportation Brought Wider Markets

Improvements in modes of transportation begun in eighteenth-century England were rapidly adopted and expanded both at home and abroad. Canals, railroads, and steamships drew the various parts of the world closer together and transported the products of the new machines more swiftly and cheaply than commodities had ever moved before. The new modes of transportation were an essential factor in the Industrial Revolution, for without the wider markets they provided, the increased production made possible by the machine would have been stringently limited in usefulness.

3. purification of impure metal, especially iron, by heating and stirring

The digging of canals in England had provided a new method of moving heavy goods cheaply. During the nineteenth century other countries perceived the advantages of this mode of inland water transportation, and great canal schemes were put into motion in other countries. . . . The Suez Canal was opened in 1869, linking the Mediterranean and Red seas and immediately becoming a vital part of the British empire's lifeline. . . .

Railroads

Of even greater importance than the canal was the railroad, which developed with phenomenal rapidity from the first lumbering locomotives of Trevithick and Stephenson.[4] In 1825 the first English railroad was opened, the famous Stockton and Darlington. The engine was driven by Stephenson himself at the dizzy speed of over four miles an hour. A signalman on horseback dashed in front to warn spectators of the approach of the iron monster, its chimney red-hot and belching forth clouds of smoke and sparks. But it was a real engine. Another line opened in 1830, this time from Liverpool to Manchester, and Stephenson's *Rocket* made what was then the terrifying speed of 29 miles an hour.

A contemporary account [by writer Samuel Smiles] of the speed of the first trains strikes us as amusing: "It was anticipated that the speed at which the locomotive could run upon the line would be about nine or ten miles an hour; but the wisest of the lawyers and the most experienced engineers did not believe this to be practicable, and they laughed outright at the idea of an engine running twenty miles in an hour. But very soon after the railway was opened for traffic, passengers were regularly carried the entire thirty miles between Liverpool and Manchester in little more than an hour."

The future of the railroad was assured. Whereas in 1838 England had only 500 miles of track, in 1890 it possessed 20,000 miles, while other European countries had made similar strides forward. . . . Of tremendous economic and

4. Richard Trevithick and George Stephenson first used steam to power locomotives for hauling.

political significance during the twentieth century was the start of other huge railroads—the Cape-to-Cairo railway, which was designed to span Africa from north to south and keep British dominion there supreme. . . .

Steamships

On the seas the steam engine, so effectively revolutionizing land travel, was also put to use to speed ocean crossings. In 1819 the *Savannah*, a sailing ship with an auxiliary engine, crossed the Atlantic in twenty-nine and one half days—but used steam for only eighty hours of that time. By 1838 ships were crossing the Atlantic entirely by steam power.

Another innovation was the use of iron in ship construction after 1840. Great Britain evolved the steel steamship at the same time that the United States was perfecting the wooden sailing ship—the famous clippers that brought back tea cargoes from the orient, whose beauty and speed have been so often praised. Despite the achievements of the splendid Yankee clippers, however, the age of wood and sail was replaced by the less romantic but more practical age of steel and steam.

The steamship was aided by various improvements: the use of steel hulls, the invention of the screw propeller which replaced the old side-wheel or stern-wheel paddles, and the innovation of compound engines, which proved more economical and efficient. These improvements in ships made possible the development of the great north Atlantic passenger service. By the last quarter of the nineteenth century large numbers of American tourists were being transported to Europe by a fine fleet of ships, and hundreds of thousands of European emigrants were being brought back to the New World. The advent of grain and refrigerator ships also played an important part in making food supplies easily available for the European countries. . . .

Not only have the transportation facilities of modern life been revolutionized; there has been a corresponding revolution in communication facilities. The year 1840 saw the inauguration of the penny post in England, while in 1875 the Universal Postal Union was created to facilitate the passage of mail from one country to another. Meanwhile, certain men, including Samuel F.B. Morse, the American, had a share in perfecting the telegraph. The first British telegraph company was formed in 1846, and in 1856 the Western Union Company was organized. Within ten years, Cyrus W. Field had successfully laid a cable across the Atlantic Ocean. Today cables span every ocean, while telegraph wires cross every continent and country, thus making the news of one portion of the globe the instant knowledge of the rest. . . . Wireless telegraphy was the invention of Guglielmo Marconi, an Italian scientist, who obtained a British patent for his discovery in 1896. He succeeded in sending a wireless message from England to Newfoundland, and in 1909 Marconi's momentous achievement in the realm of communication earned for him the Nobel prize in physics.

The industrial era could not have advanced very far without the advances in transportation and communication just described. . . . Vast quantities of cotton, rubber, jute, copper, lumber, oils, and tin—and many other materials—had to be imported. This would not have been possible without the existence of cheap and efficient transportation. Industrialism also brought about a growth of population. England and Japan in particular could not grow enough food to meet their needs. The new transportation enabled overcrowded centers of population to obtain adequate and cheap supplies of food products.

We saw earlier the reasons why industrialization came first to England. This process, which brought radical changes to that country in the years following 1750 and gave her economic supremacy for the next century and a half, inevitably spread to adjoining areas during succeeding decades. It was not to be expected that the continental countries should submit forever to England's control of the textile trade or that the United States should remain only an agricultural nation, when she had more natural resources for becoming a highly industrialized power than England herself. However, it was not until after 1870 that such leading nations as Germany, France, the United States, and Japan found themselves in a position to challenge England's industrial rule.

England enjoyed a virtual monopoly up to that time, not only by reason of her accumulation of machines, capital, and markets, but also because various political circumstances prevented rival nations from turning wholeheartedly to an industrialized economy. Germany was not united politically until 1870–1871, the United States underwent a civil war in the sixties, and Japan did not embark upon her era of westernization until the seventies. However, when industrial changes did occur in those nations, they took place in a fifteen- or twenty-year period, whereas a full century had been required for the transformation in England. Industrialism was transplanted almost *en bloc* from England, which served as a working model for all such innovations.

Late Nineteenth-Century Inventions

Alan Bott

Alan Bott describes the proliferation of inventions made during the last thirty years of the nineteenth century and the public resistance to the new and unfamiliar mechanisms. Electricity had a particularly slow and troublesome start until the mid-1890s. The telephone competed with the telegraph, and cars with horses. The century closed with inventions of the wireless, X-rays, and the forerunner of the airplane. Alan Bott, whose research focuses on social customs in the late Victorian period, is the editor of *Our Mothers: A Cavalcade in Pictures, Quotation and Description of Late Victorian Women 1870–1900.*

What was (and is) electricity? The mid-century theorists held it to be this and that in their quest after a definition adapted to a mechanistic universe which their science could explain in terms of geometry, chemistry, ballistics and magnetic attraction. In 1870 the public knew next to nothing of the invisible force concerning which Fellows of the Royal Society continued to contradict one another. It merely knew that when it went to Brighton Pier, showmen with coils upon barrows took tuppence for making it wriggle with tingling current.

It was forty years since [physicist Michael] Faraday had discovered that an electric current arose when a magnet was thrust in and out of a coil of iron wire. Thus far electric induction had given nothing to the man in the street and the woman in the home. They used the electric telegraph, but this was as often as not a portent of personal disaster—it rep-

Excerpted from Alan Bott, *Our Fathers* (London: Heinemann, 1931).

resented to the family news of death, accident, or urgent illness, through an orange envelope to which postmen gave a ritual of urgent ringing and knocking.

Resistance to New Inventions

A sedate civilisation, gaslit only in parts, in the age of steam and the century of invention, believed itself to be racing onward at almost excessive speed; as indeed it was by comparison with the England of forty years earlier, when the first trains were wonderments. Its many reactionaries fought to the last ditch against the idea of an electrified age. While they merely disbelieved in the future of steel ships, and only derided the Boneshaker cycles: while Paterfamilias, Lover of Horses and Pro Bono Publico contented themselves with letters to the papers protesting against the Jabberwockian road steamers and the inelegant steam trams, electricity symbolised to them a headless, menacing ghost which they must exorcise, lest it upset the harmony of the best of all possible worlds.

There was plenty of excuse for resentment by the self-satisfied. Our own age considers itself the speediest and most fluid ever; but in mechanical invention the last thirty years of the nineteenth century surpassed by far the first thirty years of the twentieth (although this century's contribution in scientific thought through biological invention is leading us to greater heights). Edwardians and Georgians have seen the introduction of the aeroplane, the dirigible airship, radio transmission and the wireless telephone (the cinematograph, like the gliders that preceded aeroplanes, appeared during the 'nineties—a film of the Queen driving to St. Paul's for the Diamond Jubilee was publicly shown). The late Victorians had to digest many more major inventions that were revolutionary in effect—electric light, electric trains and carriages, the dynamo and electric power station, the microphone, the telephone, the bicycle, the phonograph and gramophone, the motor car, steel ships, submarines, torpedoes, marine turbines, wireless telegraphy, the linotype and monotype, the chilled-meat refrigerator, the machine-gun, the breech-loading and magazine rifles, the modern field gun, and the mobile long-distance gun. Innovations like the fountain pen, and the typewriter perfected in the 'eighties by [Philo] Remington, seemed by comparison small fry. Transcending everything new and old in terms of importance to humanity were [Joseph] Lister's applied antiseptics, which remedied the state of things whereby every other operation in hospital brought death from gangrene, while abdominal operations could be classed among the methods of the executioner. Antiseptics and inoculation, arriving in the same decade, have saved within fifty years more lives than were destroyed in all the wars between Napoleon and Hindenburg. Yet the dear old *Lancet* (fighting as usual in the rearguard of progress) half-heartedly hit out in 1877 at the man who gave surgery its greatest benefit: "Mr. Lister has acquired the reputation of a thoughtful, painstaking surgeon, and has done some service to practical surgery by insisting on the importance of cleanliness in the treatment of wounds, although this has been done by the glorification of an idea which is neither original nor universally accepted."

Development of Electrical Inventions

Electrical invention was everywhere welcomed as long as it produced only marvels. Late in the 'seventies, a bootmaker in the Edgware Road advertised his shop by erecting outside it a huge arc light; and the crowds it drew in circus mood were so dense that traffic had to be diverted. The idea that a spectacle, and not a revolution, was being provided remained for some years after [Joseph] Swan and [Thomas] Edison separately discovered that a divided carbon thread, lit by electric current in a vacuum, would not burn itself out. The electric lamp had arrived; and Aldersgate Street Station demonstrated its practical uses before so many sightseers that police regulation was needed. His Majesty's Theatre tried the new lighting, but desisted because audiences complained of the thrumming dynamo.

Two great country houses, Hatfield and Craigside, contested claims to be the first private residence with the new light. Lord Salisbury, in the former, had earlier tried to instal Jablokhoff arc lights in the dining-room, but lady visitors found the glare impossible for eyes and complexions.

He now made his estate workmen—each new installation needed its own expensive plant—instal Edison-Swan lamps. "There were evenings," writes Lady Gwendolen Cecil in her excellent Life of her father, "when the household had to grope about in semidarkness, illuminated only by the dim red glow such as comes from a half-extinct fire; there were others when a perilous brilliancy culminated in miniature storms of lighting ending in complete collapse. One group of lamps after another would blaze and expire in rapid succession, like stars in conflagration, till the rooms were left in pitchy blackness. . . . One evening a party of guests, on entering the Long Gallery after dinner, found the carved panelling near the ceiling bursting into flames under the contact of an overheated wire. It was happily a shooting party in which young men . . . rose joyfully to the occasion, and with well-directed sofa cushions rendered the summoning of a fire engine unnecessary."

All this was in 1880. In the two following years electricity changed in public estimation from a wonderment to a god of progress that deserved fear. Paddington, Charing Cross and Liverpool Street Stations adopted the lighting. The General Post Office and the House of Commons half-heartedly followed. Liverpool, Bristol and Brighton installed it in the streets. Electric companies were formed, the City of London offered its lighting to three of them as an experiment; and protest was made to *The Times* that the City was unsuitable for the experiment, because it was uninhabited at night and "only the cats and the caretakers would enjoy the fun." Following Edison's public electric supply station for New York in 1881, a similar station was built at Holborn Viaduct. A miniature electric railway was demonstrated at the Crystal Palace, after Berlin had set the example. Electric trams on live rails came into being, and stimulated inventors to prepare the safer tramway, operated by current from overhead wires, which Kansas City introduced in 1884 but London did not copy until 1891.

An electrical Exhibition at the Crystal Palace in 1882 promoted enterprise on the one hand and reaction on the other. It set young England to learning about volts, amperes, and how to rig up an electric bell that would startle the maids in the kitchen. It was visited by representatives from all the town corporations—Birmingham, East London, Sheffield, Godalming and others—that followed Liverpool's lead in street-lighting. It helped to promote more electricity companies; and these in their turn promoted fear of monopolies. Vested interests in gas lighting, helped by timid politicians, persuaded Mr. Gladstone's government to pass an Electric Lighting Bill that gave local authorities power to buy out private supply companies after twenty-one years. English business ardour in electricity was dampened, and America was left unchallenged at the head of electrical development. This official brake was kept clamped for six years, after which the Act was amended and electrical enterprise became profitable. New methods of storage and generation then enabled companies to provide house-to-house current. By the middle of the 'nineties, every important town in England and Scotland—and for that matter, in the United States and Western Europe—had electrical current. At the century's end electric trams and trains were abundant: the "Tuppenny Tube" had been bored underground from Marble Arch to the Bank; and bigger and better dynamos were electrifying factory plants.

Telephones and Cars

The establishment of the telephone was almost as difficult. The first exchange having come to London in 1879, with lines run from the Temple to the Law Courts in Westminster, everybody from office boys to Law Lords hurried to use them. (Salisbury was again early in the field with private experiments at Hatfield, on primitive apparatus which necessitated simple phrases. I quote from Lady Gwendolen Cecil again: "Visitors were startled by hearing Lord Salisbury's voice resounding oratorically from selected spots within and without the house, as he reiterated with varying emphasis, 'Hey diddle diddle, the cat and the fiddle, the cow jumped over the moon'"). In the provinces the smaller area of towns made wiring easier. Pro Bono Publico, and the rest, reinforced by many aldermen, forthwith blew off warnings about the dangers from a network of overhead wires. It was further held that the telephone might supplant the government-owned telegraph—in 1880 the Post Office assailed the Edison Telegraph Company with an action for infringement of monopoly. The invention continued diffidently for a while. The first long-distance line (from London to Brighton) was little used. The G.P.O. promoted a service of its own, and local exchanges were universally adopted; but Manchester, Liverpool and Birmingham were not linked to London until 1890; and in 1900 telephone lines to the Continent were still a hope for the future.

The cause of the motor car suffered most in England from Sleepy Hollow reactionaries. A tricycle driven by an internal combustion engine, with benzoline vapour exploded by an electric spark inside its one cylinder, was built in London in 1885, when Gottlieb Daimler and others in France had already begun to use internal combustion for "horseless carriages." It was at once ruled that the new tricycles and the newer auto-carriage came under an Act of 1865, whereby vehicles dependent upon engines had been forbidden a speed of more than four miles an hour, and must be preceded by a man carrying a red flag to warn drivers of horses. England's hands were tied for ten years by this kind of crassness, while France and Germany developed the motor car. The first automobile race, between Paris and Rouen, was hardly mentioned by the English press except as a matter for ridicule. Even when the fantastic restriction was removed in 1896, early motor cars were jeered at, abused for the dust they raised and the horses they terrified, and condemned for their danger. Drivers were said to be daring fools who were certain of death if they kept to their rash hobby: and in the procession of cars from London to Brighton, to celebrate the end of the red-flag law, each of the high, blunt contraptions that broke down met hoots of laughter and dislike. As a result of all this, France was allowed to dominate the market in motor cars until well into the twentieth century.

The century ended with four more inventions, or applied discoveries, of great importance. Wireless telegraphy arrived; and England, who this time showed administrative foresight, welcomed and encouraged Marconi's system. The first wireless despatch was received across the Channel in 1899, the big wireless station at Poldhu in Cornwall was built a year later, and in 1901 it managed to exchange signals across the Atlantic. The Hon. C.A. Parsons, at about the same time, invented a completely new method of steam propulsion with his turbine motor, which was to find its way into most ships. [Physicist Wilhelm Konrad] Rontgen's experiments with so-called X-rays were altering the popular conceptions of matter, and causing speculation in medical science. Finally, though aeroplanes as now understood did not enter the century, the gliders of [American aviation pioneer Samuel] Langley and others forecast them. The theory of how plane surfaces behave in the air, as applied later to heavier-than-air flying machines, was evolved before [Percy] Pilcher and [Otto] Lilienthal killed themselves in their gliding experiments of 1899. Dirigible airships and wireless telephony were also forecast. Radio broadcasting, embryonic television and insulin are the only first-class discoveries in applied science thus far owned entirely by the twentieth century.

The Great Exhibition

Margaret Drabble

Margaret Drabble describes the Great Exhibition of 1851, a collection of British products displayed in a specially built crystal palace. Margaret Drabble, who teaches in an adult-education college in London, is the author of thirteen novels, including her 1996 *The Witch of Exmoor*, several plays, and critical editions about Jane Austen, Charlotte Brontë, and Thomas Hardy.

The Great Exhibition was an exhibition of science and manufacture, of design and raw materials, unprecedented in aim and achievement. Even the building which housed it, happily labelled The Crystal Palace by [the periodical] *Punch*, was a triumph of imaginative architecture. Designed by Joseph Paxton, after the model of the Great Conservatory at Chatsworth, it soared up, a glittering canopy of glass and steel; [writer Thomas Babington] Macaulay who was present at the opening came away enraptured, and wrote that it was 'a most gorgeous sight; vast; graceful; beyond the dreams of the Arabian romance. I cannot think that the Caesars ever exhibited a more splendid spectacle. I was quite dazzled . . .'

The reference to the Caesars is revealing, for the Victorians showed a Roman determination to overcome obstacles. One of the objections to the building of the Palace in Hyde Park was that it would involve cutting down a clump of three tall elms on the site—the Victorians, too, could show concern for conservation, when it suited them. So Paxton incorporated the trees in his design, and an immense transept was built to house them. They must have added to the exotic, fairy tale quality of the place. Paxton's whole concept was in fact based on nature; he is thought to have devised the

Excerpted from Margaret Drabble, *For Queen and Country* (New York: Seabury Press, 1979). Copyright ©1978 by Margaret Drabble. Reprinted by permission of the author.

rib structure from his study of the huge South American water lily, *Victoria Regina*, which he had seen at Chatsworth; its giant leaves were strong enough to bear the weight of Paxton's small daughter. Like so many of the great Victorians, Paxton was strictly an amateur, as he had no professional qualifications as architect, engineer or scientist; this was an age when the inspired amateur, his imagination unshackled by a narrow professional training or discipline, could achieve astonishing results.

Controversy Surrounded the Palace and the Exhibits

The elms were not the only excuse for opposition to [Queen Victoria's husband Prince] Albert's scheme. Some muttered that it would ruin Hyde Park, the only decent open space left in London; others feared the building, unorthodox by any standards, would collapse. A more natural fear, perhaps, was that the huge crowds it would attract might prove violent, and that it might provide an opportunity for a rekindling of the radical spirit of Chartism[1] which had inflamed the working classes in the previous decade. The Victorians were easily alarmed by the idea of a 'mob', and memories of the French Revolution lingered; more recently, Revolution had swept through Europe in 1848, and the English feared that it might be their turn next. The discontent of a badly-paid, badly-housed proletariat could not be totally ignored, many felt, though that was not how they expressed their alarm. 'I would advise those living near the Park to keep a sharp look over their silver forks and spoons and servant maids', wrote one angry colonel to *The Times*. But his fears were unfounded. The crowds were orderly and loyal, nobody took advantage of the situation to attempt to assassinate or even to shout abuse at Queen Victoria, and there was no drunken vandalism—perhaps wisely, the refreshments available did not include alcoholic beverages. The exhibits, ranging in scale from meat-paste pot lids to huge power looms, were generally considered wonderful, and the whole project, which had been financed

1. a movement by workers to gain suffrage

entirely by private money, made a large profit.

But was it an artistic success? Did it not, rather, illustrate what we think of as typically Victorian 'bad taste'? One could argue either way. Sir Nikolaus Pevsner, an expert on design, writes: 'The attendance as well as the size of the buildings and the quantity of the products shown was colossal. The aesthetic quality of the products was abominable.' These are hard words. He goes on to argue that designers had not yet learned to cope with the newly invented processes of production, such as machine weaving and electro-plating, and were applying the wrong techniques to the wrong materials. Certainly some of the objects indicate more pride in the fact that a thing *can* be done than interest in the use or beauty of the finished object—take, for example, the wonderful knife with eighty blades and other instruments, made by Rodgers and Sons of Sheffield. It was heavily decorated with gold inlay, etching and engraving—a remarkable piece of work, but neither use nor ornament. The Osler fountain of cut crystal glass was famed more for its size and weight than for its beauty; it weighed four tons. Designs for carpets and fabrics show, as Pevsner points out, a lack of restraint, a lack of plan, a picking from here and there of jumbled scraps of pattern, a confused eclecticism. Eclecticism is a word one cannot avoid long when talking of the Victorians, for it so perfectly describes their attitude to decoration; it is the art of borrowing from various sources, to suit oneself. The Victorians had a great deal to be eclectic about; easier travel and the spreading Empire, as well as new techniques, provided a vast range of new patterns—peacocks from India, carpet designs from Turkey and Persia, lace designs from France, even sphinxes from Egypt. The Victorian instinct was not to look for uniformity of style, but to jumble everything up together, at random; even a room like The Indian Room at 7 Chesterfield Gardens, which at first sight looks as though it is trying to keep to some kind of Far Eastern plan, proves on closer inspection to combine Indian, Japanese, Chinese, and European bamboo chairs. Most interiors had even less coherence, and individual designs could show several separate influences.

So the Great Exhibition had, in the world of art, an immensely useful function; it drew attention to the chaos of taste and to the evils of 'Sheffield Eternal' and 'Brummagem Gothic'. From this chaos emerged art critics such as [John] Ruskin, and designers and artists such as William Morris. The artistic directors who had helped to set up the exhibition had already declared their desire for reform; Henry Cole and Owen Jones felt that 'ornament must be secondary to the thing ornamented', and that ornament should be fitted to the object's function. The Exhibition proved a focus for their theories and a breeding ground for new theories, as well as a display of the dangers and disasters of the age. Some of the new ideas were of course already in the air—the architect Augustus Welby Pugin was in charge of the medieval court, where he had scope to exhibit his highly original and influential views on design. He was of the opinion that

> All the mechanical contrivances and inventions of the day, such as plastering, composition, papier-mâché, and a host of other deceptions, only serve to degrade design, by abolishing the variety of ornament and ideas, as well as the boldness of execution, so admirable and beautiful in ancient carved works . . .

We see here the growing revulsion against the new machine age of mass production and cheap imitation materials, and a new interest in the old arts of craftsmanship. (Today, some feel the same revulsion from plastic, nylon, and other 'unnatural' materials.) Professional designers were almost unknown in the early Victorian period; in the later half of the century, they were to flourish.

But the Great Exhibition offered far more than a spectacle of bad taste. Many of its visitors saw their first railway train there, and machinery of most kinds was still a novelty. A model diving bell, a lace machine, and a steam brewery attracted great attention. The Victorians may have liked overdecoration in luxury goods, but they had a strong sense of functional design; the sewing machine, the typewriter, the earthenware inhaler, and the gynaecological forceps remained unchanged for many years after their original conception. British engineering was the best in the world, encouraged by the efforts of men like James Nasmyth, the inventor of the steam hammer, and his pupil Joseph Whitworth, whose machine tools at the Great Exhibition were praised for 'their great beauty and power'. The nineteenth-century toolmakers have been acclaimed by modern art historians as a new race of artists, and even at the time, objects like lathes and microscopes were considered beautiful as well as useful; more significantly, many appreciated that they were beautiful because they were useful. The English, said [American writer Ralph Waldo] Emerson, love 'the lever, the screw and the pulley', and as early as 1759 the economist Adam Smith had stated that 'Utility is one of the principal sources of beauty.'

Over-decoration and embellishment never overwhelmed such inventions as the bicycle and the electric light bulb—the shape of the light bulb is so well adapted to its function that we accept it, says Herwin Schaefer in an excellent account of the functional tradition, 'as if it were a product of nature'. Significantly, more attempts were made to decorate the sewing machine and the typewriter, because they were primarily used by women, but even here the dignity of the basic design survived. Schaefer advises us, when looking for a good design, to concentrate not on luxury items such as the Osler fountain, but on ordinary objects in daily use, such as egg beaters, kitchen scales, scissors and coat hooks, bottles, pots and bell pushes. It is interesting to note that the American exhibits that most impressed the British were such things as sleighs, ice skates, racing sulkies, canoes and farm implements; necessity was proving the mother of invention and by the 1870s the Americans had taken over the world lead in machinery, as they demonstrated in 1876 at the Centennial Exhibition in Philadelphia.

The Function-Decoration Conflict
Extends Beyond the Great Exhibition

The nineteenth-century conflict between function and decoration was nowhere better expressed than in the building of the railways. The telling contrast between the elaborate

Gothic façade of St Pancras, more a cathedral than a railway terminus, and the austere simplicity of the roof and girders within is still eloquent. The Victorians themselves were conscious of such problems, and in 1852 Frederick S. Williams published a book, *Our Iron Roads*, which shows a spirited enthusiasm for the immense enterprise of the engineers, and for the beauty of their constructions. The railways have retained their excitement and glamour for some addicts, and Williams is one of their earlier admirers. Of the High Level Bridge at Newcastle, he writes:

> It is scarcely possible to imagine a more interesting and beautiful sight than it presents, with the huge span of arches diminishing in perspective, and the opening at the furthest end of the bridge showing only like a bright spot in the distance. The pillars, which carry the road, add greatly to the picturesque effect . . . such a combination of beautiful lines is seldom seen.

Here is a writer who does not despise the machine-made. He writes with equal lyricism of the Britannia tubular bridge across the Menai Strait:

> Could the reader stand upon the shores of the Isle of Anglesey, and view the entire spectacle, though but for a few moments, on some fine spring evening, he would retire with impressions of its magnificence that neither pen nor pencil can create. . . . Science and nature mingle in harmonious contrast, and receive the grateful homage of every rightly-constituted heart.

Williams clearly did not share the fears of [poet William] Wordsworth, who thought that the railways would ruin the scenery of the Lake District.

He is also impressed by sheer technical triumphs, such as the blasting of a tunnel through Shakespeare's Cliff between Dover and Folkestone, an event which attracted crowds of admiring sightseers, at the risk of their lives. It has been suggested that the fiery and dramatic paintings of John Martin, now restored to fashion after years of neglect, may have been partly inspired by the sight of the quarries and craters and scars that gashed Britain during the building of the railways; he was very fond of portraying caverns, tunnels, and falling rocks. His versions of Hell remind one of the fiery furnaces of industrial England, and his huge work, *Belshazzar's Feast*, distinctly resembles a vast railway station. Martin certainly appreciated the picturesque aspects of engineering feats, as well as their practical ones—significantly, he devoted a good deal of time not only to Biblical and classical subjects, but also to designing and drawing schemes for sewage and water supplies, embankments and colliery safety apparatus. Most Victorians were, like him, moved rather than appalled by the grandeur of the new engineering miracles, and Londoners watched the new cuttings slicing their way into the heart of the city with awe.

Yet efforts were made to landscape the railways; Williams had strong views on appropriate designs for tunnels and bridges. Tunnel entrances, he says, should show 'plainness combined with boldness, and massiveness without heaviness', which sounds sensible enough. But his book has illustrations which prove how difficult it was for the Victorians to find appropriate designs for wholly new concepts—there is a railway station that looks like a gothic chapel, a tunnel entrance with castellated towers modelled on a medieval castle, and the Britannia bridge, a triumph of modern engineering, was flanked by highly inappropriate sphinxes. Eclecticism at work, again. The bridges themselves dictated their own aesthetic laws, but when it came to decorating them, and blending them in with traditional ideas of the beautiful, the Victorians were less happy, and had less to guide them.

The Great Exhibition Inspires the Work Ethic

The Great Exhibition, which provided an opportunity for much debate on design, also created a new attitude to work, which was to prove equally significant. Work had become respectable; trade and manufacture were given the nation's blessing. Albert himself, who could have chosen to be little more than an idle and handsome figurehead, was much inspired by the romance of industry, and worked hard himself, contributing to the view that hard work is good even for the richest of us. In the words of *The Economist* of 1851, 'Labour is ceased to be looked down upon . . . the Bees are more considered than the Butterflies of society; wealth is valued less as an exemption from toil, than as a call to effort . . .' The idea of a leisured class of wealthy parasites became less popular, as the work ethic and the virtues of self help took over. Sir Felix Carbury in [novelist Anthony] Trollope's *The Way We Live Now* is shown as even more contemptible than the unscrupulous Melmotte, because, although well-born, he is a complete idler and wastrel, who does nothing but play cards, hunt, borrow money, seduce poor girls, and plot to marry rich ones. The polite world of [novelist] Jane Austen, in which families lived without visible means of support, was on the way out. Religion placed itself firmly on the side of the worker; God would help those who helped themselves. Samuel Smiles published in 1859 a book called *Self Help*, which became the Bible of the self-made man; he also published glowing biographies of men like [railway engineer] George Stephenson, and praised the great industrialists who had started from humble origins.

Commerce had become respectable, and great buildings rose to celebrate the civic pride of the great commercial centres—Cuthbert Brodrick's Town Hall in Leeds, Bunning's Coal Exchange in London, Edward Walters' Free Trade Hall in Manchester. These, one could say, were the real cathedrals of Victorian England. Ruskin and Pugin were to look back nostalgically at the gothic cathedrals of a more spiritual age, but they could not stem the flow of pride in profit, in invention, in commercial daring. The Crystal Palace glorified the golden age of prosperity. In the official catalogue, Albert wrote 'We are living at a period of most wonderful transition', and went on to sing the praises of a unified world, in which 'thought is communicated with the rapidity and even by the power of lightning'. Science, industry and art together will, he said, help us to fulfil the sacred mission of man, helped on by the stimulus of competition and capital. Endless progress, sings *The Economist*, in a fine confident moment, is 'the destined lot of the human race'.

And England was firmly in the forefront of that progress, a model to the world.

It is pleasing to note that the profits raised from the Great Exhibition went into educational projects which we can still enjoy today; again, the vision was Albert's, and the projects include the Victoria and Albert Museum, the Natural History Museum, and the Royal College of Music. Triumphant commerce did not neglect succeeding generations.

Health and Medicine

Sally Mitchell

Sally Mitchell outlines the state of health care, one element of English social life that changed little during the nineteenth century. Because germs and antibiotics had not yet been discovered, health care workers had little knowledge of the causes of disease and, consequently, of effective treatments. Mitchell cites public health studies as a major advance of the Victorian era. Sally Mitchell was a Fulbright scholar at Oxford University in England and is professor of English and women's studies at Temple University in Philadelphia. She is the editor of *Victorian Britain. An Encyclopedia.*

Life expectancy was much shorter in the nineteenth century than it is today. In England, rural people lived longer than city dwellers, and members of the upper classes were healthier than workers. Unlike many aspects of daily life, medical care made no dramatic advance during the century. Nutrition was poorly understood, and physicians had very few effective ways to treat illness. Epidemic diseases swept through crowded cities. Although the bacteria that caused some of them were identified by the century's end, it would be another forty years before cures were found.

Most people depended on traditional remedies, herbal medicine, homemade prescriptions, and the health advice passed along by household manuals and elderly women. Even in an aristocrat's country house, there was apt to be a servant—perhaps a laundress or one of the kitchen staff—whose medical knowledge was helpful not only for the other servants but also for members of the family. She made poultices for injuries and sore muscles, lanced boils, put herbs in boiling water to soothe coughs and croup. Her observation, experience, traditional herbal knowledge, and authoritative assurance were as useful as most therapies available to doctors.

Reasons for Poor Health

Some people suspected that plentiful energy and a hearty appetite were not "ladylike," as women and older girls were expected to be delicate. It was widely assumed that members of the upper class could not digest the coarse food that working people ate. Furthermore, people in the fortunate classes thought that cold, wet, and exhaustion were far more dangerous for themselves than for their servants. Evidence reveals, however, that men and women who did heavy labor were usually too old to work by the time they reached age forty; their health was depleted from long hours, poor nutrition, and the physical stress of beginning full-time employment before their bodies had matured. . . .

Household manuals explained that "bad air" and "bad smells" caused most illnesses. The observation (if not the explanation) was correct: when the air smelled bad because of rotting garbage and inadequate sewers, the as-yet-undiscovered germs that caused many diseases were likely to be present. People who followed the advice to avoid "bad air" by cleaning drains and choosing a house on high ground promoted their families' health. However, the common practice of sealing up windows to keep night air out of the house was not so good. Close indoor environments promoted the spread of airborne bacteria. Tuberculosis, in particular, was so widespread that almost any medium-sized group of people was likely to include a carrier. . . .

Infant mortality (the number of babies who die before reaching their first birthday) is one sensitive measure of a community's physical condition. Even at the end of the Victorian period, infant mortality was about ten times as high as it is today in industrialized countries. Then, as now, variations in the number of infant deaths reveal important information about poverty, housing, sanitation, access to medical care, and general health. In the early 1990s, the average infant mortality rate in the United States was about 10 per

1,000—but in some poor inner-city neighborhoods the number was more than twice as great. In Liverpool in 1899, the rate was 136 per 1,000 in upper-class areas; 274 per 1,000 in working-class areas; and as high as 509 per 1,000 in the most impoverished slums. . . .

Medical Training and Practice

The training and organization of regular medical practitioners—that is, the people we would call "doctors"—became increasingly professionalized. However, it was still possible, even by the end of the period, for people to see patients and prescribe treatments without having any formal qualifications.

Among the regular practitioners, apothecaries not only sold drugs and compounded prescriptions but also gave medical advice. Surgeons set bones, pulled teeth, and treated wounds and skin diseases. Double qualification in these two fields was common: most ordinary general practitioners until the latter part of the century were apothecary-surgeons.

Medical workers were traditionally trained by learning from someone who was already in practice. Apothecaries served a five-year apprenticeship, which had to include at least six months of hospital work. Surgeons were also apprenticed. Other boys became a doctor's "paying pupil." They read his books, watched him treat patients, and acted as his assistant. Medical students (whether apprentices or paying pupils) began in their middle teens and had a reputation for rowdiness.

Physicians, who had more prestige than other members of the profession, were the only ones who had university degrees. A medical degree from Oxford or Cambridge required students to read a great deal of Greek and Latin theory but did not provide any clinical experience. Physicians were gentlemen; their wives could be presented at court. The wives of apothecaries or surgeons could not, because those medical men were trained by apprenticeship and did manual labor. Because gentlemen (in theory) did not work for money, a physician's fee was wrapped in paper and quietly put down on a table near his hand. In aristocratic households the physician might be invited to dinner, but an apothecary-surgeon who was caring for a member of the family would have his meal with the housekeeper. . . .

By 1900, most registered practitioners entered training at age eighteen and had a five-year curriculum of classes and clinical work before passing a licensing examination. The usual degree was "Bachelor of Medicine" and the initials were "M.B." rather than "M.D." By the end of the century, however, "Doctor" was the ordinary form of address. (In the middle of the century, a man called "Dr. Arnold" was more likely to be an important clergyman who held the Doctor of Divinity degree.) Surgeons continued to be addressed as "Mr."

The Medical Act of 1858 effectively prevented women from becoming licensed by requiring that medical qualifications be earned in the United Kingdom. But two women managed to get their names on the medical register before the act went into full force: Elizabeth Blackwell, who had a degree from an American school; and Elizabeth Garrett Anderson, who found a temporary loophole in the Apothecaries' Act. For the next twenty years women tried to gain admission to medical schools. Sophia Jex-Blake and four others were admitted to Edinburgh University in 1869 but were then prevented from taking required courses. In 1874, Jex-Blake organized the London School of Medicine for Women. Sympathetic professors from several London medical schools agreed to provide the teaching. In 1878, women were admitted to all degrees—including medicine—at the University of London, and small numbers of women began making their way into the profession. . . .

The Training and Practice of Midwives

Midwives delivered most babies born during the century. Traditional midwives were trained through informal apprenticeship. They worked for several years with an older midwife, not only attending births but also learning about anatomy and herbal pharmacology. The local wisewoman who delivered babies, gave advice about infant care, helped in ordinary illness, and sat beside sick people probably knew more about women's and children's health than most physicians did.

Whether she was attended by an obstetrician or a midwife, a Victorian woman was far safer delivering her baby at home than in a hospital. Puerperal fever (also called "childbed fever") was easily transmitted in hospitals. Midwives had a much better safety record than doctors, because they typically stayed with one patient throughout the birth and for several days afterward. Doctors, who went from patient to patient, were much more likely to carry the infection. . . .

The transition from traditionally trained to medically trained midwives began in the 1860s, when the Nightingale Fund established a training course at King's College Hospital in London. Midwifery was not, however, subsumed under nursing (as it was in the United States). Although there were various dissenting voices (especially from male obstetricians), the Midwives Act of 1902 secured a continued role in England for women trained and licensed to deliver infants and provide well-baby care.

The Training and Practice of Nurses

Florence Nightingale made nursing into a popular career, but she overemphasized the faults of earlier nurses. The women hired to look after sick people in charitable hospitals or in their homes had no training, but because they stayed constantly with their patients they might be more perceptive than doctors in tracing the course of a disease and understanding the effect of certain treatments. They slept in the ward or just off it, so they were on call day or night; they cooked patients' meals and did cleaning as well as nursing care. But the pay (a shilling per day in London, plus room and meals) was relatively good for a working-class woman; pre-Nightingale nurses were not, therefore, the dregs of their class.

The earliest well-trained sick-nurses in England belonged to Protestant orders modeled after the Catholic nursing sisterhoods of Europe. St. John's House, founded in 1848, provided nurses for London teaching hospitals. After the *Times* had stirred up public agitation about horrible conditions in the military hospital at Scutari, Florence Nightingale (who had studied briefly at a Protestant nursing foundation in

Germany) was empowered by the War Office to take a party of nurses out to the Crimea. Her staff consisted of ten Catholic nuns, fourteen Anglican sisters, and fourteen hospital nurses.

When the [Crimean] War ended, a grateful public rewarded Nightingale by pouring money into a fund that she used to found a training school at St. Thomas's Hospital. The school she designed and the regimen she established determined the shape of nursing as a profession. Despite its name, St. Thomas's had no religious connections. Probationers, in training for one year, were paid a salary of £10 plus room and board. Each had her own room in a nurses' residence. Free uniforms were provided. The students were taught both by doctors and by experienced nurses and worked under supervision on the hospital wards.

When she had completed her probation, a new nurse spent three years in the service of St. Thomas's. She was paid about £20 per year (plus board and lodging) and was assigned to various duties in the hospital and elsewhere. After that, her name was put on the register. In the early years, when there were very few trained nurses, she could choose among posts as chief nurse, hospital matron, or district nursing director. "Nightingale nurses" became the founding directors of new training schools established in hospitals throughout the English-speaking world. . . .

The probationer was expected to have a good general education and some experience with housework and cookery. She was also required to have character references, including a recommendation from her clergyman. Her training, which generally lasted three years, included lectures, laboratory work, and experience on a variety of wards. Both probationers and nurses lived under strict supervision in quarters provided by the hospital. A typical day shift ran from 7:00 A.M. to 9:00 P.M., although the nurse had time off for meals and two additional hours for recreation. Maids did the scrubbing and heavy carrying, but probationers were responsible for making beds, bathing patients, carrying bedpans, and maintaining linen supplies.

After finishing her probationary year, the trainee became

a staff nurse. In that capacity she changed dressings, gave medicines, carried out doctors' instructions, and provided most of the skilled care for six or eight patients. Over her, supervising the ward, was a fully trained nurse known as a "sister." (In a U.S. hospital, she would be called a "head nurse" or "charge nurse.") A qualified sister at the end of the century earned between £30 and £50 per year; room, meals, and uniform were provided at no cost. Hospital work was laborious; but because well-to-do patients continued to be treated at home for most illnesses, many older nurses turned to private duty. Most towns of any size also had public health agencies and well-baby clinics that employed trained nurses.

Medicines and Therapies

No matter who provided the medical care, there were not many ways to interrupt the progress of an illness. (As late as the 1950s, young doctors were told that 90 percent of the practice of medicine lay in keeping patients comfortable while nature took its course.) The heroic medicine practiced by some Victorian physicians—attacking disease by purging, bloodletting, and dosing with dangerous drugs—probably did more harm than good. Practitioners often simply recommended cleanliness, rest, and nourishing food. Poor law doctors could actually write prescriptions for eggs or meat broth to build the strength of impoverished patients so their bodies could overcome disease.

Before the discovery of antibiotics and other specific chemical therapies, drugs did little to cure disease. Even today many medicines simply control symptoms; cough syrup, for example, quiets a cough but does nothing to stop the cold or flu that causes it. Nineteenth-century medical practitioners used wine, narcotic drugs, and traditional herbal preparations to promote sleep and to relieve coughs, muscle cramps, nausea, and other troubling symptoms. Opium, which could be bought without a prescription, was dispensed by doctors and also used in patent medicines and homemade mixtures. Laudanum (a liquid solution of opium in alcohol) was a common sleeping medicine, painkiller, and cough suppressant. It also prevented loose bowels. Not until the end of the century did doctors begin warning about the dangers of addiction, although many well-known people who regularly took laudanum at bedtime recognized the need to increase their nightly dose as the years passed.

Because people did not generally see doctors except for serious illness, the primary means of medical care was self-diagnosis and self-dosing. Almanacs, household guides, home medical books, and magazine advice columns all provided "receipts" for mixtures that could be used for a wide variety of symptoms and ailments. . . .

Patients who could afford it were often urged to have a change of air. This might have been the best treatment for lung problems caused by urban pollution. In addition, because people had to leave their ordinary work or household routine and spend a few weeks at the seashore or in the mountains, "change of air" was probably as effective as many twentieth-century prescriptions for stress-related illnesses. A similar function was served by visiting a spa or having special baths as part of a water cure.

Advances in Surgery

The only field of medical treatment in which the Victorians made great strides—and learned to accomplish cures that were previously impossible—was surgery. At the beginning of the nineteenth century, with no anesthetics and no antibiotics, injuries that tore the skin almost inevitably became infected. A surgeon who was strong and quick could sometimes save a life by amputating a mangled limb and cauterizing the stump; but the death rate from shock, loss of blood, and infection was so high that voluntary operations were almost unthinkable.

Chloroform was successfully used to anesthetize patients in the late 1840s. At first patients were simply knocked out before the operation, but by the late 1850s anesthetists learned how to keep them safely unconscious, giving surgeons time for more delicate and careful work. But as the use of surgery increased, so did the danger of infection. Even before bacteria were discovered, surgeons understood the need for cleanliness and used agents such as chlorine for dressing wounds. Most postoperative complications came not from the doctor's dirty hands and instruments (although that myth remains in circulation) but through epidemics of "hospital fever" caused by staphylococcus and streptococcal bacteria.

Florence Nightingale on Ventilation

In an excerpt from Notes on Nursing, *Florence Nightingale rejects the notion of "night air" and recommends sleeping with an open window.*

Another extraordinary fallacy is the dread of night air. What air can we breathe at night but night air? The choice is between pure night air from without and foul night air from within. Most people prefer the latter. An unaccountable choice. What will they say if it is proved to be true that fully one-half of all the disease we suffer from is occasioned by people sleeping with their windows shut? An open window most nights in the year can never hurt any one.

Florence Nightingale, *Notes on Nursing,* 1859. In Sally Mitchell, *Daily Life in Victorian England.* Westport, CT: Greenwood Press, 1996.

Antiseptic surgery was originated by Joseph Lister in the late 1860s. Even though not all surgeons shared his conviction that bacteria were the cause of infection, by the 1890s it was customary for surgeons to scrub their hands and boil their instruments. Both mother and child sometimes survived a Caesarean section, previously used only in heroic attempts to save the infant of a woman who was already dead or dying. Specialists could perform skin grafts, repair orthopedic defects such as clubfoot, remove ovarian cysts, and do appendectomies. Surgeons—who had been very low-ranking members of the medical profession at the beginning of the century—were becoming its most skilled and respected practitioners by 1900. . . .

Hospitals

During the nineteenth century, hospitals (and the patients in them) became increasingly important for training medical practitioners. A few medical schools built teaching hospitals. In many other places, staff doctors had paying pupils who needed hospital experience before their licensing examination. Surgeons in the leading London hospitals could demand indenture fees as high as £1,000 for taking an apprentice. . . .

Special "fever hospitals" were set up in temporary quarters during an epidemic. (Several early nursing administrators were middle-class women who gained experience as volunteers supervising a local fever hospital during one of the cholera epidemics.) As interest in medical research grew, some specialized hospitals were established. For example, philanthropist Angela Burdett-Coutts built the Brompton Cancer Hospital in the 1850s. Children's hospitals became an especially popular charity.

In addition, the treatment of mental illness grew more humane. Specialists created diagnostic labels to describe conditions that can be recognized under other names in current psychiatric literature: "melancholia" (severe depression), "monomania" (obsessive-compulsive disorders), "mania" (schizophrenia). The term "partial insanity" was used for hysteria, hypochondria, and other neurotic states. Legislation and public opinion slowly came to recognize insanity as a medical condition rather than a moral disorder. New mental hospitals had pleasant surroundings and opportunities for outdoor exercise. A good private asylum kept people from harming themselves and others through careful separation and constant supervision instead of putting patients in straightjackets or keeping them chained to the wall. For some conditions such as depression (which often ends in spontaneous remission), the new treatment seemed to provide a high rate of cure because it kept patients healthy until they felt better.

Advances in Public Health

The most significant Victorian medical achievement lay not in individual treatments or the discovery of cures but through legislating effective measures for public health. By 1837, it seemed evident that urban people were sickly. Popular images contrasted the tall, sturdy countryman to the stooped and feeble city dweller. Diseases of all sorts swept out of crowded slum neighborhoods into the dwellings of the well-to-do. After the New Poor Law went into operation, the physical condition of the rural poor also attracted notice. Edwin Chadwick's *Report on the Sanitary Condition of the Labouring Population*, published in 1842, was the first comprehensive investigation of the people's health.

Chadwick's work was supplemented by accurate statistics that could be developed once civil registration of births and deaths became compulsory in 1837. By the middle 1840s, reliable statistics could prove that poor drainage, inadequate water supplies, and overcrowded housing were related to increased rates of serious illness and early death. Edwin Chadwick also argued persuasively that poor health was the primary cause of poverty.

As a consequence of these investigations, the Public Health Act of 1848 created agencies that began many new programs. Sewers were built, pure water was supplied, slaughterhouses were moved away from city centers. Overcrowded city churchyards were closed to burials; new cemeteries were located away from heavily populated areas. The tax on soap was abolished. Standards of purity were applied to food products. Building codes required ventilation and reduced overcrowding. Factory inspectors began to study occupational diseases. Towns were required to provide regular garbage collection. School health examinations were begun. Public baths and laundries supplied space and hot water for people to wash themselves and their clothes.

The diseases that had been spread by contaminated food and water significantly diminished. Cholera ceased to be a problem after the epidemic of 1866–1867. Summer diarrhea killed fewer children and elderly people. Even viral and bacterial diseases, such as scarlet fever and tuberculosis, grew less deadly when overcrowding and malnutrition were no longer the ordinary condition of life among the poor. Although public health investigations at the end of the century still found much to criticize, people on the average lived longer and were in better physical condition than they had been in 1837.

Chapter 3

Daily Life in Victorian England

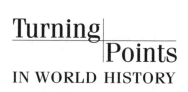

Turning Points
IN WORLD HISTORY

Victorian Farmers and Farm Laborers

W.J. Reader

W.J. Reader explains that farmers who owned their own land had decent food, adequate housing, and simple entertainment, but their lack of education made them unqualified to be social or political leaders. The lives of the laborers whom the farmers employed were sparse and strenuous. Reader reports that laborers made too little money, ate poorly, lived in small, rundown cottages, and worked long hours. Many escaped by becoming servants, joining the military, or emigrating. W.J. Reader was historian for Imperial Chemical Industries, Metal Box Ltd., and Bowater Corporation. He is the author of *Professional Men: The Rise of the Professional Classes in Nineteenth-Century England, Hard Roads and Highways,* and *The Middle Classes.*

The gentry owned the land, the farmers rented it, the labourers worked it. This was the normal pattern of English agriculture under Victoria, and it was fairly new. Its distinctive feature was the separation between ownership and cultivation. . . . The smallholders of the ancient common fields had been enclosed away over a very long period, and particularly fast in the late eighteenth and early nineteenth centuries. Some of their descendants had prospered as tenant farmers, some had gone to town, most had become labourers with no rights of cultivation beyond the garden hedge. Rural England had gone through a series of social revolutions of which the latest was quite recent. . . .

These changes were nearly all in favour of the large farmer, so that all the time small farms were growing fewer

Excerpted from W.J. Reader, *Life in Victorian England.* Copyright ©1964 by W.J. Reader. Reprinted by permission of B.T. Batsford Ltd.

and large farms more numerous, though the process was not on such a scale as to make any very drastic difference in the number of farmers. . . .

The Status of Farmers

The small farmer, scratching a living from a few acres of land, was scarcely above the labourers either in education or in general manner of life. Nor were larger farmers usually men of culture or broad views, though they might lead a life of roughish comfort and plenty. 'Farmers of the ordinary class', wrote [historian] W. Johnston in 1850, 'generally divide their time between the labours of their calling, and amusements with which neither mental cultivation nor refinement of taste have much to do.' Some amusements—field sports mostly—they were allowed to share with the gentry, but 'on a footing of understood inferiority, and the association exists only out of doors, or in the public room of an inn after an election.' Moreover, this kind of tolerance did not often extend to the shooting of game, and strict preserving was a fairly common source of ill-feeling between landlords and tenants. Hunting, on the other hand, tended to draw the two sides together, and the farmers were allowed to share in it. . . .

The farmers took little part in running local affairs. Under the old Quarter Sessions system there was not much opening for them, and there is little evidence that they took much interest. They might serve as guardians of the poor or as churchwardens, but it was beyond them, socially and educationally, to become magistrates. . . .

Farmers Lacked Respect for Education

Partly, no doubt, the trouble was the farmer's attitude to education. He might be prepared to have his daughters polished up a little, but he saw small benefit in book learning for his sons, especially if schooling looked expensive. In the fifties and sixties, when the grammar schools were acknowledged to be failing, a number of 'county schools' were set up, intended particularly for farmers' sons. One was at West Buckland in Devon, another at Framlingham and another at Cranleigh.

The county schools were proprietary boarding schools. To keep the fees down the boys lived in hostels and ate centrally, instead of being spread about in masters' houses, as at the ancient public schools. They were set up for farmers but not by farmers, and the schools' sponsors found that farmers were inclined to look on such things as new books, expensive apparatus and well-paid staff as extravagances. Even if they were willing to believe that the education and the living conditions were worth the price asked for them, they were apt to think they could get all their sons required without paying so much for it. 'Many of them', said the Report of the Schools Enquiry Commission in 1868, 'do not yet appreciate airy and well arranged schoolrooms and dormitories, single beds, abundant washing apparatus, any more than the study of French or Euclid.' An illuminating comment, this, on the way prosperous Victorian farmers were accustomed to live, as well as on their view of education.

Towards the end of the seventies the farmers of England began to feel the impact of foreign competition, especially in the shape of imports of American grain. It was all the worse because it coincided with a run of bad seasons. In the past the bad seasons would have raised the price of grain and the Corn Laws would have prevented foreigners from underselling. By the seventies the Corn Laws had gone and the prairie farmers, newly linked by rail with the Atlantic ports, could undersell in a big way. On 31st December 1879 a Monmouthshire farmer wrote in his diary: 'Being the last day of the year which is a very good thing it is. This year 1879 has been one of the wettest years any living man can remember and a very disasterous one for agriculture. Having a very bad yeald of corn & sheep rotten & doing very bad.'

The shaky grammar and spelling of this extract betray the educational limitations of even the larger farmers of the day, for the diarist, William Till, had spent a couple of years at a boarding school (1868–70) before, at the age of fifteen, he joined his father on the farm, which consisted of about 500 acres of arable and pasture land at Caerwent in Monmouthshire. By the time he was keeping his diary he had taken over the running of the farm. On an ordinary day he would get up early and, as he put it, 'set the men to rights'. Then he might spend the day in work about the farm—or he might not. He shot, he fished, he dug out badgers, he sang with the village glee club, and he visited friends and relations. Of one typical evening he records 'had tea & sundry games of wist . . . lost –/9 spent a very injoyable evening. Arrived home after a pleasant ride 3:15 a.m.'. . . .

Farm Labourers Were Poor

A few farmers were rich: many were comfortably off. Of the people whom they employed—the labourers—the one outstanding common characteristic was that they were all poor. Cash wages in some districts, just before the Crimean War, had fallen as low as 6s. or 7s. 6d. Over the next fifty years they rose, though not steadily because they varied with the general prosperity of farming. By the end of the century it was calculated by [journalist] Wilson Fox that labourers' wages in the Midlands and the eastern counties were about forty per cent greater than in 1850. . . .

Pay was always better near London and the factories than it was in, say, Somerset or Berkshire. Cowmen, shepherds and carters would always get more than ordinary labourers, especially where animals of great value were reared, but their pay was low compared with what they could get in towns, and their duties were more arduous than the unskilled men's, because the needs of animals take no account of their guardians' convenience.

Of the allowance in kind which made up some part of farm labourers' earnings the most important was usually a cottage held on a very low rent or no rent at all—and on a very insecure tenure. There might be beer, cider or food at harvest time, free carting of fuel, an allowance of milk or, in the north, half a ton of potatoes a year. These things varied very much from place to place and where their value was greatest, cash wages were lowest, so that there was no real gain from them. Money, in any case, was the labourer's greatest need. He could usually feed himself, with a pig behind his cottage and the produce of his garden, but how was he to buy clothing and especially boots? Payments for piece-work and harvesting, therefore, were extremely important to him. They were calculated according to all sorts of different local customs, and they might be worth as much as £4 or £5 a year.

The utmost that could be expected on a farm labourer's income, if he had a decent cottage, good health and not too many children, was a certain frugal comfort, which would depend very much on his wife's skill and strength of character. It was all too easy, especially for the aged and the sick, to fall into utter wretchedness, and Johnston, writing in 1850 when agriculture was depressed, remarked: 'A kind of Irish fate seems to hang over the lowest grade of the population, and they accept labour and sorrow, overcrowding and un-healthiness, as their destined portion.'. . .

Farm Labourers Lacked Decent Housing

Many cottages had one room downstairs, one above. Few had more than two bedrooms. They were unlikely to have been very well built in the first place, and they might have been neglected since, so that they would be damp, cold and draughty as well as overcrowded. Farm labourers' housing was a scandal for years—it was noticed, for instance, in a well-known *Punch* drawing of the sixties—and it was very thoroughly investigated by a Royal Commission, on which the Prince of Wales served, which reported in 1885. 'You will find', said one witness, 'between the Mendips and the fashionable watering-place known as Weston-super-Mare that you can hardly call the dwellings cottages, for some of them are only lean-to roofs up against the wall.' In one room of such a hovel, the witness said, he had seen eleven children and their parents. . . .

Conditions of this sort stirred some landowners to action. When the Prince of Wales bought Sandringham early in the sixties the estate was run-down, remote and neglected, be-cause the previous owner had lived there very little, only vis-iting occasionally for the shooting. In twenty years or so the Prince put up more than seventy new cottages, each with three bedrooms and two living rooms. Other landowners all over the country did the same sort of thing, building pairs or short rows of cottages in stone or brick. . . .

In 'open' villages where many small owners held the various properties, and especially where farmers were responsible for their men's cottages, the housing was at its most deplorable. In these overcrowded tumbledown houses the offence to morality, to the Victorian mind, was the gravest of many offences against ordinary ideas of civilized life, and the most that could be said for country cottages in general was that the overcrowding was not quite so bad as in town slums, because most families had more than one room to live in. . . .

Most Farm Labourers Were Illiterate

And in a labourer's life there was scant room for education, so that the 'yokel's' stupidity, ignorance and gullibility were a stock joke among townees. Certainly until well on in the century many farm labourers, probably most, must have been to a greater or lesser degree illiterate, because until the Act of 1870 made provision for a school within reach of every child in the land it was a matter of chance whether a country child could get to school or not. A good many squires and parsons saw to it that schools were built, often at their own expense, partly as a result of the general quickening of the social conscience and partly to make sure that the poor were taught proper notions of religion and morality. As an inscription still existing at Shalbourne, Wiltshire, puts it: 'A.D. 1843—This school was built for the purpose of giving a bible education to the Children of the Poor.' But there was no compulsion on the gentry to build or on the 'children of the poor' to attend.

For the villagers, indeed, compulsion was the other way; school had to take second place to earning. 'I once went to school for a week', said a farmer's boy of 1850. 'I know that twice ten is twenty, because I have heard other boys say so. I cannot read.' He was twelve and had probably been at work for four years or so, since boys of eight could earn 4*d.* a day at scaring birds off newly-sown corn, or by helping their fathers with odd jobs, and from that age on they would be at work whenever work could be found. As one boy put it, 'When I am not at work I do not often get bread and meat

for dinner. . . . I had rather work than play, you get most victuals when you work.'

A Hard Life for Farm Labourers' Wives

Women worked in the fields as well, though the practice was
pretty generally deplored and diminished as time went on. A
woman of 1850 said she had had thirteen children, of whom
seven grew up, and she had been accustomed to field work
for eleven hours a day at haytime and harvest. In the autumn
she would go out gleaning, perhaps from two in the morning
to seven in the evening, perhaps as much as seven miles from
home, and she would take three daughters (aged ten, fifteen
and eighteen) with her. For this effort, she would reckon six
bushels of corn a very good reward. Such habits had a disas-
trous effect on home life. 'When the wife returns . . .', says
Johnston, 'she has to look after her children, and her husband may have to wait for his supper. He may come home
tired and wet; he finds his wife has arrived but just before
him; she must give her attention to the children; there is no
fire, no supper, no comfort, and he goes to the beershop.' In
1864 an East Anglian parson visited a young woman who was
dying—'a victim of *field work*, a disgrace to the county'.
Thirty years later, in parts of Norfolk, Cambridgeshire and
south Lincolnshire, gangs of women and girls were still
being hired out to farmers at busy times, and in the north
labourers' daughters were still working on the land.

The best thing a cottager's daughter could hope for was to
go into service in a good family, and when she was between
ten and fifteen years old her parents would try to place her.
The Census Report of 1891 remarked on the fewness of
women, in country districts, at all ages from ten upwards. It
also said that almost one-third of all girls in the country, between the ages of fifteen and twenty, were in service, and
about one in every eight over the age of ten. These figures
indicate the intense pressure to get away from the villages, of
the demand for servants, and of the very limited openings
for women outside domestic service.

Life in service could be dreary and laborious, especially
where there was only one maid. The lists of servants' duties

given in Victorian works on household management are intimidating. Employers certainly expected hard work, for the idea that the lower classes (or the middle classes, for that matter) should do anything but work hard did not enter anyone's head. But in a good household the maid's job had solid advantages. A girl was well fed, clothed and housed. She would see something of a wider world and she would get some idea of how to run a house. If she were in some great mansion she would have her place—however lowly—in the ordered, ceremonious life of the servants hall, where distinctions of rank, from butler down to kitchenmaid, were meticulously observed, and she would gain some idea of good behaviour. There was always the hope that she might become an 'upper servant', though these generally came from the farmers' families rather than the cottagers', and she might marry some steady young man who would take her from poverty towards the comfort of the lower middle class. . . .

However great the hardship of the life of the country poor, it was at least less grinding from the middle of the century onwards and, on the whole, things grew better rather than worse. To take one example, by the end of the century the labourer might be riding to work on his bicycle rather than trudging on foot, and the fact that he could buy a bicycle would have astonished his grandfather no less than the existence of the machine itself. Moreover, cheap imported food, though from one point of view it imperilled his livelihood, from another standpoint worked as much to his advantage as to the advantage of the poor generally, for he had more and better things to eat than the bread, potatoes, fat bacon and beans of earlier times.

Villagers Tried to Escape

Most important of all, the doors of escape from the countryside opened wider and more attractively as time went on. . . .

Enlistment was one possibility. Emigration was another. As penal transportation ceased, the colonies became more attractive to honest men, and as sailing ships gave way to steam the discomfort and danger of long voyages grew less. The discovery of gold in California and Australia in the middle of the century drew many adventurers; others, more sober, could find land cheap or free in the United States and elsewhere. . . .

But the countryman might seek his fortune much closer at hand, and the Census figures show in what numbers he did so. In 1851, 1,200,000 men and 143,000 women were reported working on farms; in 1901, 700,000 and 12,000. Whatever anyone might say about the horrors of the towns, their unhealthiness, and the dissatisfactions of factory life, the villager was ready to take the risk.

The Transition from Agriculture to Industry

George Macaulay Trevelyan

George Macaulay Trevelyan explains how the mining and textile industries developed after the old agricultural system deteriorated. He also describes the resulting dismal living conditions in towns hastily built around the new factories in which workers, especially women and children, labored long hours under harsh working conditions. Historian George Macaulay Trevelyan taught at Trinity College, Cambridge. He is the author of *Lord Grey of the Reform Bill*, *England Under the Stuarts*, *The Age of Shakespeare and the Stuart Period*, and *The English Revolution 1688–1689*.

When George III ascended the throne on the eve of the Industrial Revolution, the English labourer was in most cases a countryman. He enjoyed not a few of the amenities of the pleasant old-world life, and often some personal independence, and some opportunity of bettering his position. For a variety of reasons, real wages had been fairly good in the first part of the eighteenth century. The labourers and the small farmers had reason for the traditional pride that they felt as 'free-born Englishmen,' and they appear to have looked up to the gentry, more often than not, without envy or resentment. This happy state of society did once in some sort exist. . . .

The 'labouring poor' in the eighteenth century had enjoyed many privileges, but they had lacked political power. This weakness proved their undoing alike in town and country, when the world of old custom, which had so long afforded them a partial shelter, was destroyed by the Industrial Revolution. When the common [fields], the cow, the garden, the

Excerpted from George Macaulay Trevelyan, *British History in the Nineteenth Century* (London: Longmans, 1924).

strips of corn land, the cottage industries, and the good wages of the early Georgian period disappeared together, the poor had no means of demanding analogous benefits under any new system. They had neither the influence nor the knowledge to plead so as to be heard, either before Parliament, or before their more immediate lords, the Justices of the Peace.

The wealthy classes then enjoyed, to a degree seldom paralleled in our history, a monopoly of every form of power. They had done more to earn and deserve it than any continental *noblesse*, but it was excessive. Because their position was unchallenged, they fell unconsciously and almost innocently into the habit of considering all national and economic problems in terms consonant with their own interest. . . .

The Breakup of Rural and City Systems

Step by step with the rural revolution, advanced the urban revolution, similar in principle and in spirit and at the outset similar in its social consequences. Just as the old theory of subsistence agriculture, associated with ancient rights, small properties and communal tillage, was being replaced by a new habit of mind that looked for the greatest net productivity of the national soil, on a basis of unfettered individual farming on the large scale—so in the towns the old theory of a 'limited' and 'well-regulated' trade, based on the local monopoly of a chartered few, subjecting themselves to a common set of rules about trade and apprenticeship, was being gradually abandoned for the new principle of open world-competition wherein all traders who could muster the capital and enterprise were invited to buy in the cheapest market and sell in the dearest, and to hire their labour wherever they liked and on what conditions each could secure. The change, in town as well as country, caused a wide cleavage of sympathy and of interest between classes which had previously shared, each in its degree, the common advantages of a fixed system of life and work; now that everyone scrambled for himself, the rich became richer and the poor poorer, and the law instead of attempting to redress the balance interfered heavily on the side of the employer. Such at least was the first phase of the new civilisation in England. . . .

The social and intellectual conditions of the England of that day would not have been enough to initiate the industrial revolution without the presence on the spot of coal and iron. Both had long been known and used, but they had not yet been used together. . . . This discovery led, by a chain of closely interrelated developments, to the whole urban revolution.

Iron-smelting moved to the North and Midlands to be near the coal. As the demand for coal grew, steam-engines, invented by James Watt in the early years of George III, were used to pump water from the mines. More iron, the result of more coal, in turn made it possible to produce more steam-engines, and men looked round for other ways to employ them, whether in locomotion or manufacture. In Watt's own lifetime his steam-engines were applied to the cotton industry. . . .

The Development of the Textile Industry

The textile revolution was the work of a wholly new order of men, risen from the ranks by their energy in seizing the opportunities of the new industrial situation. A workman who had toiled at the hand-loom in his own cottage might borrow £100 to start as a small employer with the new machines. The more enterprising of the vanishing class of yeomen invested the price of their ancestral farms in a like venture. Such are the origins of not a few families who became honourably famous in the nineteenth century.

The first generation of these men had the defects as well as the merits of pioneers. A common type of 'millowner' in the days of the younger Pitt[1] was a hard-bitten North-country working-man, of no education and great force of character, taking little stock of his social or political relations with the outer world, allowing neither leisure nor recreation to himself or to his hands, but managing somehow to convert the original £100 that he borrowed into a solvent 'mill,' the prison-house of children. . . .

The cotton industry, though not absolutely created by the new machinery, derived thence almost its whole importance. Between the accession of George III and the passing of the

---

1. William Pitt was a member of Parliament and later prime minister, 1783–1801.

Reform Bill its output increased a hundred-fold. Already by 1806 cotton was said to supply a third of the total British exports. The industry was concentrated in South and Central Lancashire, because the port of Liverpool was convenient to a trade depending on the import of raw cotton and the export of the manufactured article; because there it was near cheap coal; and because the climate of the damp Atlantic seaboard is peculiarly suitable to fine spinning.

The first mills, worked by water-power, were established on the upper reaches of the Pennine[2] streams. But throughout the long war with France, Watt's steam-engines were replacing water-power, and the industry was carried on by altogether more modern methods. This meant a change from small to large mills, real capitalist employers, great assemblies of working-people and an increase in the proportion of skilled mechanics,—circumstances all of which prepared the way for improved conditions of life in the future. The employees, now accumulated in one mill by hundreds instead of by scores, could not long fail to combine for economic and political action. The new type of large millowner had a secure financial position, more education and sometimes more enlightenment. Individuals of this class introduced factory conditions which inspectors in a later time could enforce as standards. And when the age of Factory Acts[3] came, it was easier to inspect properly one big mill than many small ones.

If the cotton industry showed England the way into some of the worst miseries of the industrial revolution, it also showed the way out, because it passed most rapidly through the period of semi-capitalised and half-organised industry, with its mean cruelties, into full-blown capitalism where the workpeople, the masters and the State could readily take stock of each other.

Working Conditions in the Early Textile and Mining Industries

But before the age of Factory Acts, the condition of women and children in both small and big mills was as a rule very

2. mountains near the border between England and Scotland   3. four Factory Acts—1833, 1844, 1847, 1850—each limiting the working hours for women and children

The New Factory Town

In his 1854 novel Hard Times, *a satire of industrial society and utilitarianism, Charles Dickens creates the fictitious but recognizable Coketown, notable for its grim ugliness and the inhumane conditions its inhabitants endure.*

Coketown, to which Messrs. Bounderby and Gradgrind now walked, was a triumph of fact; it had no greater taint of fancy in it than Mrs. Gradgrind herself. Let us strike the keynote, Coketown, before pursuing our tune.

It was a town of red brick, or of brick that would have been red if the smoke and ashes had allowed it; but as matters stood it was a town of unnatural red and black like the painted face of a savage. It was a town of machinery and tall chimneys, out of which interminable serpents of smoke trailed themselves forever and ever, and never got uncoiled. It had a black canal in it, and a river that ran purple with ill-smelling dye, and vast piles of building full of windows where there was a rattling and a trembling all day long, and where the piston of the steam-engine worked monotonously up and down like the head of an elephant in a state of melancholy madness. It contained several

wretched. Mothers and children worked from twelve to fifteen hours a day under insanitary conditions, without either the amenities of life which had sweetened and relieved the tedium of family work in the cottage, or the conditions which make factory life attractive to many women to-day. The discipline of the early factories was like the discipline of a prison. Small children were often cruelly treated to keep them awake during the long hours, which shortened their lives or undermined their health.

The men were in little better case. Often out of employment, they were forced to sell their wives and children into the slavery of the mills, while they themselves degenerated in squalid idleness. The hand-loom weavers had flourished until the early years of the nineteenth century, weaving the increased product of the new spinning mills. But the coming of the power-loom destroyed their prosperity; their wages large streets all very like one another, and many small streets still more like one another, inhabited by people equally like one another, who all went in and out at the same hours, with the same sound upon the same pavements, to do the same work, and to whom every day was the same as yesterday and tomorrow, and every year the counterpart of the last and the next. . . .

You saw nothing in Coketown but what was severely workful. If the members of a religious persuasion built a chapel there—as the members of eighteen religious persuasions had done—they made it a pious warehouse of red brick, with sometimes (but this is only in highly ornamental examples) a bell in a bird-cage on the top of it. The solitary exception was the New Church; a stuccoed edifice with a square steeple over the door, terminating in four short pinnacles like florid wooden legs. All the public inscriptions in the town were painted alike, in severe characters of black and white. The jail might have been the infirmary, the infirmary might have been the jail, the townhall might have been either, or both, or anything else, for anything that appeared to the contrary in the graces of their construction.

Charles Dickens, *Hard Times*. 1854. New York: New American Library, 1963.

fell, they went on to the rates as paupers, and drank the dregs of misery, until after long years their old-world employment altogether disappeared.

The older branch of the textile industry, wool, was more widely spread over the island than its younger and half-foreign sister, cotton. But its chief centre remained in the dales of the West Riding of Yorkshire. Wool was subject to the same general conditions of employment as cotton, and underwent in the end the same kind of transformation. But the change came more slowly in wool. Although the spinning-jenny had in the last years of the eighteenth century gone far to destroy the spinning of wool by women and children in rural cottages, the power-loom was introduced for the weaving of worsted and wool several decades later than for cotton. In the early years of the century, therefore, the woollen weavers suffered little from the introduction of machinery, although the fluctuations of trade caused them much distress.

Coal-mining was an ancient industry, but its development in the age of 'iron and coal' was prodigious, and a large part of the population now worked underground. Women were used there as beasts of burden, and children worked in the dark, sometimes for fourteen hours.[4] The men laboured under conditions that showed but little regard for health or human life. In Durham and Northumberland it was not the custom before 1815 to hold inquests on the victims of the innumerable accidents. Payment was not on a cash basis, owing to the 'truck' system,[5] and the oppression by the 'putties' or subcontractors for labour. These things and the condition of the miners' cottages, which were generally owned by their employers, too often rendered the life of the miner [in the 1820s] 'brutish, nasty and brief.'

If things were thus in the great textile and mining industries, they were no better in shops and smaller businesses where the new semi-capitalised industry was breaking up the old apprentice system and the 'regulated' trade. Indeed in many small or less highly organised concerns, where Trade Unionism failed to take root, 'truck' payments and 'sweated' wages and hours continued till the end of the nineteenth century, though they were worse when it began.

Unemployed Rural Poor Swarm to Factory Towns

The new urban proletariat was swelled in numbers and depressed in standard of life by constant arrivals of fresh swarms of impoverished rustics, driven by stress of famine from the English and the Irish country-side. Any attempt of workmen to combine for a living wage consonant with the rise of prices was illegal under Pitt's Combination Acts (1799). . . .

Before tracing the political history of the new era, it remains to notice some of the moral and intellectual influences

4. As late as 1842 the Royal Commission on Mines, that first threw light on the life of underground England, brought out such facts as these from a Lancashire woman: 'I have a belt round my waist and a chain passing between my legs, and I go on my hands and feet. The water comes up to my clog tops, and I have seen it over my thighs. I have drawn till I have the skin off me. The belt and chain is worse when we are in the family way.' It was also shown that children under five worked alone in the darkness.   5. a form of barter, in which workers were paid in goods

to which men and women were subjected, when, uprooted from the pieties and associations of the old rural life, they drifted to the new factories to find work.

First they had to be housed, if only in the private and temporary interest of the employer. Consideration for the public and forethought for the future were absent from the planning of the new town. The man for the employer's purpose was the jerry-builder, who designed the outward aspect of the new civilisation. Street after street sprang up, each more ugly, narrow and insanitary than the last. They were barracks for cheap labour, not homes for citizens.

Citizens, indeed, the workmen were not. They had no word in the government of England, and no civic position in the local area which they had come to inhabit. If they happened to be lodged within a chartered town, they lived under a close corporation and its municipal magistrates. If they were outside such precincts, they were under the rural Justices of the Peace and the antiquarian relics of the Court Leet. Neither urban nor rural authorities were called upon to provide for health, lighting, decency or education in a new factory quarter. They were content to quell riots and to arrest trade unionists, seditionists, deists, frame-breakers and other criminals.

The municipal corruption of the eighteenth century had lost the civic traditions and the public spirit of mediæval corporate life. The sudden growth of the new factory quarters hardly disturbed the complacency of the long inactive oligarchs, who were so well accustomed to neglect their old duties that they were not likely to attend to the new.

It is perhaps the greatest of our national misfortunes that the modern English town arose too rapidly and with too little regulation, either sanitary or æsthetic. The bodily and spiritual health of future generations was injured in advance. A type of city was allowed to grow up which it was fatally easy to imitate as the model for the whole industrial development of the new century, until the great majority of Englishmen were dwellers in mean streets, 'divorced from nature but unreclaimed by art.' When, indeed, in the course of the nineteenth century, local government was made to attend to its duties, by being subjected partly to democratic election and partly to an elaborate system of central control, large provision was made for health, convenience and education. But ugliness remained a quality of the modern city, accepted by the public conscience in spite of [essayist John] Ruskin and his successors. It has yet to be dislodged.

Working-class life [in the 1820s], divided between the gloom of these dreary quarters and the harsh discipline of the workshop, was uncheered by the many interests that now relieve the lot of the town dweller. Few of the workmen or their wives could read; the children had the factory and the slum, but not the school or the playground; holiday excursions and popular entertainments were rare, except some sporting events of a low type, such as setting on men, women or animals to fight. In the vacant misery of such a life, two rival sources of consolation, drink and religion, strove for the souls of men.

Child Labor in the Cotton Mills

Anonymous

The report of the "Committee on Factory Children's Labour," 1831–1832, includes an interview with Samuel Coulson, father of girls who worked in the cotton mills; the report reveals the long hours and the severe conditions of his daughters' employment. The editors introduce the report with information that led to child labor in cotton mills and follow it with political attitudes that led to worker protection. Editors Mary Ann Frese Witt and Charlotte Vestal Brown teach at North Carolina State University, Roberta Ann Dunbar at the University of North Carolina, Frank Tirro at Yale University, and Ronald G. Watt at Duke University.

There are a number of reasons for English precedence in industrial development. By the early eighteenth century Englishmen (with the Dutch) had the highest standard of living in the world. After approximately a century of applying innovative techniques, English agricultural producers were able to supply food cheaply and in abundance while still making a profit. This efficiency in agriculture also liberated a large percentage of the working population for other pursuits. English government compared with continental monarchies was inexpensive, and the low tax burden left most of the money in the pockets of those who earned it. There was consequently a good deal of money available for investment and consumption. Moreover, whereas absolutist monarchies on the continent regulated economic life closely, productive enterprise in England was relatively free; personal initiative and experimentation were encouraged. Finally, in the coming age

Excerpted from Mary Ann Witt et al., *The Humanities: Cultural Roots and Continuities*, 2nd ed., vol. 2, *The Humanities and the Modern World*. Copyright ©1985 by Houghton Mifflin Company. Used with permission.

of the machine, England was particularly favored with its enormous deposits of a cheap fuel, coal.

The breakthrough in industrialism first came in cotton, a cloth industry that, compared with wool or silk, was very new. Because of its low cost relative to that of wool and silk, the market for cotton cloth was large, and it happened that cotton could be worked more easily by machine than by hand. By the late eighteenth century the demand for cotton cloth both in England and abroad was such that the raw material came into short supply. [American inventor] Eli Whitney's cotton gin remedied the major bottleneck in production of raw cotton, and the plantation economy of the American South soared from the 1790s on.

The mechanization of cotton production encouraged invention and investment in other areas of the economy. By the end of the eighteenth century the English had developed a relatively efficient steam engine, were able to mine coal and manufacture steel in impressive quantities, and were increasingly utilizing new chemical discoveries for industrial purposes. The nineteenth century in Europe was marked by the continued progress of British industry and by the desperate efforts of continental and American competitors to imitate and catch up with Britain.

Social Effects of Industrialization

The social consequences of industrialization were enormous. Within decades hundreds of thousands of workers moved into the industrial centers, overwhelming the capacity of the cities to absorb them. Shanty towns grew up on the outskirts where the new workers lived in crowded unsanitary conditions. The machines not only demanded regimentation of work but also reduced the need for skill or physical force. Especially in the cloth industry most operations involved in mechanized production could be performed by children, who were cheaper to hire than adults. By the middle 1820s a small boy working two looms could produce fifteen times more than an adult laborer working by hand.

Unable to support the family even with both mother and father working, parents were forced to send their children into the factories. Children four and five years of age worked from twelve to sixteen hours, six days a week, for pennies. Often forbidden to sit down during their hours of work, they were subject to the brutality of the overseer for the slightest infraction. In the case of babies too young to work, desperate parents, unable to pay for babysitters, resorted to "Mother's Helper" to drug the baby from early morning until late at night when they returned home. In the seething tenements of workers' quarters, twisted bodies and early death were common.

An Interview with a Father of Child Laborers

Included in the report of the "Committee on Factory Children's Labour," 1831–1832, was the following interview with a certain Samuel Coulson.

At what time in the morning, in the brisk [busy] time, did those girls go to the mills?

In the brisk time, for about six weeks, they have gone at 3 o'clock in the morning, and ended at 10, or nearly half past at night.

What intervals were allowed for rest or refreshment during those nineteen hours of labour?

Breakfast a quarter of an hour, and dinner half an hour, and drinking a quarter of an hour.

Was any of that time taken up in cleaning the machinery?

They generally had to do what they call dry down; sometimes this took the whole of the time at breakfast or drinking, and they were to get their dinner or breakfast as they could; if not, it was brought home.

Had you not great difficulty in awakening your children to this excessive labour?

Yes, in the early time we had them to take up asleep and shake them, when we got them on the floor to dress them, before we could get them off to their work; but not so in the common hours.

Supposing they had been a little too late, what would have been the consequence during the long hours?

They were quartered in the longest hours, the same as in the shortest time.

What do you mean by quartering?

A quarter was taken off.

If they had been how much too late?

Five minutes.

What was the length of time they could be in bed during those long hours?

It was near 11 o'clock before we could get them into bed after getting a little victuals, and then at morning my mistress used to stop up all night, for fear that we could not get them ready for the time; sometimes we have gone to bed, and one of us generally awoke.

What time did you get them up in the morning?

In general me or my mistress got up at 2 o'clock to dress them.

So that they had not above four hours' sleep at this time?

No, they had not.

For how long together was it?

About six weeks it held; it was only done when the throng was very much on; it was not often that.

The common hours of labour were from 6 in the morning till half-past eight at night?

Yes.

With the same intervals for food?

Yes, just the same.

Were the children excessively fatigued by this labour?

Many times; we have cried often when we have given them the little victualling we had to give them; we had to shake them, and they have fallen to sleep with the victuals in their mouths many a time.

Had any of them any accident in consequence of this labour?

Yes, my eldest daughter when she went first there; she had been about five weeks, and used to fettle the frames when they were running, and my eldest girl agreed with one of the others to fettle hers that time, that she would do her work; while she was learning more about the work, the overlooker came by and said, "Ann, what are you doing there?" she said, "I am doing it for my companion, in order that I may know more about it," he said, "Let go, drop it this minute," and the cog caught her forefinger nail, and screwed it off below the knuckle, and she was five weeks in Leeds Infirmary.

Has she lost that finger?

It is cut off at the second joint.

Were her wages paid during that time?

As soon as the accident happened the wages were totally stopped; indeed, I did not know which way to get her cured, and I do not know how it would have been cured but for the Infirmary.

Were the wages stopped at the half-day?

She was stopped a quarter of a day; it was done about four o'clock.

Did this excessive term of labour occasion much cruelty also?

Yes, with being so very much fatigued the strap was very frequently used.

Have any of your children been strapped?

Yes, every one.

Despite the terrible conditions of life suggested in reports like this, many historians maintain that, on the whole, conditions of the laboring poor in England improved with the Industrial Revolution. Many of the poor preferred the urban slums to those in the rural districts where their misery was compounded by chronic underemployment and hunger.

Changes in Beliefs About Government's Role in Protecting Workers

Indeed, while no doubt regretting the sufferings of the poor, an important group of English and continental thinkers called the liberals believed that these were minor evils compared with the greater good attained by industrialization. Espousing the Enlightenment values of liberty and equality, thinkers like Adam Smith and David Ricardo argued that there was a kind of law of human nature: if individuals were allowed to follow their own self-enlightened interest, the general good and liberty of all would best be served. The state should interfere as little as possible with the exercise of individual judgment, aside from keeping order and protecting property; the economy as well as other aspects of society should be in the control of private citizens. Wages would always tend to the subsistence level because, when workers rise above this, they have more children who devour the surplus, thus forcing the family income down again. However, in a free society, the liberals argued optimistically, individuals with initiative have the opportunity of leaving this condition and joining the ranks of the successful.

Although thinkers of this stamp violently opposed it, public opinion in the 1830s and 1840s finally forced the English government to pass legislation to remedy the worst abuses. As the continent came to industrialize, government there, too, stepped in to ameliorate the condition of workers to a degree. Some of the major proponents of this legislation belonged to a new breed of liberals. These thinkers had come to realize that, if liberty and equality were truly the goals of a society, the major threats to those principles did not come so much from the government as from private pressures. A worker's freedom was essentially limited to starving or accepting the conditions offered him by an employer. The role of government, as they began to conceive it, was that of a mediator, which through its laws would prevent the oppression of one individual by another. The ideal remained, as earlier, to foster individual freedom, but the experience of the first fifty years of industrialism had shown that, paradoxically, freedom had in certain respects to be restricted by legislation in order to maximize it for everyone. The new liberals also moved gradually to the position that the lower classes must also be given the vote. Political power was not, as for earlier liberals, a privilege achieved by the successful; rather, it was a basic right. Thus, the newer liberalism endeavored to incorporate the workers into the establishment.

Life in Victorian Prisons

Philip Priestley

Using the biographies of ordinary prisoners and the records of prison authorities, Philip Priestley examines life in Victorian prison cells. Prisons were built for a system called separate, which meant solitary confinement for every prisoner. The system requires inmates to adjust to sparse, dark cells, cold, and absence of human interaction. Philip Priestley has been involved in prison rehabilitation and has written curriculum and self-help books. He is the author of *New Careers, Justice for Juveniles, Social Skills and Personal Problem Solving*, and *Community of Scapegoats*.

The cell was to be the physical hub of the new prisoner's unfamiliar future. Its size and shape and purposes were the products of a bitter historical battle between two ideas: between separate confinement and silent association, from which the advocates of separation had at first emerged victorious during the 1830s. Their victory was celebrated in the construction of a government penitentiary at Pentonville in 1842, and in the rash of imitative building that spread across the country in the years that followed.

To the prisoner who knew nothing of this history, the cell was no more than a special kind of room. 'Imagine to yourself,' we are invited by Frederick Brocklehurst, 'a whitewashed cube 7 feet by 13, with a barred window of ground glass at one end, and a black painted door at the other, and you can form some idea of the dimensions and appearance of a prison cell.'

Brocklehurst belonged to the recently formed Independent Labour Party. Its Manchester members insisted on ex-

Excerpted from Philip Priestley, *Victorian Prison Lives: English Prison Biography, 1830–1914* (London: Methuen, 1985). Copyright ©1985 by Philip Priestley. Reprinted by permission of Methuen and Co.

ercising rights of assembly and free speech on the Boggart Clough, an historic open space and popular meeting place in Manchester. For defying a local order banning meetings on the Clough Brocklehurst, together with a colleague, Leonard Hall, was committed to the borough gaol for one calendar month in 1896. Strangeways was a local prison, in whose construction 'the model of Pentonville' was 'pretty closely adhered to . . . Colonel Jebb having had the approval of all the designs'. The intention, as in all these designs, was to create what a penitentiary chaplain called 'a noble building—the very reverse of gloomy' and such as to show at once to a man that he was entering 'a prison of instruction and of probation rather than a gaol of oppressive punishment'.

A quite different message was spelled out by the cellular arrangements at Chatham, Dartmoor, Portland and Portsmouth, where men were sent to complete their sentences of penal servitude labouring on large-scale public works projects. Jabez Balfour's cell at Portland was 'nothing but a small corrugated iron kennel with a stone or slate floor . . . seven feet long, seven feet high, and four feet broad'. It reminded one gentleman of 'a small second-class state room on board an emigrant ship'. Convict 77, a person of humbler station in life, thought his 'smaller than the third class compartment of a railway carriage'. But whatever their social origins, many convicts saw the cell as a dismal terminus. 'Oh, don't put me in there,' cried Mrs Maybrick, 'I cannot bear it.' Her cry was one that echoed and re-echoed around the stone walls of the prison house. Helen Gordon heard it years later at Strangeways: 'a scream of horror—re-iterated, imploring—rising in notes of entreaty—"Don't put me in there," over and over again, until the voice changes from entreaty to impotent anger till the limit is reached—there is terror of the thing feared, and the terror of lost self-control'. Mrs Maybrick's entreaty fell on deaf ears. 'For answer', she says, 'the warder took me roughly by the shoulder, gave me a push and shut the door.'

The Lighting and Signaling Systems

Inside the locked cell, the first impression was one of darkness; the gloom in Mrs Maybrick's was relieved only 'by the dim light of a window that was never cleaned'. 'Outside, the day may be blue and gold,' said Oscar Wilde, 'but the light that creeps down through the thickly-muffled glass of the small iron-barred window beneath which one sits is grey and niggard. It is always twilight in one's cell, as it is always midnight in one's heart.' Reading, where Wilde was held, was a local gaol reserved for not so serious offenders; even less light penetrated to the penal servitude prisoners. 'Daylight never entered' Convict 77's cell at Portland, 'except through the aperture under the door,' and at Dartmoor the limited illumination came via a 'narrow window of thick rough plate glass' which gave onto the *interior* of the prison. Only 'immediately close to the window' was there 'light enough to see anything distinctly'. Until quite a late date the Dartmoor cells were lit at night by candles, but at Millbank the standard equipment was a 'small gas-jet protruding from the wall about 4 feet from the ground'. The unauthorized use of the gas for self-asphyxiation, and of the jet itself for suspending nooses, led to its reinstallation behind a 'tiny thick ribbed glass window, inserted in the wall outside'.

But if light was supplied through these openings—'as grudgingly as food,'—there were others through which generous measures of supervision were possible: 'alongside the door was a loophole similar to those usually seen in old castles for arrow slits, and in fortified outworks for musketry firing. . . . Anyone walking along the corridor could see at once the inmate of the cell and what he was doing, and had a full view of him both when at work or in bed.' Another singular device for keeping watch on prisoners was 'the eye that never slept'. This was a 'cunningly contrived spy hole' in the centre of the cell door, sometimes made to resemble a human eye, 'complete in every detail, pupil, iris, eyelashes, eyebrow, etc. It was not only painted but carved, to add to the realism of the thing.' 'No matter how you would place yourself in your cell, standing, sitting, or lying down, that cursed eye seemed to follow you'. Below the spy-hole, in some cells but not all, there was 'a trap door, eighteen inches by twelve, cut in the door itself', which could be opened only from the outside, and used both for passing things through and for inspection.

The slits and spy-holes were meant to be looked through in one direction only, and in a way that robbed the observed prisoner of privacy, but other contrivances were provided which allowed him or her to communicate with staff in the main body of the building. In some cells there was to be found 'a thin lath of wood, 3 foot long, 2½ inches wide, and ¼ inch thick; one half painted on both sides black, and the other bright red.' One-who-has-endured-it 'was at a loss' to understand the purpose of this 'mysterious wand' until an officer explained, 'When I wished to speak to a warder for any purposes, I was to put out the red end from the inspection aperture, to cause him to come to me.'

More mechanically advanced was the 'gong in the corridor, the handle of which is just inside, and to the right of the door'; 'when the gong is rung, a wooden slip attached to the handle just outside the door, is projected into the corridor, having on it the number of the cell in bold characters, and should the warder happen to be aside when the gong sounds, his attention is called to the sign directly he enters the corridor'.

Two kinds of distress most commonly prompted recourse to these signals: sickness of all sorts, and an urgent need to use the closets. If the prisoner was fortunate, his 'signal was immediately attended to, and he was carefully let out'. On this point, the members of the 1879 Penal Servitude Commission were assured by 'officers that ample facilities are given' for men wishing to go to the closets. But after 'personal inquiries made of some prisoners at Pentonville' they came to the conclusion that they were 'not quite satisfied that there is no ground'—note the delicate double negative—'for complaints in this respect'. . . .

Suffering Cold and Stench

In the real world of the cell, one of the most pervasive causes both of sleeplessness and of bodily suffering in general was the cold. 'Oh, Rossa,' a Fenian comrade groaned to him one day, 'the cold is killing me.' Rossa was already only too familiar with 'the horrible sensation of cold in the morning in those cheerless Pentonville cells. It was not so much the intensity of the cold, for probably the cold was not so intense, as the abominable feeling of always waking cold, and the hopeless and helpless feeling that there was no prospect of going to sleep again, and no possible way of getting warm till the bell rang and you were allowed to get up and put on your clothes.' 'For two months' George Jacob Holyoake 'was never warm.' William Barrow spent the night 'shivering in bed.' And so did anarchist David Nicoll, because whereas the 'plank beds at Pentonville are solid, the planks nailed closely together; at some jails there is a space of an inch between every plank through which the cold air can creep.'

Elsewhere, 'any water spilt took days to dry up,' or 'frequently froze . . . overnight'; 'hands and feet were covered with chilblains'; fingers 'had large cracks in them.' Helen Gordon, a suffragette, suffered from a coldness that was 'gradually penetrating– every afternoon the prisoner knows that an hour after exercise her body will become gradually petrified.' And at Portland 'it was so cold in winter that the very warders of the night patrol used to make their rounds of the peep-holes with blankets wrapped about their heads and shoulders. But if *they* suffered from the cold,' asks Balfour, 'what was it to us prisoners?'

Complaints about the cold at Pentonville were ironic in view of the efforts that had been made in its design and construction to avoid extremes of temperature. The first report of the commissioners for the prison, published in 1843, was less than two pages long, but room was found in it to boast that 'The perfect ventilation of the cells, and the means of maintaining an equable and proper temperature, have been successfully accomplished, and cannot fail to have a beneficial effect on the health of the prisoners,' and all 'at a cost of less than one half-penny per cell for 24 hours . . . in the coldest weather of the current winter'. Hepworth Dixon was predictably moved to criticize 'the costly extravagances of the model cell, with its scientific ventilation—its elaborately adjusted temperature, kept at the nicest point of comfort by means of valves, which let in warm air or cool air as the case may require.'

Many prisoners from 1849 onwards were confined, however, not in 'model' cells but in the corrugated iron 'kennels' of the convict establishments. Ticket-of-leave-man for instance had a 'vagabond' next to him who was 'not only a moral but a physical nuisance; the effluvium which was exhaled from his body . . . found its way through the chinks of my cells and disgusted me'. And if men were obliged to make use of their pots in the night, the results were equally offensive: 'when an occurrence of this kind happens, which, owing to the nature of the food, it does very frequently, the fact is made known by a nasal telegram, almost over the whole ward, announcing an addition to the already over-tainted atmosphere.' 'You grow gradually sensible,' wrote the writer of *A Letter from a Convict*, 'as the morning draws on, that you are in the midst of a great cesspool. I speak strongly, but with truth.' It was a general complaint, due to the fact that 'there was no adequate means of escape for the foul air that collected in the central hall of the prison, and the smell there of a morning was enough to knock you down.' 'It is no uncommon thing', claims Oscar Wilde, 'for warders, when they come in the morning out of the fresh air and open and inspect each cell, to be violently sick.' At Liverpool, the stench was 'unbearable, especially in the morning. To keep down putrid fevers—indeed to render the corridors at all passable—it is found necessary to burn chloride of lime in them incessantly, as well as in the day-rooms and eating rooms.'

Prisoners Invent Methods to Communicate

Besides the cold and the smells, the killing thing about solitary was, of course, the absence of ordinary human contact. The 'scattered words' spoken by Fenian Michael Davitt during his first ten months at Millbank 'would not occupy twenty minutes to repeat.' Stuart Wood 'craved for human companionship . . . for the sound of a human voice not raised to threaten, but just to utter the most absurd commonplace; to catch and respond to the twisted, frightened smile of understanding that springs from suffering endured in common.'

In the absence of verbal contact, other means were tried. 'A soldier waiting trial next door' to Dr McCook Weir 'kept knocking all day, and frequently far into the night. In fact, he and his next door neighbour kept up a dumb conversation in this manner, and a double rap for "goodnight" was almost as distinct and impressive as the words themselves.' The noise of these knockings could be heard all over the prison: 'the rappings, and the mysterious code by which the prisoners communicate, sound through the building like an imprisoned woodpecker tapping to be free.'

It was in fact possible for 'telegraphing' to be 'carried on between two prisoners though four or five cells might intervene—that is, provided the fellow receiving the message pressed his ear against the wall, making, as it were an airtight connection.' Also, there was a time when 'the W.C. system used to be the favourite avenue of communication. Emptying the bowl of its water, they converted the refuse pipes into speaking tubes. By this morally disgusting and physically dangerous means a prisoner used to carry on regular conversations with any one or all of the other seven prisoners connected with the drainpipe of his cell.' 'Under the pail system', says Brocklehurst with relief, 'this is done away with now.'

In the penal servitude prisons at Chatham, Portland and Dartmoor none of these ingenious expedients was necessary; the fabrication of the compartments out of thin corrugated iron made cell to-cell conversation a simple matter of convenience: 'a man with good ears can listen to his neighbour's yarns even without the aid of a "chat-hole." It is the custom however, for prisoners to bore a small hole through the partition, near to the ground, through which the chat takes place.' The one prisoner lies down on the ground and talks and listens, with his mouth or ear to the chat-hole; his neighbour sits at the window, which opens onto the landing along which the officer in charge walks. If he approaches, a knock from the watcher causes the chat to be suspended until he has passed, when it commences again.'

An alternative mode of communication, albeit a slow and non-reciprocal one, was to scratch messages on the cell tins. The meal tins in which food was brought to the cells provided a mobile medium of communication because they were not personal to each prisoner but part of a common stock which circulated daily. Some men simply scratched their names on them; 'Black Prince, King Theodore, Swansea Pete, Black Jim, Poor Bill from George Street'. Some of the specimens collected by Brocklehurst from tins in Strangeways reflected essentially corporeal concerns: 'Wouldn't you like a pork pie?' 'Plenty of beef and beer for the brothers Loney on the 29th of August.' Most often though, the messages of this genre consisted of simple but cheerful exhortation. O'Donovan Rossa 'came to read "cheer up"—"cheer up", so often' that he felt himself 'growing sympathetic towards the writers'. 'It is perhaps', concludes Brocklehurst, 'the strangest postal system extant. The warders are the postmen, and, instead of postage stamps, the "broad arrow" is the only sign of Her Majesty's approval.'

Finding Solace in Pets

Denied proper human intercourse, there were prisoners who sought solace instead from an unlikely quarter—the indigenous fauna of the prison cell. Chicago May made overtures to some flies, and 'tried to make friends with a couple of these insects, which ventured into my prison. If only I could have had some sort of an animal to care for and love, it would have been of the greatest help in keeping my mind occupied.' George Bidwell 'never destroyed any kind of insect' which found its way into his cell—'even when mosquitoes lit on my face I always let them have their fill undisturbed, and felt well repaid by getting a glimpse of them as they flew, and with the music of their buzzing.' Manchester Merchant, on the other hand, had befriended 'a tremendous spider' which he kept in his soap box; 'I then made a raid upon the other occupants of my cell (the flies), which as I caught I deposited in the soap box. Such was the manner in which I relieved my distressed condition for some days, until fly hunting became monotonous.'

Prisoners did have more acceptable pets. Michael Davitt had a blackbird at Portland, 'through the kindness of the governor.' 'He would stand upon my breast as I lay in bed in the morning and awaken me from sleep. He would perch on my plate and share my porridge. Towards evening he would resort to his perch, the post of the iron bedstead, and there remain, silent and still, till the dawning of another day.' Davitt's blackbird was also the occasion of his prison writing. 'One evening as "Joe" sat upon his perch, it occurred to me to constitute him chairman and audience of a course of lectures: and with him constantly before me as the representative of my fellow creatures, I jotted down what I have substantially reproduced in the following pages.' Perhaps appropriately, George Bidwell had a rat 'that was easily taught,' and he trained it 'to stand upright on his feet, with his head up like a soldier.' So pleased was George with his account of this friendly and talented rodent, that he persuaded brother Austin to include it in *his* memoirs as well—word for word the same, and unacknowledged. But these objects of affection also created possibilities for the display of other and less attractive human emotions. A prisoner at Portland 'was greatly wrapped up in a mouse that nestled in his breast by day, and careered about his cell by night. Happening one day to leave it behind him in his cell as he went out to work, the warder, with stupid cruelty, drowned the mouse. Its master was heart-broken, sat moodily in his cell and refused to do a stroke of work. The governor himself tried to soothe him, but he was inconsolable, and gave warning that if he ever met that warder he would murder him!' Basil Thomson says that 'although it is contrary to the rules for pets to be kept, the warders used to look the other way when mice were in question. I had long observed that pet birds and mice kept violent men out of mischief.'

Resignation

All of these methods for combating the ordeal of solitary confinement were at best partial ones. In order to cope more effectively with their sentences, in order 'to get through with the minimum of mental and physical injury,' prisoners had to turn in on themselves to find the resources they required. One well-used route to survival lay through a straightforward acceptance of the situation. 'Satisfied, after a time, that what is cannot be helped, that no anxiety on their part can undo the past or affect the future, they put aside all thought both of past and future, and live only for the present, making the best of everything. . . . This power of living for the present seems to be possessed by all alike.' It was certainly possessed by Mrs Maybrick; she called it 'the opiate of acquiescence . . . the keeping of my sensibilities dulled as near as possible to the level of the mere animal state which the Penal Code, whether intentionally or otherwise, inevitably brings about.' But beneath these outward shows of conformity there was usually concealed a mixture of private responses. 'As he grows accustomed to imprisonment,' says an anonymous convict, 'much as a woman may become accustomed to being kicked, a quiet, immeasurable contempt for legality and "authorities" and "regulations" and "discipline" dominates and never leaves him.'

Political prisoners were more likely to be sustained, not by personal hatred, but by their political convictions; a feeling that they suffered in a noble cause; and a sense of distance from the common criminals amongst whom they were condemned to pass so many years of their lives. 'I kept myself a free man in prisons,' insists O'Donovan Rossa; 'while they had my body bound in chains, I felt that I owed them no allegiance, that I held my mind unfettered—that I was *not* their slave.'

There was also for long-sentence and repeated offenders, a process of habituation which softened and made the privations of imprisonment seem, if not more acceptable, then at least less intolerable. Stuart Wood says: 'I wept in the shadows of my cell and longed to die; but as the weeks crept on I wept less and less; the process of hardening had set in.'

Chapter 4

Ideas That Changed Values, Views, and Events

Turning | Points
IN WORLD HISTORY

Bentham's Utilitarianism

Richard D. Altick

Richard D. Altick explains Jeremy Bentham's theory of utilitarianism, a social philosophy that dominated the thought and practice of the Victorian middle class. Bentham and his ideas influenced government administration and the justice system throughout the Victorian period. Richard D. Altick was a professor of English at Ohio State University in Columbus. He is the author of several books, including *The Scholar Adventurer, The Art of Literary Research*, and *Victorian Studies in Scarlet*.

Two ideologies molded early and mid-Victorian social and cultural life: Utilitarianism and Evangelicalism. . . . Utilitarianism in its practical applications had its maximum impact two decades later. But both left their ineradicable imprint upon the whole of the Victorian period. . . .

Utilitarianism, the secular member of the pair, is also called "Benthamism," a virtual synonym, but in strict usage referring to the pure form of the philosophy held by the doctrinaire enthusiasts who gathered about Jeremy Bentham. Another alternate name, most often used to designate the creed of the Benthamite members of Parliament and their supporters, is "Philosophic Radicalism." In ordinary practice, all three terms were used almost interchangeably, as they are in modern historical writing and will be in these pages. Most broadly and loosely applied, they refer to the socio-economic-political ideology and set of values held by the Victorian middle class—to the entrepreneurial mentality which dominated the period and adopted these tenets to rationalize its actions and aims, habits and prejudices.

By whatever name it is called, Utilitarianism was a hybrid

Excerpted from *Victorian People and Ideas: A Companion for the Modern Reader of Victorian Literature*, by Richard D. Altick. Copyright ©1973 by W.W. Norton & Company, Inc. Reprinted by permission of W.W. Norton & Company, Inc.

philosophy partaking equally of eighteenth-century French rationalism and eighteenth-century English materialism. It was introduced into the mainstream of post-Napoleonic thought by Jeremy Bentham, a rich, amiable, eccentric bachelor whose lifelong occupation was devising master syntheses of economic, political, and social thought. . . .

The Utilitarian Philosophy

The tag phrase indelibly associated with Utilitarianism, "the greatest happiness for the greatest number," was borrowed from Joseph Priestley, the late-eighteenth-century Unitarian theologian and discoverer of oxygen. Its Hobbesian[1] assumption was that self-interest is the prime, in fact the only, motivation behind human conduct, and that the achievement of pleasure and the avoidance of pain alone constitute that self-interest. It subscribed, as Nassau Senior, a leading exponent and apologist, put it with disarming candor, to "an arbitrary definition of man, as a being who invariably does that by which he may obtain the greatest amount of necessaries, conveniences and luxuries, with the smallest amount of labour and physical self-denial with which they can be obtained in the existing state of knowledge." Utilitarianism was, therefore, wholly hedonistic; it made no allowance for the promptings of conscience, or for the humane impulses of which the Shaftesburyan ethic[2] had made so much a century earlier—the forces of generosity, mercy, compassion, self-sacrifice, love. Benthamite ethics had nothing to do with Christian morality.

The only determinant of personal or social action, in any given situation, was the demonstrated preponderance of "good" results over "bad" results. The demonstration was mathematical, by means of what, in the Benthamite argot, was known as the "felicific calculus" or "moral arithmetic."[3]

1. based on the political philosophy of Thomas Hobbes, who advocated absolute monarchy as a means of controlling the inherently selfish nature of human beings
2. based on the ethic of politician Anthony Ashley Cooper Shaftesbury 3. Had it been available to them, the Benthamites would have happily fed all their questions of moral and social choice into a digital computer. They almost had one. A single-minded contemporary named Charles Babbage spent sixty years and £20,000 of his fortune as well as £17,000 of government money trying to perfect a calculator, and he nearly succeeded. Parts of the two machines he constructed are in the Science Museum in South Kensington, London.

The formula for deciding whether or not to adopt a given choice of action, be it an individual deed or a law affecting millions, was simplicity itself:

$$\text{PLEASURE} \qquad vs. \qquad \text{PAIN}$$
$$a + b + c + d + e + f \qquad\qquad a + b + c + d + e + f$$

where the letters represent six categories of anticipated effects: intensity, duration, certainty, propinquity (the closeness of the effect to the person(s) involved), fecundity (the degree to which the primary effect will be followed by secondary effects of a similar kind and extent), and purity (the absence of undesirable side-effects). These six qualities were to be taken into account in deciding any individual's best course of action; when a body of people was involved, a seventh quantity, the number affected, was added to the computation. The "good" results, or pleasure (defined by Bentham as "*profit*, . . . or *convenience*, or *advantage*, *benefit*, *emolument*, *happiness*, and so forth"), were compared with the painful results ("*mischief*, or *inconvenience*, or *disadvantage*, or *loss*, or *unhappiness*, and so forth"). When the correct weightings were assigned each factor and the balance struck, the heavier side of the scale determined the action. The sole criterion was quantitative, the arithmetical relationship between units of "pleasure" and units of "pain." Neither the quality of the supposed effects nor the possibility that individuals might differ in their notion of happiness or the degree of their altruism affected the Benthamite calculation. Presumably every human being on earth prized nothing but material values. Nor was any account taken of the happiness of those who did not belong to the greatest number. They doubtless had to accept their sacrificial position on the scale's high beam with whatever disinterested resignation they could muster.

Utilitarianism Required Complete Representation

But how was a social group to decide what constituted the greatest happiness for the greatest number? The answer was government by a representative legislature. For this reason, the Benthamites advocated universal suffrage as well as the

John Stuart Mill Rejects Benthamism

Bentham inspired Victorian politician and philosopher John Stuart Mill to become a reformer. Later Mill rejected Benthamism, as the following excerpt explains.

[John Stuart Mill] describes how, from the age of fifteen when he first read Bentham, he had one object in life: 'to be a reformer of the world'. He was that peculiar product of the nineteenth century, a professional reformer; prepared to make reform an almost full-time occupation, a career, even a crusade. By dint of the agony of his own spiritual experience when he came to abandon the rigid creed of his father, he perceived the fallacy in Benthamism: its debased conception of human happiness as a mere arithmetical sum of physical pleasures. He learnt that happiness is a state of mind and being, a condition of spirit, and not the total result of merely seeking pleasure and avoiding pain. This discovery led him to revolutionize Benthamism, for the distinction between higher and lower pleasures undermined the whole basis of the materialist philosophy of utilitarianism: 'better Socrates dissatisfied', as he put it, 'than a fool satisfied'. His honest good sense rebelled against the notion that push-pin is as 'good' as poetry if it gives the same 'amount' of pleasure. From this fundamental change much else followed. It followed, for example, that human liberty means more than just leaving the individual alone to pursue his own selfish pleasures, and is a social pursuit of 'the greatest happiness of the greatest number' by deliberate and possibly coercive measures. It followed, too, that legislation must have a more positive function in society than Bentham had allowed: it must seek to enable men to exercise their natural capacities, use their talents, and develop their personalities, untrammelled by artificial legal impediments and evil economic conditions.

David Thomson, *England in the Nineteenth Century: 1814–1914*. Baltimore: Penguin, 1950.

five other Chartist[4] principles, all of which, as a matter of fact, Bentham had advocated. They regarded the First Reform Bill as an initial step toward the far-off day when Parliament would be an infallibly accurate mirror of the wisest wishes of all the people. But they recognized that, for the present, the voters and their elected representatives would be far from agreeing on the best course of action in a given situation. The felicific calculating machine was a sure guide only if it were accurately programmed, and it could be so programmed only if every man whose personal interests were fed into it knew what they really were and what relation they bore to the interests of society. That final insight into self-love vis-à-vis social welfare could come only with universal education, which would teach every man how to define his motives through the use of reason. Pending the comprehensive reconciliation of self and society, the carrot and stick had to be provided, as we will note later on, by legislation.

The system of moral arithmetic illustrates the pedantic dependence on formula, the confidence in the universal and uniform operation of theoretical moral forces, which ruled the Utilitarian mind. . . . Benthamism was Newtonian mechanism applied to ethics. It was not accidental, then, that Benthamism played an important role in the early history of what came to be known as social *science*. The claims to scientific authority which came to be advanced by the branches of learning gathered under that name were largely derived from the Benthamite assumption, supported by similar assumptions in contemporary French thought. . . .

The Results of Benthamism

What, apart from rationalizing the spirit of competitive capitalism, were the chief results of Benthamism? For one thing, the Utilitarians instigated many legislative and legal reforms. Jeremy Bentham's lifelong ambition had been the complete overhaul of English law and administration. . . .

Bentham's true monument is the whole of British (and to

---

4. The Chartist movement was a working-class movement advocating six principles that gave workers better representation and voting rights.

a great extent American) executive government, both central and local. He was a founder of the science of public administration, in which non-partisan, tenured professionals put legislation into action and constantly supervise the results. By centralizing in London governmental functions which had hitherto been performed, if at all, by local authorities—the new Poor Law administration was an initial case in point—the Benthamites achieved uniform standards and relatively efficient operation, insured by inspection. . . .

An equally important Benthamite reform, accomplished in close cooperation with the Evangelical humanitarians, was the revision of the penal code. In the third decade of the century, somewhere between 200 and 223 offenses were punishable by death. (The authorities differed on the exact number, as well they might, given the chaos of the statutes.) Although it is true that in such circumstances some juries were reluctant to convict and some judges reluctant to impose the full penalty—only one out of every seven offenders convicted on a capital charge was sentenced to hang, and only one out of every six capital sentences was carried out—the possibility of being hanged for a petty crime was very real. [Member of Parliament Samuel] Romilly had begun the slow work of prodding Parliament to trim the list as early as 1808, but his only immediate successes were in respect to pocket-picking (reduced to an offense punishable by transportation for life) and stealing cloth worth more than five shillings from a bleaching ground. After 1825, however, the rate picked up as a direct consequence of the Benthamites' growing influence, and the death penalty ceased to be attached to such crimes as forgery, housebreaking, stealing more than five shillings' worth of goods from a shop, sheep-stealing, damaging Westminster Bridge, and impersonating an inmate of the Chelsea Hospital for old and disabled soldiers. When Victoria became queen in 1837, only about ten capital crimes remained on the books.

But the most important Utilitarian legacy, and the most ironic in view of the popular identification of Benthamism with laissez faire, was the later Victorian trend toward state action. After the Manchester School and their intellectual mentors, the political economists, became a spent force, that side of the Benthamite creed which inclined toward enlarging the functions of government carried the day. Beginning with laws which were essentially protective (factory and public health acts, for example), the Benthamite spirit impelled successive Parliaments to move government into the additional role of provider. The state became responsible for the care of paupers, the destitute sick, lunatics; it set up schools where they were lacking and more closely supervised those that religious groups had established; it allowed local authorities to assess levies for public library buildings.

The Reform Acts Expanded Democracy

Norman Gash

Norman Gash argues that England gradually extended voting rights to a larger percentage of its people without clashes and violence among the social classes. Widespread unemployment among the workers had instigated reformers to organize in the early part of the century and in the 1840s. Consequently, politicians in Parliament passed the three reform acts of 1832, 1867, and 1884 because they feared losing their seats if they did not. Ironically, men who neither saw universal suffrage as an ideal nor trusted the illiterate to have power greatly expanded democracy even though still short of one person one vote. Norman Gash has been lecturer in modern history at the University of London and the University of Leeds in Yorkshire. He is the author of *Politics in the Age of Peel, Reaction and Reconstruction in England*, and *The Prime Ministers*.

It could be said with reasonable assurance that the three British nineteenth-century parliamentary reform acts established the broad principle of political democracy, leaving the finer details and the separate problem of female suffrage to be solved in the twentieth century by the legislation of 1918, 1928 and 1948.

What this generalization obscures, however, is the odd circumstance that the acts of 1832, 1867 and 1884 were passed by men who had no belief in the kind of political democracy implicit in universal suffrage and equality of electoral districts and who feared that the introduction of such a system would lead to the tyranny of the illiterate many over

Excerpted from "Parliament and Democracy in Britain: The Three Nineteenth-Century Reform Acts," from *Pillars of Government and Other Essays on State and Society c. 1770–1880*, by Norman Gash. Copyright ©1986 by Norman Gash. Reprinted by permission of the publisher, Edward Arnold.

the cultured few and of a numerical majority over the interests of minorities. For the greater part of the century the view of most politicians, and indeed of most educated people, was that the parliamentary vote was a trust and that the proper exercise of that trust called for a certain degree of education and social responsibility. Direct advocates of democracy—the radical reformers of the early part of the century, the Chartists[1] of the 1840s, and the extreme radicals of the age of [liberal William] Gladstone and [radical liberal MP Joseph] Chamberlain—never found much substantial support in the House of Commons.

There is another difficulty in accepting parliamentary reform as a smooth evolutionary process moving in successive stages towards a clearly defined goal. It is this. The three acts were carried by sharply contrasting methods and with sharply contrasting motives. . . .

This rather mundane reflection, if it is to be persuasive, needs to be established in a wider context. In 1831 it was clear that Lord [Charles] Grey's ministry (the first in which the Whigs as a party had held office for a quarter of a century) would have to bring forward a parliamentary reform measure if it was to survive. It had no guaranteed majority in either House of parliament and whatever it did, reform was certain to be raised early in the first session as one of the more important political issues. That the country generally had expectations of reform in the winter of 1830–1 is a commonplace. Yet it is worth noting that these expectations did not amount to a large degree of popular pressure until the cabinet had actually put their proposals before parliament. The contemporary charge that Grey first created public excitement by his bill and then used that excitement to justify the bill had an element of truth. . . .

Grey, of course, had been identified with the cause of parliamentary reform ever since the 1790s. The boldness of the 1831 bill, however, arose from his conviction that the reform question could only be settled for his generation if the pub-

1. a party of political reformers, chiefly workingmen who advocated universal suffrage, secret ballot, annual elections, payment of members of parliament, no property qualifications for members, and equal electoral districts

lic was offered as full and generous a measure as possible. Grey did not miscalculate the degree of public fervour he was able to rouse on behalf of his bill. What he underestimated was the degree of opposition he would encounter in parliament and from the king. . . .

The fierce contest over this first great reform of the electoral system not surprisingly produced a debate on fundamentals unmatched by any of its successors. It was, if one may use the phrase, the most 'principled' of the three nineteenth-century reform acts. It was fought out by a determined but unhappy cabinet which had gone too far to withdraw and a determined but often despairing opposition which was never able to offer a satisfactory alternative reform of their own. A paradox of the whole reform process was that the violence of the party battles was in inverse proportion to the extent of the actual changes proposed. Though no precise statistical calculation is possible, the probable result of the first Reform Act was to add about 300,000 to the existing electorate of about 500,000. Some estimates make the increase even smaller. In any case it was substantially less than in 1867 or 1884.

What caused the bitter debate in 1831–2 was, of course, the fact that this was the first successful attempt by any British government to carry out a major change in the electoral system. It was a crucial event because it set a precedent. Even so, what was intended by the cabinet was no more than a pruning, purification and enlargement of the existing electoral structure. The motive behind the measure was to strengthen the aristocratic constitution by widening its political basis. It was emphatically *not* a democratic measure. It was, as Lord Grey insisted, a conservative measure in the truest sense. . . .

The reform crisis of 1866–7 offers an almost total contrast to that of 1831–2. In the first place the great precedent had been set; the principle that it was proper for the legislature to review the system by which it was elected had been given respectability. Since 1832 in fact there had been many discussions in parliament on the need for further reform, if only to remove the imperfections left or even created by the act of 1832. Bills had been introduced by successive ministries of opposed political complexion in 1859 and 1860, only to founder on opposition or apathy. There did not, however, seem any strong feeling in the country on the question. . . .

What decided the timing of the next instalment of parliamentary reform were personal and party considerations. Of these the most important were the death in 1865 of the veteran Liberal prime minister Lord [Henry] Palmerston who had been a consistently conservative influence in domestic politics; the desire of the elderly Lord John Russell, who had personally introduced the 1831 reform bill (the only political triumph he had ever enjoyed), to atone for the frustrations of his subsequent career; and Gladstone's somnambulistic intuition that parliamentary reform was a popular cause he ought to take up.

The bill these two Liberal leaders produced, though moderate, split their party and brought about the entry to office of a Conservative ministry which lacked a majority in the House of Commons. . . .

The ultimate determination of the Conservative cabinet to pass a reform bill of their own was based less on what was happening in the country than on a calculation of party advantage. Three motives seem to have been operating. First, to settle the reform question now that it had been inconveniently raised by their opponents. Next, to remain in office as long as possible—a natural desire in a party which had been almost uniformly in opposition since 1846. Lastly, to demonstrate to the public that parliamentary reform was not a party issue and that the Conservatives as well as the Liberals were entitled to take up the question. To this must be added a determination, particularly strong in [Benjamin] Disraeli (the ministerial leader in the Commons) to discredit his personal rival Gladstone and keep the Liberal party divided. There was, on reflection, little to be lost and perhaps something to be gained by changing an electoral system which only once since 1832 had returned a Conservative majority—and that perhaps in exceptional circumstances.

Nevertheless, to embark on legislation without control of the legislature is a hazardous business. The cabinet's policy involved them in abrupt and sometimes contradictory changes in their detailed proposals and a steady surrender to chance majorities in the House of Commons. The end result was an act more extensive than had ever been intended by either party and one whose precise effects could only be a matter of guesswork. It resulted from a process of constant and extraordinary improvisation on the part of a few ministers. Their bemused followers scarcely knew to what they were committing themselves other than it was a measure recommended by their own leaders rather than one introduced by the hated Gladstone. . . .

In its final form a genuine household suffrage, freed from any restrictions such as the payment of rates, became the basis of the new borough[2] franchise. The practical results were startling. Over a million new voters were added to the electorate, representing for the whole United Kingdom an increase of 80 per cent and for England and Wales an increase of 88 per cent. The increase was all the more dramatic for being concentrated in the boroughs, where the electorate more than doubled. . . .

The character of the 1867 act, at once drastic and lopsided, made a further adjustment within the foreseeable future almost inevitable. The exclusion of the country dweller from the household franchise was logically indefensible; and the inadequacy of the 1867 redistribution of seats threw into sharper relief the steady growth of urban and industrial population outside the parliamentary boundaries of the borough constituencies. . . .

The third Reform Act has in general received far less scrutiny from historians than its two predecessors. Yet it was in many ways a remarkable measure. The delay in bringing it forward was its first curious feature. Certainly there was no great demand in the country for yet another instalment of electoral reform. . . . The justification for Gladstone's bill lay in wider considerations—the unbalanced state of the franchise and the changed attitude of Victorian public opinion towards another downward extension of the electorate.

2. a town that sends a representative to parliament

Whatever their private misgivings, politicians now had to show a proper deference to the fashionable view that the mass of the British people had shown themselves worthy of political responsibility. What Gladstone called 'the enfranchisement of capable citizens' became a piece of conventional wisdom against which it was morally indecent and politically dangerous to argue—a political cliché elevated above rational criticism. Even the Conservative peers in the House of Lords only threw out Gladstone's first bill on the argument that it should have been accompanied by a suitable measure for redistributing the constituencies. The real parliamentary struggle did not come therefore over the extension of the franchise, even though the bill as eventually passed added another 80 per cent to the already enlarged electorate created by the 1867 act. It came over what was to the parliamentary parties the more important tactical issue of the new parliamentary constituencies.

A second oddity about the act was that the whole interparty dispute was settled rapidly, secretly, and authoritatively by the two party leaders, Gladstone and Lord [Robert] Salisbury. They then pushed the bill through parliament in a quite astonishing demonstration of party discipline—or, as some might unkindly say, party subservience. The House of Commons, which had debated at such length the 1831-2 bills, and almost dictated the form of the 1867 act, was in 1884-5 little more than a rubber-stamp. What counted were the decisions arrived at privately by six men, of whom only three really mattered—Gladstone, Lord Salisbury, and the Liberal electoral expert [Sir Charles] Dilke. . . .

Certainly Gladstone's insistence, against all precedent, on a unified reform measure for the whole United Kingdom, was in sharp contrast to the tepid and conventional remarks he made about the 'peasantry' of England and Wales (whereby he meant the landless rural labourers) as 'capable citizens' who should now be admitted to the franchise. It was precisely the inclusion of Ireland in the government's bill which aroused greatest unease in the Liberal ranks. There had been no mandate for it at any of the party conferences and it produced the most powerful and prophetic passages of the reform debates in parliament. . . .

As for Lord Salisbury, the considerations which governed his actions were almost entirely tactical. Though he did not like the extension of the suffrage, he knew it could not be prevented and as party leader he declined to tie his followers to a losing cause. What Gladstone had oratorically described in 1866 as 'the great social forces which move onward in their might and majesty' could not be stopped in 1884 if the Liberal government of the day was determined to advance their progress. . . .

The moral to be drawn from these three reform episodes is not perhaps an elevated one. In all three crises party and personal advantages played a considerable part: an underly-

---

The Reform Act of 1832 Excludes Women

On November 5, 1832, the newspaper Observer *reported an incident in which a woman made a claim to vote, but was denied. The report highlighted the reality that women were not yet allowed the same voting rights as men.*

At the Court of Revision for Middlesex, held at Stepney, on Monday, it appeared by the list of St. Anne's Limehouse that a lady had made a claim to vote. She had paid her shilling, the overseers inserted her name in the list, and then objected to it.

Mr. Palk, the barrister said that the legislature had not enfranchised the ladies (a laugh). A friend of the lady said she was a most zealous reformer; that during the discussion on that important measure she debated the question at every tea party she attended (laughter); and that she was an advocate for universal suffrage, and vote by ballot (laughter); and that she had a right to participate in the blessings of a measure which she had lent a willing hand, and an active tongue to promote (laughter). Mr. Palk regretted his inability to increase the lady's political privileges, and trusted that she would not visit her displeasure upon him, but direct it against the legislature (a laugh). He struck her name out of the list.

Marion Miliband, ed., *The Observer of the Nineteenth Century: 1791–1901.* London: Longmans, Green & Co., 1966.

ing one in 1831–2, a dominant one in 1866–7, and a large one in 1884–5. Yet one must distinguish between motives and consequences. British political evolution in the nineteenth century has incurred the reproach that democratic reform came too slowly and lagged behind social progress. There is much to support this view. Large as the additions to the electorate had been between 1832 and 1884, they still left Britain with something perceptibly short of full democracy. Only two adult males in three in England and Wales, three out of five in Scotland, five out of ten in Ireland, had the vote. It was the second, third and fifth decades of the present century, within the lifetime of many still living, which saw the establishment of the principle of one man, one vote, together with the admission of women to the franchise on equal terms with men, which is commonly held to mark the perfected political democracy.

The first three reform acts now regarded as milestones along the road to that achievement were then no more than—and were intended by their authors to be no more than—modifications of the traditional pre-1832 system. . . .

Yet there is a case also for the contrary view: that this slow and piecemeal approach towards democracy proceeded at least as fast as, if not faster than, social development. Much of the conventional justification among late-Victorian politicians for extensions of the franchise rested on little more than a string of comfortable assumptions. They talked of 'the respectable working-man' (to mention the disrespectable 'residuum' soon became unfashionable), of 'capable citizens' (with little attempt to define 'capability'), of 'trusting the people' (though they did not say with what). This vocabulary was based on not much evidence other than the absence of violent popular disorders after the middle of the century (with Ireland always the admitted exception) and on the practical continuation in power of an aristocratically dominated ruling class. It was this apparently remarkable social stability, even more striking when contrasted with the continent of Europe, which made it possible for each of the two great political parties in turn to propose, or at least not vociferously oppose, substantial additions to the electorate on which they both depended for parliamentary office. . . .

It would in fact be difficult to show that the newly en-franchised masses had either exhibited their fitness for the vote or were qualified for its exercise on any previously ac-cepted criteria. Nor did the rise of a cheap, sensational na-tional newspaper press under such new-style proprietors as [Alfred] Harmsworth Northcliffe hold out much encourage-ment for the future. Robert Lowe's famous remark after the 1867 legislation, that 'we must educate our masters' (more accurately 'compel our future masters to learn their letters') applied with even more force to the 1884 act. The first com-pulsory education act was passed in 1870, three years *after* the second Reform Act had created a working-class majority in the boroughs. In the rural areas the early inefficiencies of the educational system and the notorious difficulties of en-forcing attendance of country children needed for small jobs on farms, made it unlikely that the new electorate was much affected by formal state education until the generation after 1900. One of the more reflective British prime ministers, Stanley Baldwin, who had been born in the year of the sec-ond Reform Act and had watched all this process as he grew up, said in 1928 that 'democracy has arrived at a gallop in England and I feel all the time that it is a race for life. Can we educate them before the crash comes?'

Even so, there was probably some advantage in the course taken by parliamentary reform in Victorian Britain, narrow, selfish, short-sighted and muddled though the process had been. It is often a charge against aristocratic or oligarchic so-cieties that they rarely surrender power until they are forced and that then it is too late for the concession to produce any benefits. In an oblique fashion the British reform acts, spe-cially those of 1867 and 1884, had the merit of coming when there was no particular demand for them by those who stood to be enfranchised. As Professor Norman McCord has sug-gested in one of the more perceptive articles on the nineteenth-century reform acts which have appeared in re-cent years, not only were those acts typically English in their untidy 'muddling-through', on no discernible basis of prin-ciple, but *because* of that, they avoided any direct class conflict of the kind which has damaged the stable evolution of democracy in other countries.

If that point is accepted, one further comment may be allowed. Political parties do not as a rule earn much praise from political theorists. Yet in their pursuit of self-regarding ends, it may be that the Liberal and Conservative parties of the Victorian age contributed more than they intended to the general good.

The Theory of Evolution Challenged Creationism

David Newsome

David Newsome explains how advances in science, particularly Charles Darwin's theory of evolution, caused doubt and loss of religious faith among Victorian intellectuals and clergymen. Because Darwin's research contradicted the Old Testament model that species were created by God, intellectuals and church leaders faced a dilemma. According to Newsome, some resigned as clergymen, some modified their interpretation of Scripture, and others held fast to old beliefs. David Newsome, social historian and biographer, taught ecclesiastical history at Emmanuel College, Cambridge, and at Wellington College. He is the author of *On the Edge of Paradise*, *The Parting of Friends*, and *The Convert Cardinals*.

On the Origin of Species by means of Natural Selection did not burst upon a world wholly unprepared for cosmic revelations. *The Vestiges of Creation* had become something of a best-seller, 25,000 copies having been bought in Britain before Darwin's work was known. It lacked the weight of convincing research, however, to cause great anxiety. More disturbing, although at the same time exhilarating to many, were the developments in the study of archaeology stimulated by the geological researches of Lyell and others. Archaeology became the popular science of mid-Victorian England—awesome in its challenge to the Mosaic[1] cosmology but, in its revelations of the gradual evolution of technology from the use of flint, bronze and iron to the astounding achievements of their own time, a

1. relating to Moses and the writings attributed to him

Excerpted from David Newsome, *The Victorian World Picture*. Copyright ©1997 by David Newsome. Reprinted by permission of Rutgers University Press. (Endnotes in the original have been omitted in this reprint.)

demonstration to Victorians that their belief in progress was being triumphantly confirmed. . . .

Scientific advance creates its own momentum. Geology stimulated studies in archaeology; and as the century progressed, archaeology in turn stimulated researches into anthropology, ethnology, and philology, each contributing its knife-thrust into those still clinging to fundamentalist, Old Testament accounts of the Creation. . . .

Darwin's *Origin of Species* Caused a Major Reaction

It would appear from the careful, almost devout, tone of [*Origin of Species*] and from Darwin's own (surely naïve) statement towards its conclusion that he saw 'no good reason why the views given in this volume should shock the religious feelings of any one', that he was unprepared for the onslaughts that awaited him. [Thomas] Huxley was more realistic. 'I am sharpening up my claws and beak in readiness,' he assured his friend. How effective those claws and beak were, in his allegedly blistering riposte to Samuel Wilberforce, Bishop of Oxford, at the meeting of the British Association [for the Advancement of Science] at Oxford in 1860, has been for many years a matter of debate. Wilberforce, in a moment of misjudgement, had concluded a not very convincing defence of orthodoxy against the implications of Darwin's theories with what he thought would score a smart debating point, posing the question (to whom directed, no one could accurately recall) whether 'it was through his grandfather or his grandmother that he claimed . . . descent from a monkey?' Various versions of what Huxley actually said in reply have been offered; and [geologist and historian] J.R. Green, who was present, claimed an exact recollection which, when subsequently transcribed, suggests a far more finished piece of prose than could actually have been either uttered or committed to memory at the time:

> A man has no reason to be ashamed of having an ape for his grandfather. If there were to be an ancestor whom I should feel shame in recalling, it would rather be a man—a man of restless and versatile intellect, who, not content with an

equivocal success in his own sphere of activity, plunges into scientific questions with which he has no real acquaintance, only to obscure them by an aimless rhetoric, and distract the attention of his hearers from the real point at issue by eloquent digressions and skilled appeals to religious prejudice.

More recent investigations, based largely on press reports, have cast doubts on whether Huxley ever said anything of the sort. According to the report in *The Athenaeum*,[2] the truly effective reply to Wilberforce's speech came not from Huxley at all, but from Joseph Hooker.

What is not a matter of doubt is that Darwin had seemed to deliver body blows to Christian orthodoxy in three main respects. In the first place, his careful analysis of the transmutation of species made it impossible to adhere to the traditional view of 'special creation'—the notion that at some historic moment God determined that birds should be birds, beasts should be particular beasts, and that man should be man. Secondly, the process by which organisms developed and modified, through adaptation, was not according to some benevolent design, but in response to the exigencies of chance. What determined the survival and evolution of one species and the death of another was natural selection. 'Nature', as Basil Willey has explained [in "Darwin and Clerical Orthodoxy"], '. . . takes advantage of the favourable variations, and suppresses the unfavourable; creatures that happen to put forth variations advantageous to them in the struggle, survive and perpetuate themselves; the rest perish."

The third disquieting element was Darwin's picture of the amorality of nature: the survival of the fittest, suggesting that it was certainly not the meek who inherited the earth. Darwin was not intending to say that there was no possible role for God in this, admittedly unbiblical, scenario. As Walter Cannon has pointed out [in *Victorian Studies*], Darwin rejected Design, but he did not repudiate the concept of some underlying purpose in the way in which *Homo sapiens* evolved. Inevitably, however, the rejection of the account of

2. a literary and artistic review, later called the *New Statesman*

the Creation in Genesis fostered an escalating scepticism. If there was no Adam and Eve, there was no Garden of Eden. If no Eden, there was no Temptation, and no Fall of Man. If no Fall of Man, what became of original sin and the requirement of redemption? So, a thirteen-year-old schoolboy named George Macaulay Trevelyan [future historian] reasoned, from hearing that Darwin had proved the Bible to be untrue, 'the fabric of Christian doctrine instantaneously fell away in ruin.'

How far this sort of thinking percolated to the 'man in the pew' is difficult to gauge. *The Origin of Species* is a very substantial volume, and although elegantly written, it is by no means simple reading. But the substance of Darwin's teaching and of Huxley's own contribution—*Evidence as to Man's Place in Nature*—was widely known. There can be little doubt that the theory of evolution was popularized among the earnest self-improving members of the Mechanics' Institutes,[3] whose reaction was likely to be similar to the young Trevelyan's. But not all churchmen were discountenanced. The Catholic [John Henry] Newman, for example, distanced himself from an attempt by one of his co-religionists in 1868 to undermine Darwin's conclusions.

> I do not fear the theory so much as he seems to do [he wrote] . . . It does not seem to me to follow that creation is denied because the Creator, millions of years ago, gave laws to matter. He first created matter and then he created laws for it— laws which should *construct* it into its present wonderful beauty, and accurate adjustment and harmony of parts *gradually* . . . Mr Darwin's theory *need* not then be atheistical, be it true or not; it may simply be suggesting a larger idea of Divine Prescience and Skill.

It is interesting to note that [Anglican churchman Charles] Kingsley, Newman's great adversary, came to precisely the same conclusion. Earlier than either of them, only months after Darwin's book had appeared, the young [theologian] F.J.A. Hort, who was to play a not insignificant role

3. schools providing education for working men

years later in correcting some of the errors of the Tübingen school [of biblical criticism], wrote to his friend Brooke Foss Westcott: 'Have you read Darwin? How I should like a talk with you about it! In spite of difficulties, I am inclined to think it unanswerable. In any case it is a treat to read such a book.' What each of these three men were saying, at least by implication, was 'your God is too small'. The extraordinary picture presented by Darwin, far from diminishing the stature of God, enlarged it. Certainly the barber whom the young [future statesman and essayist] A.J. Balfour visited in the 1860s—full of the chatter of his kind—thought that it was all very exciting: 'the doctrine of evolution, Darwin and Huxley and the lot of them—hashed up somehow with the good time coming and the universal brotherhood, and I don't know what else.'

Major Intellectuals and Clergymen Lost Their Traditional Beliefs

For the majority of the clergy, it is probable that the advent of Darwinism immeasurably intensified their anxieties. They were being presented with questions they were unable satis- factorily to answer. Many will have swallowed their own doubts and misgivings and put a brave face on things. [Poet Alfred Lord] Tennyson's father, long before Darwin, did his duty as a parish priest, while having lost his faith. [Clergy- man and essayist] Leslie Stephen, on the other hand, could not live a lie. He ceased to officiate as a priest when he found that he no longer believed; but he was quite certain that many of his Cambridge contemporaries 'shared my scepti- cism, but continued to be clergymen'. They were 'rational enough to see that the old orthodox position was untenable . . . but also thought that religious belief of some kind was necessary or valuable'. Perhaps not without a little struggle of conscience, they took heart from the advice which the cynical and sceptical Roger Wendover gave to the over- scrupulous Robert Elsmere in Mrs Humphry Ward's novel [*Robert Elsmere*]: 'Good God, what nonsense! As if any one inquired what an English parson believed nowadays, so long as he performs all the usual antics decently!'

The loss to the Church of many men of stature who—in different circumstances—might have been expected to become its staunchest defenders, cannot, of course, be measured. While Leslie Stephen abandoned his Orders without a struggle, [biographer and historian] J.A. Froude felt it necessary to make a loud noise about his loss of faith. [Biographer and essayist] Mark Pattison continued to officiate half-heartedly, but he became soured and peevish; and the Rugby[4] of Arnold, Tait and Temple—the nursery of talented, ardent young Christians—produced more than its fair share of disenchanted souls, [philosophers and writers] A.H. Clough, Matthew Arnold himself, Henry Sidgwick and T.H. Green the most celebrated among others. Green found a new cause in preaching a religion of humanity; Sidgwick felt an intense sense of responsibility lest his own scepticism should influence others, and was totally honest about his personal sense of loss. 'I still hunger and thirst after orthodoxy,' he wrote in 1862, while yet in his early twenties; 'but I am, I trust, firm not to barter my intellectual birthright for a mess of mystical pottage.'

When Clough and Matthew Arnold lost their faith, they seemed to lose too all sense of joy, never really to be recovered. They both became wanderers, as Arnold expressed it in *Stanzas from the Grande Chartreuse:*

Wandering between two worlds, one dead
The other powerless to be born,
With nowhere yet to rest my head.

But then, one never quite knows with Arnold. Did he, as [writer] George Landow suggests, have a secret wish—in spite of his predilection for 'metaphors of isolation and help-lessness'—to find himself wandering back home? [Critic] R.H. Hutton suspected that Arnold was 'never quite at his best except when . . . delineating a mood of regret'. This was not quite joylessness, but rather a sort of melancholy joy in the midst of pain.

4. The Rugby School of Christian Education for Christian Men, the place where Rugby football originated; Thomas Arnold was headmaster, 1828–1842, followed by A.C. Tait and Frederick Temple.

None of these men was an atheist. They had no wish to try to prove that God did not exist, even if that were possible. Some agnostics believed, with Huxley, that the release from Christianity enabled one to aspire to a superior moral code. In an article on 'Science and the Bishops' in 1887, Huxley wrote:

> Theological apologists who insist that morality will vanish if their dogmas are exploded, would do well to consider the fact that, in the matter of intellectual veracity, science is already a long way ahead of the Churches; and that, in this particular, it is exerting an educational influence on mankind of which the Churches have shown themselves utterly incapable.

Was there a future for human kind in the beyond? Some of the agnostics hankered after some convincing evidence of life after death. Huxley was not one of them. He unburdened himself at length to Charles Kingsley in 1860, pointing out that he neither denied nor affirmed the immortality of man; and as for ultimate judgement of man's actions, why should it be necessary—he asked—to believe in anything so improbable when, in this life on earth, 'the gravitation of sin to sorrow is as certain as that of the earth to the sun'? He had frankly been revolted, at the recent funeral of his little son, by the words of the officiating minister: 'If the dead rise not again, let us eat and drink, for tomorrow we die.'

> I cannot tell you how inexpressibly they shocked me . . . What! because I am face to face with irreparable loss . . . I am to renounce my manhood, and, howling, grovel in bestiality? Why, the very apes know better, and if you shoot their young, the poor brutes grieve their grief out and do not immediately seek distraction in a gorge.

Religious Reactions Varied at the End of the Century

. . . During the 1870s and 1880s, unbelief was reaching its peak. [Satirist] W.H. Mallock's 'Mr Leslie' in *The New Republic* (1877) observed to the assembled company: 'I certainly think that our age in some ways could not possibly be worse.

Nobody knows what to believe, and most people believe nothing.' The protracted conflict over the election to Parliament in 1880 of the avowed atheist Charles Bradlaugh, who refused to take the required oath 'on the faith of a Christian', degenerated almost into farce, to the embarrassment of [prime minister William] Gladstone's ill-starred second administration. It lasted until 1886, by which time the whole country was talking about it and taking sides, the working classes on the whole firmly supporting Bradlaugh. In the same year, Sidgwick recorded in his diary: 'I do not think the spirit of the age, in its most religious phase, is really Christian; I think it is Theistic.'

This may have been wishful thinking on the part of a somewhat disillusioned agnostic. In fact, through these same decades and well into the next century, all the Christian churches were showing signs of a new vitality. From some quarters there was a decided counter-attack. Unquestionably, too, Christian defences were being reappraised and reorganized. Much of what had seemed shocking to Christians at first had had time to be absorbed and appreciated for its positive rather than its potentially destructive significance. Darwinism, for instance, by the close of the century had become so much part of the accepted thinking within the Establishment that Darwin's remains were interred in Westminster Abbey. In 1894 Huxley had cause to marvel at the extent to which the old conflicts had subsided. The British Association had met again in Oxford, and Huxley reported on events to his lifelong friend, Joseph Hooker:

> It was very queer to sit there and hear the doctrines you and I were damned for advocating thirty-five years ago at Oxford, enunciated as matters of course—disputed by no reasonable man!—in the Sheldonian Theatre by the Chancellor.

This had required from the churches some shifting of ground; and for the most part they had responded, the notable exceptions being the Evangelicals and the Weslyan Methodists. One traditional argument in particular—the notion that the abandonment of Christian belief would inevitably lead to moral collapse—was less confidently asserted. At least for the educated classes, this would no longer serve. J.E.C. Welldon, later to become Bishop of Calcutta, was ill-advised enough in 1885, in the hearing of Henry Bradshaw, the University Librarian, to state publicly that the spread of unbelief in Cambridge had been invariably accompanied by 'loss of morality'. Bradshaw knew the undergraduates well. They were as honest, decent and caring as they had ever been. He also knew Sidgwick well, whose influence in Cambridge was little less than that of T.H. Green in Oxford. Sidgwick might have encouraged agnosticism, but never a lowering of morals. So Bradshaw gave Welldon a little lesson in morality in return. 'Well, Welldon,' he said. 'You lied; and what is worse, you knew you lied!'

Darwin Contributed to Religious Doubt

Noel Annan

Noel Annan explains the effect of Darwin's *Origin of Species* on Victorian thinking. He argues that Positivism, with its emphasis on reasoning and logic, had already raised doubts about traditional Christianity. The advent of evidence and proof, on which Charles Lyell's and Darwin's works are based, further undermined religion's claim to truth. Evangelical churches denied the value of facts and proof and proclaimed the value of faith, a position most scholars found unconvincing. Annan also argues that Darwin changed traditional ideas regarding time and space. Noel Annan, provost of King's College, Cambridge, and lecturer in politics, is the author of *Leslie Steven: His Thought and Character in Relation to His Time*.

Science is a word for ever changing its meaning in popular imagination. It still conjures up for us, as it did for the Victorians, the romance of man making discoveries and taming Nature, and like them we take pride in our scientific geniuses. They were also proud of their artisans, as we admire technologists, for translating the scientific discoveries into marketable products. But we realize, as they did not, that the development of science and technology rests on a vast base of institutions. We realize what technological effort is required to transform the brain-child of a team of university or industrial or government research scientists into a mass-produced product; what ingenuity and organization is required to market such products; and what complex investment by banks and corporations is needed to finance new

Excerpted from "Science, Religion, and the Critical Mind: Introduction," by Noel Annan, in *1859: Entering an Age of Crisis*, edited by Philip Appleman, William A. Madden, and Michael Wolff. Copyright ©1959 by Indiana University Press. Reprinted by permission of Indiana University Press.

projects. We know how scientific invention is for ever changing the structure of industry and transport—still more the welfare, culture, and way of life—of both highly industrialized and under-developed countries. Today science is part of politics. For better or for worse nation-states have begun to invest in science and technology and to organize them as part of the national power complex.

A century ago no such picture could have formed in the minds of the Victorians. [Historian George] Haines tells in his essay of a country in which science had scarcely begun to be taught. . . .

Science, then as now, was feared. Today while we see in it the hope of human welfare, we fear it as the agent of our destruction. But it is not the subject itself but the use to which nation-states put it that we fear. In 1859 the Victorians were hardly beginning to take account of the political and international implications of science, but they were deeply suspicious of its effect upon individuals. Science was suspected of being a moral danger. [Essayist John] Ruskin pointed to one type of corruption—the corruption of the craftsman. [Theologian John Henry] Newman, and after him [Victorian writer] Matthew Arnold, pointed to another—the impoverishment of the individual's mind if he were permitted to specialize in science and set aside the liberal arts. But in the popular imagination the greatest danger seemed to be whether science was going to contradict the whole tradition of European thought by substituting a totally different account of what life on this planet had been, was, and ought to be. How could the findings of science be reconciled with the history, the morality, the ideals, and the faith of Christian England? . . .

Positivism Caused Religious Doubt Before Darwin

The *Origin of Species* was not, of course, the sole great dissolver of faith in mid-Victorian England, and we would misinterpret the age if we saw it as such. To see the celebrated controversy between science and religion a century ago in perspective we must stand back from the 'fifties and relate Darwin's book to a tradition of thought already long developed. The *Origin of Species* was simply another stage in the development of the positivist tradition—a tradition that owed something to [seventeenth-century philosopher Francis] Bacon but first took shape in the writings of [philosophers Thomas] Hobbes, [John] Locke, and [mathematician Isaac] Newton. For over two centuries it was to be the most consistently powerful intellectual movement in England. . . .

Positivism was both a method and a disposition of mind. It claimed to be scientific because it applied to human behaviour the methods of inductive and deductive reasoning that Newton had hallowed. The interplay of these methods . . . was put forward as the soundest way of discovering truth about all subjects. Today we think of knowledge as a set of different subjects, each with its own discipline; but when in 1852 Cambridge, responding to demands to broaden its curriculum, instituted the Natural Sciences and the Moral Science Triposes,[1] the names reflected the implicit assumption that knowledge was a unity. In the nineteenth century, moreover, science meant pre-eminently the discovery of new laws: great immutable hypotheses necessarily replete with profound cosmological implications. There was nothing new in such extrapolation. From Newton's laws not only had a new physical universe been constructed; psychology and even economics and religion were infused with Newtonian inferences. And so, as each new scientific law in Victorian times was propounded, men tried to apply it to society or the universe. [Poet Alfred] Tennyson, whose sensibility was so acutely tuned to the dilemmas of his generation, was of course doing this when he immortalised in *In Memoriam* the relation of thermodynamics to the ancient tale of the loving purposes of God towards man.

There was every reason why such ideas should take root easily. The eighteenth-century tradition of rationalism had assumed that the words "scientific" and "rational" were synonyms. The business of living in society—of choosing between right and wrong, of choosing your objectives, of choosing between different courses of action, of choosing the means to achieve your goals—was described as a ratio-

1. examinations required for a degree

nal, and, as men grew wiser, a scientific process. It was irrational to prefer pain to pleasure; it was ascetic or unnatural to aim at unattainable goals; it was superstitious to perform actions, such as rituals, which were not directed towards a specific end. Circumstances, "other people," and the situation in which you found yourself of course influenced your conduct. But you could prevent circumstances dictating to you by acquiring facts about your situation and inferring—scientifically—from them how best to act. What prevented men from doing this? What impeded the march of mind and the progress of civilization? Ignorance, false doctrine, and anachronistic[2] institutions. Here the positivist disposition of mind deeply disturbed the conservatives and the orthodox: they were faced by something much more sweeping and alarming than a movement for political reform.

New Attention Paid to Facts and Evidence

At the same time positivists recognized that the social sciences could not hold a candle to the natural sciences when it came to making claims that incontrovertible truths had been discovered. The basic premise about society—that its health and wealth rested on the pursuit of rational self-interest—was said to be implicit in Nature herself and to be confirmed by the most striking achievement in all the social sciences—the body of related conclusions about human behaviour constructed by the classical economists. And yet, difficult as it was to refute these conclusions, the abstract and deductive nature of the argument detracted from its prestige. The conclusions of [philosopher Jeremy] Bentham or [French philosopher Auguste] Comte or [writer Henry] Buckle were not demonstrable to the same degree as those of Lyell.[3] Lyell's work contained hypotheses in plenty but they rested on facts. Was there a branch of knowledge about human beings that could produce facts of comparable strength and validity? . . .

This new scientific treatment of evidence put Biblical history outside the orbit of any but professional scholars, and as

2. out of proper order   3. Charles Lyell published *Principles of Geology* in 1830. In it he provided factual evidence that geological changes occur slowly, thus making the earth much older than had previously been thought.

a result bewildered and enraged the mass of the clergy in mid-Victorian England. . . .

Lyell's geology was all grist to the positivist mill, and the idea of development—the idea that the world and all that is in it has radically changed over the centuries and that nothing, not even our knowledge of God, is given once and for all and is immutable—was current long before 1859. Darwin confirmed more rigorously what positivism had for long asserted—that the history of the world is the history of progress and that there was no need of supernatural intervention during the ages to account for whatever had happened. The descent of man was incorporated into the positivist cosmology and the picture painted by the new scholars of Natural History was set up to mock the old picture of Creation which the churches implicitly upheld.

And yet we should be equally wrong to minimise the shock made by the publication of the *Origin of Species*. No doubt [writer] Francis Newman, [novelist] George Eliot, and others had lost their faith because they found Christian morality as preached by the churches deficient. No doubt [writers] J.A. Froude and Baden Powell were more affected by the Higher Criticism of the Bible[4] than by science. . . .

Darwin's *Origin of Species* Brought Crucial Changes in Thinking

But Darwin remains a crucial name and 1859 a crucial year. The *Origin of Species* became the foundation of a new history of the world. [Bishop John William] Colenso's statistical enquiry into the arithmetic of the Pentateuch,[5] which so enraged his brother bishops, was influenced by Darwinism as well as by the Higher Criticism. The issue was not simply whether scholars might re-interpret the Bible but whether the beloved story of man's Creation and the Flood was rub-

---

4. a collection of treatises by scholars who considered the Old Testament a collection of human documents—tribal histories, genealogies, digests of laws, erotic songs, biographies, and folk myths—not divinely inspired or authoritative 5. Bishop Colenso's *The Pentateuch and Book of Joshua Critically Examined* (1862) denied the authenticity of the Moses books. Colenso was temporarily excommunicated for writing the book.

bish. Darwin not only offended the Fundamentalists among all Christian communions . . . but all those attuned to believing in a world in which God was continually at work in a material way—in a world which He planned. Was Natural Selection part of God's design? . . .

A great chasm seemed to have opened between God and Nature. Darwin introduced the idea that *chance* begot order in the world, and today, whether in atomic physics or in the genetical properties of the nucleic acids, chance still rules in terms of any single individual particle, however much the laws of mathematical probability work in respect of any groups of particles. To the Victorians the metaphysical significance of this situation seemed of appalling importance. As [English professor Basil] Willey shows, it seemed to many of them that God had been banished from the world and that the new account of Creation foretold a spiritual and moral destiny for the human race incompatible with the story of God's dealings with man as depicted in the Bible. Belief in Divine intervention in the affairs of men was widespread and disasters in Nature were often held to be instances of God's justly provoked wrath. How could this be if mechanistic blind chance alone prevailed in the order of Nature? Despite the fact that Darwin denied that he intended to trespass on theological pastures, and despite the fact that he was to dissociate his work from [philosopher] Herbert Spencer's adaptation of the principle of evolution, the churches fell upon him. The rumpus perhaps was inevitable, but it turned out to be singularly unfortunate for the churches. As sometimes happens when the established order in society decides to force an issue and crush a lone danger, the dissident suddenly appears to gather strength from the soil itself and emerges as the leader of an army triumphant with banners flying. . . .

Churches Rejected Evidence and Proclaimed Faith

Undoubtedly the churches had become more sharply opposed to science than they had been a century before. . . . Yet of the dozen other factors that one could mention, which led to the conflict of science and religion, none is as important as the rise of Evangelicalism. The movement that began with [Methodist minister John] Wesley and revived both the Nonconformist[6] communions and the Anglican Church scorned the value of evidences and proofs and wagered all on the conviction of faith. The question was no longer, "How do we believe?" but "Do you believe?" It reduced the Christian religion to "God's scheme of salvation," an historical-theological account of the Fall, of man's universal need for redemption, of Christ's atoning sacrifice, of man's justification in God's sight by faith in this sacrifice, and of an afterlife of reward or punishment. It told this story in simple, literal, and personal terms. The transcendent Father, majestic in wrathful justice, could be propitiated by belief in Jesu, the Son, the pitying Saviour, the sinner's friend—an intensely personal and corporeal God. Evangelicalism transformed practical religion and the nation's morality. By the very simplicity of its Christian message it affected the lives of many people who underwent an intense religious experience—even the lives of many of those who disliked the Evangelicals. But this same simplicity rendered it terribly vulnerable to the new weapons in the positivist armoury; and it is not, I think, an exaggeration to see Victorian theology in retrospect as a tireless, and at times almost desperate, attempt to overcome the appalling weaknesses which this simple faith presented to positivist criticism. . . .

Darwin's Effect on Ideas of Time and Space

The most obvious effect of science upon religion was thus to change the character of theology and hence the character of Christianity itself in England. . . . A less obvious, yet far more important, offspring of Darwin's work was the way in which it revolutionised our ideas of Space and Time. It is difficult for us to conceive how fast men's *imagination* in those days was bound by Europe and European history. For almost a century geology and archaeology had been extending the length of world history and as early as 1836 [scientist] Boucher de Perthes had argued that mankind and ex-

6. Protestant religious groups that dissented from the Anglican Church

tinct mammals were contemporaries. But not until 1859 was this hypothesis accepted by scholars, such as Falconer and Prestwich, and it was to take many more years before such notions were emotionally accepted. . . .

Darwin upset this tidy and self-contained cosmos. He created a vast new time-sequence in which man played a minute part. He linked man to Nature, and organic matter to inorganic matter, in an unbreakable chain. . . . When Darwin published his book few doubted that the culture of the present was superior to that of the past, and the culture of England surpassed all others in the present.

Chapter 5

Social and Cultural Changes

Turning | Points
IN WORLD HISTORY

Educating Women and the Working Class

William S. Knickerbocker

William S. Knickerbocker explains the incremental changes that extended education to new groups. He explains that before schools were established for working classes and women, reformers asked if education should be utilitarian or cultural, religious or secular, if government should fund schools, and if women should depart from traditional roles. William S. Knickerbocker taught at Emerson College in England. He is the editor of *Twentieth Century English, Classics and Modern Science*, and *Culture and Anarchy by Matthew Arnold*.

"Educate or govern," wrote [essayist] John Ruskin, "they are one and the same word."

During the sixty-four years of Victoria's reign, a time of hazardous transition, education in England supplemented parliamentary action as a substitute for revolution, for achieving national change without catastrophic violence. The instruction of the masses, the opening of higher education to women, the establishment of educational institutions for workingmen, and the rebirth of spirit in public schools and universities tended to break down the barriers between classes and to bridge chasms between minds. Educational processes quietly radiated, creating an intellectual climate which vastly favored creative attitudes towards renovating the national social order. Victorian education became England's alternative to successive *coups d'etat*[1] manifested by

1. the sudden overthrow of government by a usually small group of persons in or previously in positions of authority

some other European nations.

Utility or culture—which? New educational institutions tended to abandon the humanistic tradition which had been preserved in England since the revival of the classics [during the Renaissance], to reject traditional literary bases of education, and to substitute the study of science and of technological machines and processes. Emergence of new educational concepts created a conflict. Aggressive attacks upon the study of the classics aroused resistance by traditionally educated scholars who, in the situation thus evoked, voiced their faith in the formative power of literature, a philosophy of education resident in old established English seats of learning. They resisted the threat to time-honored ways of life, a threat engendered by revolutions abroad and by economic uncertainties at home. They met criticism of their own ideals and the rivalry of newer institutions by militantly recommending the idea of culture to preserve qualities of character and of human dignity which radical experimenters were too prone to ignore or destroy.

Of the two old universities, Oxford more valiantly resisted innovations, and therefore bore the brunt of the struggle. Cambridge was more elastic, more active in developing its inheritance in stressing physical science, less committed than was Oxford in devotion to literary studies as the organizing discipline of higher learning. Defending and extending the idea of culture, the humanization of man in society, were directly undertaken by some Oxford humanists, the most notable of whom were [John Henry] Newman, [Matthew] Arnold, and Ruskin.

The Need to Educate the Poor Classes

Unprecedented effects resulted from extending education to hitherto excluded classes. Indispensably a phase of Victorian democracy, . . . popular education enormously increased the numbers of those who could read and write, altered the nature of conditions of authorship and multiplied the phases of national life hitherto untouched in English literature.

Efforts to instruct the lower classes through teaching poor children to read the Scriptures and moral tracts (humanitarian by-products of eighteenth century Methodism) were scattered and unorganized. From 1700 to 1798, twenty "Charity Schools" were founded to provide the rudiments of instruction to the poor, but they too elicited little public interest until they found a champion in Sarah Trimmer[2] whose *Reflections upon Charity Schools* (1792) called attention to their inadequacies while making a plea for their improvement and increase. Maria Edgeworth's[3] *Practical Education* (1798) proceeded further and provided Clapham evangelicals[4] with an educational manual for their humanitarian zeal. For four years (1802 to 1806), Mrs. Trimmer continued her campaign in her magazine *The Guardian of Education*. Some development of the schools resulted from the work of Thomas Stock and Robert Raikes (1780) who succeeded in removing these separated experiments from the wastefulness of amateurism and converting them into the supervised schemes known as "the ragged schools."

Perhaps the intentions of these humanitarians was to rescue children of the lower classes from the blight of gin whose sodden effects were so tellingly depicted by [painter William] Hogarth. The limited scope of instruction in reading, writing, and a little arithmetic bore fruit in unanticipated results; for once taught to read the poor did not, of course, restrict their reading to the Holy Bible or to pious tracts like Hannah More's *The Shepherd of Salisbury Plain*. They avidly read, in too many instances, whatever came within range of their understanding, including (to the horror of the faithful) infidel and subversive printed matter hawked in the streets—inflaming their sense of discontent with conditions approved by their benefactors. Reaction and suspicion followed as a consequence when [American politician Thomas] Paine's *Rights of Man* and *The Age of Reason* circulated freely among the newly literate poor so that public opinion feared that the mere ability to read was probably more a menace than a blessing—an attitude which became

2. author of the popular children's book *The History of Robins*   3. Maria Edgeworth was an Irish novelist, remembered for her excellent presentation of child life in her novels.   4. fundamentalists who remained within the Anglican church and pursued humanitarian causes

patently evident during the disturbances in England accompanying the progressive violence of the French Revolution. More than one contemporary vigorously questioned, or denounced, all efforts to instruct the poor. Yet extensive popular education as a panacea for the growing problems of ignorance, poverty, and crime lingered in the minds of some who uneasily saw the threatened deterioration of England. [Poet William] Wordsworth, turning to this problem, ventured to descant on its solution in his *Excursion* [Book VIII]:

O for the coming of that glorious time
When, prizing knowledge as her noblest wealth
And best protection, this imperial Realm,
While she exacts obedience, shall admit
An obligation, on her part, to *teach*
Them who were born to serve her and obey;
Binding herself by statute to secure
For all the children whom her soil maintains
The rudiments of letters, and inform
The mind with moral and religious truth,
Both understood and practiced—so that none
However destitute be left to droop
By timely culture unsustained; or run
Into a wild disorder; or be forced
To drudge through a weary life without the help
Of intellectual implements and tools;
A savage horde among the civilized,
A servile band among the lordly free.

Wordsworth's lines anticipate Victorian faith in the edifying power of educating the masses. In somewhat cumbersome verse, he phrased in idealistic sentences the vision which inspired [Andrew] Bell and [Joseph] Lancaster in establishing free schools for elementary instruction. Their efforts were consolidated in 1811 by the creation of the National Society for Promoting the Education of the Poor and, three years later (1813), the British and Foreign School Society. Quietly, from 1799 to 1816, Robert Owen was conducting his "New Institute for the Formation of Character" at New Lanark. Wordsworth's lines seem to indicate his sympathy with these movements and with Lord [Henry] Brougham's agitation to have the government assume the burden of educating the poor: an agitation which, after several years of unremitting energy, triumphed in moving Parliament to appoint a Select Committee to Investigate the Education of the Lower Classes of the Metropolis (1816). In 1818, after publishing his pamphlet "Letter to Sir Samuel Romilly . . . Upon the Abuse of Charities [Schools]" he saw his bill passed for a comprehensive Survey of Educational Charities. Brougham tirelessly worked to supply the unprivileged classes with practical information on a wide variety of topics through the tracts circulated by his Society for the Diffusion of Useful Knowledge, competing with the newly founded Bible Society, which distributed inexpensive editions of Holy Scripture among the literate poor. In 1835 [Robert] Chambers founded his periodical, *Information for the People*. The establishment of a training school for teachers at Battersea (1833) and the parliamentary grant of £20,000 for People's Schools marked the beginnings of organized, publicly supported, extension of education to the children of the lower classes.

Educating Laborers

Education of laborers proceeded in a similar hesitating manner. The first of the "Mechanics Institutions," established in 1800, was followed, after almost a quarter century (1823), by The London Mechanics Institute (which later became Birkbeck College). In 1825, Brougham published his pamphlet, "Practical Observations Upon the Education of the People, Addressed to the Working Class and Their Employers." In the same year [poet] Thomas Campbell wrote a letter to *The Times* proposing an English university, open to all regardless of creed or social status, modeled on the German university at Bonn. This led, two years later (1827), to the founding of London University. Because this new institution eliminated religious tests for admission, devout Anglicans feared it would spread infidelity and forthwith established King's College, London (1831), to offset its baneful influence. London University did not require residence for its degrees but provided opportunities for examination given in various parts of the kingdom.

Even these provisions did not adequately solve the problem of threatened disaster to the social fabric caused by economic strains and distresses which were dramatically manifested by the anti-Corn Law[5] and Chartist[6] agitations of the thirties and forties and reached their climax in the continental revolutions of 1848. In a passionate speech in the House of Commons on April 19, 1847, [essayist Thomas Babington] Macaulay displayed his anxieties over the severe strains on public security caused by farm hands and artisans in their riots, hay burnings, and ugly threats. "This, then, is my argument," he exhorted his hearers, "it is the duty of government to protect our persons and property from danger. The gross ignorance of the common people is a principal cause of danger to our persons and property. Therefore, it is the duty of government to take care that the common people shall not be grossly ignorant."

In this context, [reformist and writer Charles] Kingsley's *Alton Locke* is a revealing social document. Perhaps Macaulay's notion of education, narrowly conceived for merely prudential reasons, may have moved [Thomas] Carlyle in his alarming sketch of the condition of England, "Chartism" (1848), to recommend a more humane motive: "Who would suppose," Carlyle wrote, "that Education were a thing which had to be advocated on the ground of local expediency, or indeed on any ground? As if it stood not on the basis of everlasting duty, as a prime necessity of man. It is a thing that should need no advocating; much as it does actually need. To impart the gift of thinking to those who cannot think, and yet who could in that case think; this, one would imagine, was the first function a government had to set about discharging."

Organizing Elementary Education

From 1848 to 1862 William Ellis founded his Birkbeck Schools and in 1862, Robert Lowe, an Oxford don, gave

---

5. The Corn Laws regulated grain trade and restricted imports of grain.   6. Chartists were political reformers, chiefly workmen.

Utilitarian School of Facts

In Hard Times, *Charles Dickens's satire on industrial society and Utilitarianism, Thomas Gradgrind and Mr. McChoakumchild run a school that allows no learning other than facts. The following scene illustrates the methods they used to instill the value of facts and the worthlessness of imagination.*

"Girl number twenty," said the gentleman, smiling in the calm strength of knowledge.

Sissy blushed, and stood up.

"So you would carpet your room—or your husband's room, if you were a grown woman, and had a husband—with representations of flowers, would you?" said the gentleman. "Why would you?"

"If you please, sir, I am very fond of flowers," returned the girl.

"And is that why you would put tables and chairs upon them, and have people walking over them with heavy boots?"

"It wouldn't hurt them, sir. They wouldn't crush and wither, if you please, sir. They would be the pictures of what was very pretty and pleasant, and I would fancy— "

"Aye, aye, aye! But you musn't fancy," cried the gentleman, quite elated by coming so happily to his point. "That's it! You are never to fancy."

"You are not, Cecilia Jupe," Thomas Gradgrind solemnly repeated, "to do anything of that kind."

"Fact, fact, fact!" said the gentleman. And "Fact, fact, fact!" repeated Thomas Gradgrind.

"You are to be in all things regulated and governed," said the gentleman, "by fact. We hope to have, before long, a board of fact, composed of commissioners of fact, who will force the people to be a people of fact, and of nothing but fact. You must discard the word Fancy altogether. You have nothing to do with it. You are not to have, in any object of use or ornament, what would be a contradiction in fact. You don't walk upon flowers in fact; you cannot be allowed to walk upon flowers in carpets.

Charles Dickens, *Hard Times.* New York: New American Library, 1961.

considerable time to the work of improving elementary education by his Revised Code.

Matthew Arnold's appointment (1851) as one of three inspectors of schools reveals the importance the government placed upon elevating the quality of popular education. Though his biographers cannot dispense with this phase of his life, they have tended to slight it as prosaic and tedious; yet a more realistic view of his experience discloses that, in spite of the drudgery and fatigue the school inspections entailed, they provided opportunities for learning at first hand the conditions of a swiftly changing age, freeing him from the confined outlook resulting from his sheltered upbringing. His duties continued through thirty of the most important years of his life (1851 to 1882) and exacted much from him in the constant travel his duties demanded. But he was compensated by the opportunities offered him, in moving him to write essays which flooded the whole view of contemporary education of the English people with insights which only one with his background and quality of mind could render. The Newcastle Commission, appointed in 1859, delegated him to investigate schools in France, Holland, and Switzerland—an experience which enabled him to see in some perspective the defects and the needs of English publicly supported schools. His report, "The Popular Education of France with Notices of That in Holland and Switzerland" (1861), placed the subject on a plane higher than the solely prudential one which had moved Brougham and Macaulay. It appeared the year that the Taunton Commission was appointed: that commission sent him abroad a few years later to continue his investigations which he presented in another report, "Schools and Universities on the Continent" (1868). By comparing it with [philosopher] Herbert Spencer's *Education, Intellectual, Moral, and Physical* one may see how Arnold's concept of culture infused educational theory with an ideal missing from the great empiricist's proposals. In some measure, it was incorporated in the great Education Act of 1870 constructed by Arnold's brother-in-law, William Forster. Ten years later, in 1880, the Compulsory Education Act definitely legalized the improvements in popular education and made education generally mandatory throughout the realm. The appointment (1894) and the report (1896) of the Bryce Commission, with the enactment of the Education Acts of 1902 and 1903, corrected and adjusted provisions of the 1870 act.

Difficulties which Wordsworth had not foreseen in his *Excursion* passage, quoted above, had arisen through the six decades of Victoria's reign. Should popular education be financed and supervised by voluntary, or by governmental, agencies? Should religion and religious doctrine be an integral part of its program? Should education of the people be confined to the instruction of "skills" or should it primarily seek the development of moral character? "What was proposed in the Acts of 1902 and 1903," wrote [sociologist] Beatrice Webb, "applying to England and Wales only, was that all schools which provided elementary education up to a certain standard should come on the rates, and be controlled by the public authority; but that such of them as had been provided by a religious denomination should be permitted to choose leaders of their own creed, provided that they were efficient in secular subjects, and that, subject to a conscience clause, there should be religious teaching according to the creed of the denominational school."

New Educational Opportunities for Women

In some sense, not too clearly discernible, professional and higher education of English women in the nineteenth century accompanied the movement for popular education. The "monitorial" system on which Bell and Lancaster relied, using older children to instruct younger, yielded to the need for adult teachers, properly trained in the skill of instruction. This opened new doors for women. Individual women, here and there, like [authors] Harriet Martineau and George Eliot,[7] were sufficiently intrepid to venture into fields of higher learning generally then regarded as solely the sphere of men. But teacher training colleges offered an avenue of useful employment for women—apart from the traditional

7. pseudonym of Mary Ann Evans, author of the novels *Silas Marner* and *Adam Bede*

post as governesses in private families—in which they found scope for public service. From this beginning, they broadened their demands for opportunities in higher education and, stimulated by the growing strength of the woman's movement in the Victorian era, slowly succeeded in securing the establishment of women's colleges and the right to enter the universities, including Cambridge and Oxford.

The circumscribed educational field for women was a legacy of the previous century. Dr. [Samuel] Johnson had devised a a triad of educational aims for women: cleverness in learning foreign languages, interest in science, and the general acquisition of quotable facts. These were to make her more attractive as maiden and more convenient and durable as wife and mother. This was a more sensible view than the sentimentalized notion then prevailing, celebrated in [Samuel Richardson's novels] *Pamela* and *Clarissa Harlow*, which persisted well into the nineteenth century and was, indeed, illustrated in the good queen herself. It was also reflected in the tender verses of Laetitia Landon, Felicia Hemans, and Jean Ingelow. Mrs. Anne Jameson's *Heroines of Shakespeare*, in its unexcised, original version, frankly stressed the frailties of women who, by various arts of wit and suffering, held up a mirror for Victorian female virtues; it was a moral masterpiece, edifying for women in a world limited to pleasures of the parlor and the martyrdoms of marriage.

Traditionalists Oppose the Women's Movement

Mrs. [Sara] Ellis's series of conduct-books, *The Women of England*, delineated the whole course of Victorian woman's behavior, from babyhood to the blessedness of the boudoir, gravely exhorting mothers to rear their daughters for careers of patient waiting until won by suitors (or, if not wooed, to endure mutely the long-suffering of inconspicuous spinsterhood); and thereafter as Griseldas[8] in the role of wife and mother. "The first thing of importance," Mrs. Ellis wrote in *Daughters of England*, "is to be inferior to men—inferior in

---

8. having patient, long-suffering fortitude, based on the comedy *Patient Grissil* by Thomas Dekker

mental power in the same proportion that you are inferior in bodily strength. . . . I confess I do not see the value of languages for a woman," she continued, questioning also the usefulness of the knowledge of science for women beyond making her an "intelligent listener" to men. As for the general acquisition of knowledge, she conceded that a knowledge of facts, however miscellaneous, might be handy "in connection with the proper exercise of a healthy mind," and "necessarily lead to a general illumination." Mrs. Ellis, like the many other women who shared her views, was moved to write in order to preserve and extend the ideal of the "proper female" in a generation whose literary tastes were appeased by the dainty gift books and annuals laden with verse, fiction, and scribblings which satisfied this ideal. It went further, saturating the minds of minor novelists, now forgotten, who conceived their women characters in this atmosphere of "namby-pambyism."[9]

In this milieu and for this public, the young Alfred Tennyson alembicated[10] some of the moods and themes of poets of the preceding romantic generation—of Wordsworth, [John] Keats, [Percy Bysshe] Shelley, and even of the sentimental [Lord] Byron of "Childe Harold"—electing himself the poetic voice of this dominant gynecocracy.[11] Harmoniously in tune with current sentimentalizing of the proper female, he remained faithful to it throughout his life; not even Thackeray's revision of the concept in Becky Sharp,[12] or contemporary women who demonstrated its inadequacy, restrained him in depicting it in *The Princess*. So long as Victoria was Queen, so long was he faithful to her view of woman's status. A glimpse of that view may be seen in the letter written by Mrs. Martin, the Queen's companion, in 1860: "The Queen is most anxious to enlist everyone who can speak or write to join in opposing this mad wicked folly of Women's Rights, with all its attendant horrors, on which her poor, feeble sex is bent, forgetting every sense of womanly feeling and propriety."

9. that which is insipid, sentimental, and weak   10. purified or altered   11. rule by women   12. the main character in William Thackeray's *Vanity Fair*

Women's Educational Opportunities Increase at Midcentury

Woman's status began to be warmly discussed shortly after Victoria's accession. Critics attacked the notion that women preferred to be sheltered, anemic, deprived of careers. Women struggled for revision of ideas concerning education for their sex despite scepticism, ridicule, and stubborn resistance. By 1848 they succeeded in gaining recognition of their claims: in that year, the year Tennyson published his satiric "medley" *The Princess*, Queen's College, London, opened its doors for the liberal education of women, followed by the Bedford College for Women in the following year. Two graduates of Queen's College, Frances Mary Buss and Dorothy Beale, became notable pioneers in the movement. Others who participated in various ways were Sophia Jex-Blake, Anne Jemima Clough, Emily and Octavia Hill, Emma Cons, Barbara Leigh Smith, and Emily Davis who, in 1864, won a long fight to secure admission of girls to London University Local Examinations, and in 1869 founded the Women's College at Hitchin which, in 1875, moved to Cambridge and became Girton College. The National Union for Improving the Education of Women of all classes was organized in 1871 and was followed, the next year, by the Girls Public School Company. Seven years later, in 1879, London University opened its degree examinations to women; in 1881 women's colleges were founded at Oxford and, in 1884, Oxford permitted women to examinations in some of its Final Schools.

Public opinion grudgingly shifted during the decade of the eighties. [Composers] Gilbert and Sullivan's *Princess Ida* was a timely parody of Tennyson's *Princess*. [Philosopher] John Stuart Mill's *The Subjection of Women* had done its work in persuading many Liberals to adopt more sensible views. George Eliot had eminently demonstrated that a woman was as competent as any of the other sex in fundamental brainwork in philosophy or in fiction. In all fields of intellectual and social action Victorian women were becoming annually more conspicuous in contributing to knowledge and to ways of solving political and economic problems. By 1901, the year of the Queen's death, among the increasing number of notable women—whose achievements were destined not only to expose the inadequacies of Mrs. Ellis's views but were to reveal how a woman, no less "genteel," could attain happiness in marriage while engaged in the severest forms of research—was Beatrice Webb. Her autobiography, *My Apprenticeship* and *Our Partnership*, is a prime source-book for Victorian education in some of its later phases. It discloses how an industrious, persevering, intelligent woman continued the efforts, by scientific methods, of Jeremy Bentham, John Stuart Mill, John Ruskin, Robert Owen, and William Morris in assisting the mind of England to confront and solve emerging industrial and economic problems.

Victorian Women Expected to Be Idle and Ignorant

Charles Petrie

Charles Petrie explains that upper-class Victorian women, governed by rigid societal rules, neither worked nor acquired education, unlike women in previous times. According to Petrie, a Victorian woman prepared for a marriage which gave her status if she landed a prosperous husband from a higher class. When she married, she was completely subservient to her husband; if she found herself in an intolerable marriage, she had no recourse for divorce. Charles Petrie served as editor of *Outlook, English Review, Empire Review,* and worked on the staff of the *Illustrated London News.* He is the author of *The Chamberlain Tradition, The Four Georges: A Reevaluation of the Period from 1714–1830,* and *William Pitt.*

In no respect was the Victorian Age more markedly different from the periods which preceded and succeeded it than in its attitude towards women. . . . The bustling dames of the age of Chaucer, of Elizabeth I, and of the Civil War had long since passed away. In their time spinning and weaving, the care of dairies, and the management of large estates while husbands were away at the wars, at the Court, or concerned with their judicial duties, had been the responsibility of ladies in the manor-houses up and down the country, and the direction of large numbers of servants and retainers, combined with the entertainment of distinguished visitors, had called forth executive powers of no mean order. . . . Even until well on in the eighteenth century women of the upper

Excerpted from Charles Petrie, *The Victorians* (London: Eyre & Spottiswoode, 1960).

classes were still personally interested in the management of their estates. . . .

The Industrial Revolution increased both the population and the wealth of the country, and it became the sign of a man's importance that he kept his women-folk in idleness; that they were not compelled to work was the outward and visible sign of the success of their husbands and fathers. The example spread through the middle-class, until work for women became a misfortune and a disgrace. Only financial ruin sent a girl out of her home to seek employment, in which event she was pitied by others and she pitied herself.

This had, as has been mentioned, not always been the case, and women's industrial work in the previous century was by no means limited to the textile and smaller domestic industries. In addition there were numerous crafts and trades in which they were engaged, either on their own account or as married women assisting their husbands. It was still the age of small scale businesses, and in many trades the skilled worker was both craftsman and merchant, producing goods at home and selling direct to the consumer; such workers, both men and women, formed a considerable section of the shopkeeping classes. Where the workshop was attached to the home it was customary for the whole family to work together in the craft. Goldsmiths' daughters, for example, were frequently expert in designing and chasing, while furniture makers, stone masons, and engravers brought up their daughters to assist them in carving, sculpture, drawing, and graving. The craftsman's wife was not infrequently so familiar with her husband's business as to be 'mistress of the managing part of it', and she could therefore carry on in his absence or after his death. Marriage was, in fact, a business partnership. . . .

Victorian Women Prepared for Marriage, Not Work

During the period of the Industrial Revolution the tendency was for women's activity in the business sphere to decrease except in the trades conducted chiefly by women. This was due firstly to social changes following on the increase in wealth, and secondly to the reorganization demanded by the new commercial and industrial conditions. When the home became separated from the business premises women ceased to take their old interest in their husbands' affairs, and so lost the experience which they would otherwise have gained; moreover, the development of large scale business, combined with the need for greater capital, made it increasingly difficult for women, even in their own trades, to set up in business on their own account

It is only necessary to contrast the vigorous life of the seventeenth and eighteenth century business woman, travelling about the country in her own interests, with the sheltered existence of her Victorian descendant, to realize how much the latter had lost in initiative and independence by being protected from all real contact with life.

Few aspects of modern society are as well documented as the middle-class woman of the nineteenth century, with whom contemporary fiction so largely dealt. The Victorian heroine was an almost standardized product, and her functions were courtship and marriage. Novels like [William Thackeray's] *Vanity Fair* began with the day a girl left school and they generally ended with her wedding. From infancy all girls who were born above the level of poverty had the dream of a successful marriage before their eyes, for by that alone was it possible for a woman to rise in the world. Ethel Newcome [in Thackeray's *The Newcomes*], the daughter of a manufacturer descended from a weaver, married Lord Farintosh, and so entered the charmed circle of the aristocracy, and even Rosamond Vincy [in George Eliot's *Middlemarch*], whose father was a provincial silk manufacturer and whose mother was a vulgarian, was not considered to have done too badly in marrying a doctor who was cousin to a lord. One reason for this cultivation of the aristocracy of course was that it was more stable in the Victorian Age than it had ever been before or was ever to be again. . . .

'To get ready for the marriage market a girl was trained like a race-horse. Her education consisted of showy accomplishments designed to ensnare young men. The three R's of this deadly equipment were music, drawing, and French administered by a governess at home, or, for girls below the aristocratic and the higher professional ranks, by mistresses in an inferior boarding-school.'[1] Miss Pinkerton's academy as described in *Vanity Fair* was probably typical of the more ambitious girls' school. Amelia Sedley for six years studied music, drawing, orthography,[2] every variety of needlework— in all of which, according to Miss Pinkerton's testimonial she 'realized her friends' fondest wishes'—and geography, which she apparently less completely mastered. Formal walks, stigmatized by Alfred Garth in [George Eliot's] *Middlemarch* as 'such a set of nincompoops, like Mrs Ballard's pupils, walking two and two', gave the only outdoor relief from the prison of the schoolroom.

The artificiality in the relations of the sexes where the upper and middle classes were concerned outlasted the Victorian Age, for it continued to exist to no inconsiderable extent until the outbreak of the First World War. If a woman went in a hansom[3] alone with a man who was neither her father nor her husband, nor old enough to be her grandfather, her reputation was irretrievably lost. The ruling convention was directed against unmarried men and women ever being alone together unless they were engaged, and not always then, for it would appear to have been tacitly assumed that on the slightest provocation the Victorian male would take advantage of the Victorian female, who would then suffer the fate described by contemporaries as 'worse than death'. If an engagement was broken off the girl suffered in consequence, while divorce was never mentioned in polite society.

The effect of these taboos was to drive the young man of the classes in question to somewhat sordid intrigues in other quarters. Readers of [Elizabeth Gaskell's] *Mary Barton* and [Thackeray's] *The Newcomes* will remember how young Carson and Barnes Newcome treated the girls of a lower social status than their own. Youths in their teens were apt to take rank among their fellows according to their alleged triumphs over what were generally termed 'scivvies' or shop-girls, and such conditions were not good for either party, while in the presence of women of their own rank in life they were too often diffident and tongue-tied. It would be rash to dogma-

1. W.F. Neff, *Victorian Working Women*, p. 190   2. spelling   3. a two-wheeled carriage

tize in these matters, but it is difficult to resist the conclusion that the Victorian segregation of the sexes in what was then termed 'polite society' occasioned just as many *liaisons* of one sort and another as have marked more recent generations, even if not so much was said about them.

Girls Educated by Governesses or in Boarding Schools

As the Industrial Revolution developed it became the respectable thing for middle-class households, as well as for the aristocracy, to have a governess, and in the Victorian Age she became a firmly established institution. Her importance is proved both by the census figures, and by her frequent appearance as a heroine or in some minor capacity in the novels of the period. In the census of 1851 over twenty-one thousand women appeared as governesses, and the field of their employment was rapidly spreading. Mark Pattison, giving evidence before the Schools Inquiry Commission fourteen years later, explained that the daughters of the aristocracy, the upper middle-class, professional men, and the clergy were educated mainly by governesses, but those of the middle-class proper received their tuition in boarding-schools: other witnesses of broader experience reported that the fashion of educating girls at home had spread downward in the social scale, and that owing to the inadequacy of suitable schools farmers and tradesmen had governesses. . . .

Whether she had been away at boarding-school, or had imbibed such learning as a governess could impart, the Victorian girl of the class which we have been considering continued her education, such as it was, until she married. Nor was this education entirely intellectual, for many young women were physically tortured with an instrument called a backboard, which was a board worn or fastened across the back to give erectness to the figure. It is true that the English girl of the mid–twentieth century often walks badly, but her grandmother was drilled as if she was a grenadier of Frederick William I of Prussia. Miss Pinkerton recommended to Amelia when she left school the 'undeviating use of the backboard for four hours daily during the next three years, for the acquirement of that dignified deportment and carriage so requisite for every young lady of fashion'.

Then there was music, and it was an article of faith with mothers and daughters alike that it was an infallible method of attracting a husband. Once the Victorian girl was seated at the piano with an enraptured swain bending over her, and turning the pages, while she sang, the battle was half-won, so music was a very important weapon in her armoury. The daughters of Sir Pitt Crawley 'took exercise on the pianoforte every morning after breakfast'; Blanche Amory in *Pendennis* to quote her unsympathetic stepfather, was 'screeching from morning till night'; Rosamond Vincy in *Middlemarch* went on studying after she had left school, and practised her repertoire of 'Meet Me By Moonlight', 'Black-Eyed Susan', and similar songs. Needlework, drawing, and painting flowers were also considered good bait in the husband-fishing business. The Oxford Movement[4] gave great impetus to such activities, and the embroidering of altar-cloths was considered a most ladylike occupation. Many of the goods so produced found their way to church bazaars, where they were sold to helpless young men; much of this female handiwork was known as 'the Jews' basket' because the proceeds of the sale were devoted to the conversion of the Jews. Curates, in particular, especially if they were well-connected, stood to profit by this, and they were the recipients of innumerable purses, pen-wipers, portfolios, and even braces. Honeyman, in *The Newcomes*, is an excellent example, for he received objects so diverse as flowers, grapes, jelly, lozenges, a silk cassock, and even a silver tea-pot filled with sovereigns.

What the eligible bachelor had to put up with was indeed formidable, and Lord Farintosh was no exception. 'Every daughter of Eve was bent on marrying him. . . . Everybody hunted him. The other young ladies, whom we need not mention, languished after him still more longingly. He had little notes from these: presents of purses worked by them;

4. a movement within the Church of England that sought to link the Anglican Church more closely to the Roman Catholic Church

and cigar-cases embroidered with his coronet. They sang to him in cosy boudoirs—mamma went out of the room, and sister Ann forgot something in the drawing-room.'

Victorian Males Demanded Innocent, Ignorant Wives

The real tragedy was that although the Victorian girl was skilled in the art of acquiring a husband, she was, unlike her predecessors in earlier centuries, given no training of any sort in her practical duties as a wife, and this was the case even in many lower middle-class families. She was quite untrained in household management, and generally unable to control her servants. She had no idea of the value of money, and too often squandered what her husband gave her. Even in the very important matter of child-bearing she had to learn by experience with all the physical and psychological shocks which this implies.

The blame for this state of affairs largely rested with the Victorian male. Innocence was what he demanded from the girls of his class, and they must not only be innocent but also give the outward impression of being innocent. White muslin, typical of virginal purity, clothed many a heroine, with delicate shades of blue and pink next in popularity. The stamp of masculine approval was placed upon ignorance of the world, meekness, lack of opinions, general helplessness and weakness; in short, a recognition of female inferiority to the male. [In Charles Dickens's novel] David Copperfield's Dora was a 'pretty toy or plaything'; Rosey Mackenzie [in Thackeray's *The Newcomes*] was a 'pretty little tender nurseling, like a little song-bird . . . a tremulous, fluttering little linnet'. [In Thackeray's *Vanity Fair*] Amelia Sedley's weakness was 'her principal charm—a kind of sweet submission and softness, which seemed to appeal to each man she met for his sympathy and protection'. Men in the presence of women modified their conversation, and there was a definite line drawn concerning what an unmarried girl could hear. The conversation of Queen Elizabeth I would have horrified the female subjects of Queen Victoria. Not only was the impure barred, but also anything requiring intelligence, and, above all, politics were not for women, save in the very highest ranks of the aristocracy. It was little wonder that men took refuge in their clubs from the type of women for whom they were largely responsible.

Marriage Required Subservience but Offered Financial Security

Most Victorian women accepted almost any sort of marriage that was offered them, and the only relief many of them enjoyed was a prescriptive right to indulge in hysterics in moments of crisis. The number of women who shrieked in fits of hysterics through the pages of novels and poems is legion, and as they were pregnant most of the time they possessed what they considered an excuse. Even when the children came their mothers had no idea of controlling them save by appealing to their emotions.

On her marriage a girl usually passed from dependence upon parents to submission to a husband. [In George Eliot's novel *Middlemarch*, Tertius] Lydgate wanted to find in marriage 'an accomplished creature who venerated his high musings and momentous labours, and would never interfere with them'. The conception of marriage as a partnership was quite unknown, and Charlotte Brontë wrote in *Shirley*, 'A wife could not be her husband's companion, much less his confidante, much less his stay'. One of the favourite scenes with contemporary novelists was the husband waiting until the very eve of ruin to tell his wife of the desperate state of their affairs.

The law reflected this subservience of the female to the male, for it gave women very little protection. In the middle of the nineteenth century an unattached woman of twenty-one could inherit and administer her own property, over which even her father had no power, but on marriage she was legally an infant, and as a wife she had no right to her own clothes. Her personal, as well as her real, property passed into her husband's possession, and without his permission she could not make a will concerning even her personal property, while cases were not unknown where a husband went so far as to will his wife's property to his own illegitimate children. The legal custody of children belonged to the father, and until 1840 a small infant dependent upon a mother could be taken from her. A husband had an absolute right over the person of his wife; he could lock her up, and he could compel her to return home if she ran away from him. On the other hand she did possess a few compensating advantages. Her husband had to support her, and this right could be enforced in both the ecclesiastical and magistrates' courts. He was also liable for her debts, even those contracted before marriage, while she could not sue or be sued for contracts, nor enter into them.

It was exceedingly difficult for a woman to get out of matrimony. It is true that on the ground of adultery, cruelty, or unnatural practices she could obtain a separation *a mensa et thoro*,[5] but a proper divorce with freedom to re-marry was a very different matter. Prior to 1857 it required an Act of Parliament, with an investigation resting by usage with the House of Lords alone, and it was granted to a woman very seldom, and only in cases of aggravated adultery, an isolated act or two apparently not being considered unbecoming in the Victorian husband. Also the price was prohibitive, being in the neighbourhood of six or seven hundred pounds. Of course it was open to a woman to break her chains by committing adultery herself, and so forcing her husband to divorce her, but this was to condemn herself to social ostracism for the rest of her life.

Nurses Led the Way to Change

Where women were concerned, as in practically every other aspect of life, the Victorian Age was revolutionary. The change for the better may be said to have started with the nursing profession. In the early years of the reign English nurses were only too often drunken, profligate, violent-tempered, and brutal in language, and Sairy Gamp in [Charles Dickens's] *Martin Chuzzlewit* was, it is to be feared, a typical specimen. Florence Nightingale has left it on record that when she informed her parents of her ambition to become a nurse 'it was as if I had

5. literally, "from table and bed"; a partial divorce forbidding cohabitation but having no effect on the marriage

wanted to be a kitchenmaid', but her departure for the Crimea lit a torch that was never to be put out. Slowly and surely the status of nursing was raised, and this led women to clamour for professional and business opportunities.

Slowly they got their way. During the latter part of the Victorian Age teaching steadily rose in status through the reforms of secondary schools and the extension of university degrees to women. In 1872 the Girls' Public Day School Company was founded to provide good and cheap day-schools for girls, and six years later the Maria Grey Training College was founded. London University gave a B.A. Degree to women in 1878; Cambridge opened the triposes[6] to them in 1881; and Oxford allowed them to pass the examinations in 1884. In short, the idle and useless middle-class woman of the earlier part of the reign was by the end of it well on her way to becoming what her descendant is to-day.

6. examinations for a B.A. Degree

Victorian Reading Habits Reflected Popular Tastes

John W. Dodds

John W. Dodds assesses the taste of Victorian readers and the availability of books. He finds that serious readers chose books on religion, history, and geography over fiction, while those reading for entertainment preferred novels featuring murders, horrors, and seduction. Moreover, Dodds reports that at midpoint in the nineteenth century England had fewer lending libraries than other countries. John W. Dodds taught English at the University of Pittsburgh in Pennsylvania and Stanford University in California. He is the author of *Thomas Southerne, Dramatist* and *Thackeray: A Critical Portrait*.

What books did Englishmen read in the 1840's? What kind of libraries did people have access to? What represented a good sale for a successful work? What was the size of an average edition? Who were the popular authors? How well received in this decade were the writers who were to become known as the Great Victorians, and what were the now-forgotten names which were then household words? With books, as with magazines, the answers to these too-little-explored questions take one to the heart of early Victorian culture.

To begin with, there were several factors controlling the distribution of books. The size of the reading public beyond the newspapers and cheap magazines was limited. Out of a total population of over 18,000,000, 40 per cent of the adults could not write their own names. Moreover, the cost of a standard three-decker novel was 31s. 6d.—astronomical enough to keep it off the shelves of any but the well to do and to throw the burden of circulation upon the lending libraries. As we shall see, there were notable efforts during these years on the part of many publishers to make cheap editions of good works available to the modest purse, but for the most part sales, according to modern standards, were small, and the profits of authorship in most cases not large.

The Choices of Serious Readers

English book-reading habits were essentially serious. Of the 45,000 books listed by the *London Catalogue* as published between 1816 and 1851, 10,300 were works on divinity. Sermons were bought, and presumably read. [John Henry] Newman's *Tract 90* (of controversial interest to be sure) sold 12,000 copies before it finally went out of print in 1846. And in 1847 the publisher Virtue made a profit of £4,000 from the publication of a series of lectures delivered by one Dr. John Cumming at Exeter Hall on the subject of the Apocalypse. In a list of 117 new books noted in the Athenaeum[1] on October 23, 1841, thirty-nine were on religious subjects, eleven were poetry, ten medical, thirteen travel, and only sixteen were novels. Religion aside, the *London Catalogue* listed more books of history and geography than of fiction: 4,900 as against 3,500. Indeed there were almost as many books of drama and poetry (3,400) as of fiction. Some 2,500 medical books found print in this period; 1,850 of biography; and 2,450 of science. There were 1,400 in the category of "moral sciences"—which included such diverse subjects as philology and domestic economy. The arts had 2,460 titles. Books at this level were bought, by and large, for their edifying and informing effect rather than their entertainment value.

Editions were not large. The chief sale of popular works was confined to the circulating libraries and book clubs, and averaged from 500 to 2,000 copies—the first being a good sale for a work of reasonable merit, the second an extraordinary sale for a work of a very popular author. Only 2,500

1. a literary and artistic review, later called the *New Statesman*

copies of [William] Thackeray's *Henry Esmond*, for example, were printed in 1852.

On the other hand, large numbers of certain expensive books were sold if they happened to catch on. The first two volumes of [Thomas B.] Macaulay's *History* (at 32s.) ran through five editions and 18,000 copies within six months of its first publication. [Publisher] Longman's wrote Macaulay a check for £20,000 in royalties (some of them an advance) on Volumes III and IV within eleven weeks after publication. And in December, 1849, [publisher John] Murray held his annual trade sale at the Albion Tavern. In one evening the trade agreed in advance to take, among others, the following books:

Lord Campbell's *Chief Justices of England* (2 vols.):	2,000 copies
Layard's *Nineveh and Its Remains* (2 vols., 36s.):	1,400 copies
Byron's *Works* (1 vol.):	1,400 copies
Borrow's *Lavengro*[2] (3 vols., 31s. 6d.):	1,300 copies
Grote's *History of Greece* (Vols. V and VI, 32s.):	750 copies
Curzon's *Monasteries of the Levant* (2d ed., 15s.).	750 copies

Choices of Those with Popular Taste

. . . At the other end of the intellectual scale were the "gothic" novels, many of them published first in parts and later in volume form, scribbled by the score for belowstairs readers, full of stereotyped horrors, seductions, and fearsome midnight adventures. Even the names of their authors have been lost in the cloacae[3] of literary history, and the books have gone down the drain of time just as completely as have their opposites, the streams of "edifying" bilge. But like the "improving" literature, these counterparts in the 1840's of the Minerva Press are evidence of a taste which must be reckoned with if one is not to oversimplify the history of national reading habits. Many of the titles never reached the dignity of being listed in the otherwise complete *London Catalogue:* Mrs. Elizabeth Bennett's *Gipsey Bride; or, The Miser's Daughter,* (1844), and *The Broken Heart; or, The Village Bridal* (1844). Thomas Frost's *The Black Mask; or, The Mysterious Robber* (1850), and *Paul the Poacher*

2. a novel with the subtitle "the Scholar-the-Gypsy-the Priest"   3. a sewer or latrine

(1853). Malcolm J. Rymer's *Woman's Life; or, The Trials of the Heart* (1844–45). Thomas Peckett Prest's *Fatherless Fanny; or, The Mysterious Orphan* (1841); *The Maniac Father; or, The Victim of Seduction* (1842); and *The Skeleton Clutch; or, The Goblet of Gore* (1842).

Of the sixty-one novels that Thomas Prest wrote between 1841 and 1851, his version of the Sweeney Todd legend under the mild title of *The String of Pearls* (*A Romance*) was the most spectacular. In one form or another this horrific tale of the demon barber and his victims continued to titillate Victorian readers for generations. Complete with all the possible gruesome details, the story dealt with a barber who jettisoned his better-fed customers through a trapdoor into the basement, where they were dismembered and baked into meat pies—pies the flavor of which was beyond praise, and which were devoured eagerly by lawyers and their clerks and apprentices in Bell's Yard. . . .

At this distance it is difficult to determine the extent to which all this stuff was read. The list of titles is overwhelmingly long, however, and if one can judge by the sales of [Edward] Lloyd's penny dreadfuls, in which form many books of this kind first appeared, the market was huge. Human nature being what it is, it may be suspected that not a few of these thrillers were smuggled into sedate households by younger readers.

At a more respectable level there were novels and romances for all tastes. The influence of [Sir Walter] Scott was strong, and the historical romance had a great vogue, from Bulwer Lytton to [Benjamin] Disraeli to William Harrison Ainsworth and G.P.R. James. Ainsworth wrote in 1849 that a one-shilling reissue of his earlier *Rookwood* "promises wonders—nearly 6,000 were subscribed in the City alone yesterday. This exclusive of agents, etc., which will treble that amount." The indefatigable James wrote, over a long career, a total of 199 volumes (seventy-five novels), of which the first editions usually ran 1,000 to 1,500 copies. When he got three to four novels ahead of his publishers, Smith and Elder, they asked him to restrict his annual output, whereupon he indignantly parted company with them. Disraeli's

Coningsby went through three editions in three months. Charlotte Brontë's *Jane Eyre*, published in three volumes in October, 1847, reached a fourth edition by 1850. The average run of Bulwer Lytton's novels was 2,250 to 2,700 (the last for *Harold*). For those who liked novels of the sea there was the prolific [Frederick] Marryat (who died in 1848); and for those who preferred farce plus military adventure, Charles Lever. And the superficial "fashionable" novel, of the silver-fork school, lived on into the forties in the glittering, facile stories of Mrs. Gore. Mrs. Frances Trollope continued to support her family by turning out an average of two novels a year. Her son Anthony had just begun to publish his first stories in modestly sized editions which as yet made no great splash in the world of letters. . . .

Most of Herman Melville's books appeared in England in advance of their publication in the United States. Murray recorded that he printed 5,000 copies of *Typee* and sold 4,104; of *Omoo*, 4,000 copies and sold 2,512. Only 100 copies were printed of *Mardi*, and of *The Whale* (later *Moby Dick)* in 1851, only 500 copies. But reissued in a 2s., 6d. series, *Typee* sold 4,000 copies in 1847 and *Omoo* 2,500 the same year. *Mardi*, in 1849, was praised by the English reviewers, though Sir Walter Farquhar wrote to Lord Ashley that the tone of Melville's books "is reprehensible throughout . . . they are not works that any mother would like to see in the hands of her daughters, and as such are not suited to lie on the drawing-room table."

The Popularity of Dickens and Thackeray

Dickens, of course, was the Great Novelist of the time, with Thackeray, in point of general popularity, panting behind a poor second. While [Dickens's] *Dombey and Son* was selling its 30,000 copies per monthly issue in 1846–48, [Thackeray's] *Vanity Fair* did no better than 7,000. Dickens had become the national literary hero while Thackeray had been struggling anonymously in the magazines as Michael Angelo Titmarsh. Not until *Vanity Fair* did Thackeray begin to hear himself mentioned in the same breath with Dickens, and then only by the relatively few and perceptive. Their later rivalry was a personal and artistic one only. Thackeray sold his thousands, and made more than a comfortable living, but Dickens sold his tens of thousands.

It was the custom of popular authors in those days to bring out each year, for the Christmas trade, a separately published story. *The Chimes*, Dickens's Christmas book of 1844, sold 20,000 copies at once; his *Christmas Carol*, a year earlier, had been in its sixth thousand by December 24. Before the year 1844 was over it sold some 15,000 copies. His *Battle of Life*, in December, 1845, sold 23,000 copies within twenty-four hours. Thackeray, on the other hand, sold 3,000 copies of the first edition of *The Kickleburys on the Rhine*, his Christmas book for 1850, and 2,000 of *Mrs. Perkins's Ball*, his offering for 1847.

[Dickens's] *David Copperfield* and [Thackeray's] *Pendennis* were both appearing in monthly parts in 1849—each of them autobiographical. There again Dickens's lusty vividness, his carefully brewed recipe of humor, pathos, and melodrama, triumphed in popular favor over Thackeray's quieter, mellower, retrospective method. Thackeray's admirers among the judicious were many, but numbers of the critics carped at the preponderance of his "unpleasant" characters (he had no conventional heroes); and the public preferred the juicy vitality of Dickens's eccentrics to Thackeray's more critically humorous commentary on life. The Victorians knew satire and liked it; humorous exaggeration they delighted in; tears were a benediction to them. But irony, which was the heart of Thackeray's method, left them uneasy. Blacks and whites were more comfortable than grays.

A curious legend has grown up that the Victorians were a restrained and sedate people, living in an atmosphere of gloomy if bustling activity. Nothing could be further from the truth. The energy which was their dominant characteristic included a high and romantic relish and gusto. Nothing proves this more clearly than the abandon with which the middle classes (who were buying the books) gave themselves to the woes and delights of fictional heroes and heroines. Such a public figure as Dickens wrote always under a sense of high responsibility to the accepted conventions of middle-class morality; books that were read aloud at the family fireside must be free from any possible offense. But once protected by an assurance that no book of a respected author could bring a blush to a young lady's cheek, readers were quite willing to let themselves wallow in a sentimental carousal. Nor was this unbuttoning of the emotions limited to the obscure or the ignorant. [John] Forster, [Walter Savage] Landor, and Tom Hood all wept over the death of Little Nell in the *Old Curiosity Shop*. [Actor William] Macready begged Dickens to save her life, and when the fatal stroke fell he said that it "gave a dead chill to my blood." Daniel O'Connell broke into tears, said "He should not have killed her," and threw the book out the window. . . . The Victorian heart was easily lacerated. Both laughter and tears lay near the surface. . . .

It is impossible to estimate the relationship between the sale of a book and its number of readers in the 1840's, except to say that the latter would be proportionately greater than today. This was especially true of the three-volume, guinea-and-a-half novels, which depended almost entirely upon the circulating libraries for their support. From Mudie's [circulating library] and similar enterprises at one end of the scale, through the libraries of the 720 Mechanics' Institutes with their 120,000 members and 815,000 volumes of books, down to the modest bookshelves of the coffeehouses, which were finding it increasingly advantageous to supply books as well as newspapers for their customers—all were in the business of making reading matter available to those for whom the purchase of a single novel would have meant an extortionate expenditure.

But if the middle-class reader would accept cheap reprints, he who read a book in the forties could also buy. In 1851 the *London Catalogue* listed 1,400 volumes issued by publishers in cheap "libraries" at a cost of one to six shillings. . . .

Reading on the Railway

The development of the railways encouraged the sale of books of all kinds. Until 1848 no systematic attempt had been made to supply passengers with either books or papers at the railway stations. In that year W.H. Smith got the exclusive right to sell books and papers on the Birmingham Railway. His first bookstall was at Euston Station. Shortly he had the franchise for the entire London and Northwestern System. By 1849 the station library at the Paddington terminus contained 1,000 volumes, chiefly works of fiction. Here, for the charge of 1d., a passenger had free access to the use of the library while waiting for trains, and for slightly more could take a volume with him on his journey, turning it in at his destination. To meet this new demand [publisher] Routledge launched his *Railway Library*—novels by [James Fenimore] Cooper, [G.P.R.] James, [Nathaniel] Hawthorne, James Grant, [Alexandre] Dumas, and others. Murray advertised his "Literature for the Rail"—"works of sound information and innocent amusement."

An article in the *Times* of August 9, 1851, by one Samuel Phillips, a staff writer, gives an illuminating answer to the question "what do people read on railways?" Phillips's "Literature of the Rail" was the result of a week's exploration into railway termini. He first found that, with few exceptions, unmitigated rubbish encumbered the bookshelves of almost every bookstall he visited in London. As he proceeded north, however, he saw "a wholesome change. At the North-Western terminus [Euston] . . . we poked in vain for trash. We asked for something 'highly coloured.' The bookseller politely presented us with Kügler's *Handbook of Painting*." . . .

Ladies, he discovered, were not great purchasers of good books at railway stations. "This season they have been greedy in their demand for *The Female Jesuit*. . . . If they do by chance purchase a really serious book it is invariably a religious one. There is a regular sale on the line for what are termed Low Church books."

Phillips found as he went farther north that "Yorkshire is not partial to poetry." And "it is difficult to sell a valuable book at any of the stands between Derby, Leeds, and Manchester. Religious books hardly find a purchaser at Liverpool, while at Manchester, at the other end of the line, they are in great demand. . . .

The Availability of Libraries

What kinds of libraries were available to the Englishman in the 1840's? Almost none for the use of which he did not have to pay a fee or from which he could borrow books. The elaborate and lengthy *Report from the Select Committee on Public Libraries,* ordered printed by the House of Commons in 1849, revealed some discouraging comparative facts. France, it was discovered, had 107 public libraries with an aggregate of nearly 4,000,000 volumes; the Prussian States, 44; Austria, 48; and even the United States 81 public libraries of 5,000 volumes and up. To all these admission was granted unrestrictedly, while in Great Britain there was only one library equally accessible: the Chetham Library in Manchester. There were no free lending libraries in Great Britain of any kind. At Oxford no books were ever removed from the Bodleian Library, and only M.A.'s and those of higher degrees were allowed to use the books when in the library. An undergraduate could not even read the books in the Bodleian unless he got special permission. In 1849 Cambridge gave to undergraduates the privilege of taking books out of the University library on the recommendation of the college tutors. . . .

The British Museum, with its 435,000 books (in 1849) was of course the most important library in London. It also was the subject of a Parliamentary investigation in 1849, at which Thomas Carlyle testified and was sharply critical of the reading arrangements. He thought that novel readers and the insane ought to be put off by themselves, so as not to distract serious readers. The reading room of the British Museum (like the present one) did attract some curious visitors. Charles Knight, describing the room and what he called its "inmates," observed that "some queer enough customers are among them, God knows. . . . The briefless barrister, the clergyman who cannot get a living, the doctor whom no patient will trust, the half-pay midshipman, all betake themselves to some branch of bookmaking. . . . No lights were allowed in the reading room, for fear of accidents. On many a day dark, rolling fogs sent people home long before closing time.

Culturally then, in spite of the fact that there were published in the United Kingdom in the ten-year period some 32,000 books, England was highly stratified, and had succeeded in making good books very difficult for the ordinary man to borrow. In 1850 William Ewart, who had talked Parliament into appointing the 1849 Committee on Public Libraries, saw through the Commons the first Public Libraries Act. It was little more than a bill to enable town councils to establish libraries and museums and it applied only to municipal boroughs in England. But it was an attempt to improve a bad situation, and it became law—over the protests of the ubiquitously cantankerous Colonel Sibthorp, who said that this was merely an attempt to impose a general increase of taxation. He did not like reading at all, he declared publicly, and had hated it when at Oxford.

Pictorial Publications Created a Mass Culture

Patricia Anderson

Patricia Anderson traces the evolution of illustrated publications priced for working people and argues that between 1832 and 1860 their proliferation created the first English mass culture. She describes both entertaining and informative publications: in particular, the penny dreadfuls, religious and self-improvement periodicals, temperance tracts, advertising, illustrated news, and home-decorating prints. Writer and historian Patricia Anderson has published articles in numerous journals, including *Studies in Art Education*, *Journal of Newspaper and Periodical History*, *Visual Resources*, and *Victorian Periodicals Review*.

In 1840 a commentator on the 'popular literature of the day' offered readers of the *British and Foreign Review* 'a collection of statistical notes' on the magazines and journals that then circulated amongst working people 'to an extent undreamed of' only a decade earlier:

> Seventy-eight weekly periodicals are enumerated, of which nearly two-thirds are issued at the price of one penny, none exceeding twopence: twenty-eight of these are devoted to miscellaneous matter; seven to more political subjects; fifteen to the publication of novels, romances and tales; sixteen to biography of celebrated individuals; four to scientific intelligence; three to drama; two to medicine; two are collections of songs, and one registers the progress of the Temperance cause. More than two-thirds of these have the attraction of illustrations.

By 1859 such material had so greatly proliferated that our much-quoted contributor to the *British Quarterly Review* was moved to remark upon what had become a veritable 'flood' of 'cheap literature' and 'tempting' illustrations.

This rapid and unprecedented growth in the number of inexpensive and, by 1840, usually pictorial publications was fundamental in expanding the common cultural experience of working people. And, because the expansion was dramatic, continuing, and wide-reaching in effect, we can with good reason think of it as the transformation of popular culture. The first phase of this transformation had begun in the early 1830s with the mass circulation of the *Penny Magazine* and one or two other publications such as the *Saturday Magazine* and the unillustrated *Chambers' Journal*. By 1860, with even higher circulations and wider appeal, the *London Journal*, *Reynolds's Miscellany*, and *Cassell's Paper* had brought this initial phase to its fullest development. Illustrated miscellanies thus formed the nucleus of working peoples' experience of the printed image between 1832 and 1860. But other artefacts and their associated imagery also gained in number and importance during this period; and together with magazine illustration such imagery made up almost the whole of the English worker's expanding pictorial world.

The transformation and expansion of popular culture was not just a matter of an increase in the quantity and kind of information, entertainment, and illustration available to working people. It was also a social shift whereby workers joined a wider cultural formation that was not restricted to a single age-group, gender, or class. As the previous discussion of magazine readership indicated, working people had by mid-century chosen to become part of a larger and more diverse group: the mass. In making this choice they indicated their consent to the conventional social values represented in many mass-circulation books and magazines. Such consent served their own purposes and did not negate developing class differences or the economic, social, and cultural inequalities from which these differences arose. As we will see, by the 1850s the printed imagery both of generalized social and political protest and of an emergent, although not fully formed, working-class consciousness existed side by side within the English worker's expanding pictorial world. Meanwhile that world held increasingly less of the imagery of power, privilege, and high culture. . . .

Both Entertaining and Informative Material Becomes Available

The printed imagery which had become a common feature of most working lives was myriad in number, varied in form and content, and representative of several cultural levels, any of which might be present within a single artefact such as a magazine, or even within an individual illustration. Here, then, we can only sample a limited selection of the more commonplace kinds of popular printed image and in passing gather something about the diverse ways that such images reflected and combined with other forms of cultural expression and lived experience.

It seems clear that the bulk of the illustrated printed matter that became affordable and readily available for working-class consumption between 1832 and 1860 was either entertaining in a primarily escapist way, or factually informative but still in some measure diverting. For example, serial fiction belonged to the first group; fashion news, popular biography, and so on to the second. As we have seen, the offerings of the *Journal*, *Miscellany*, and *Paper* covered all, or nearly all, of the possible range of inexpensive pictorial entertainment. But, while these three publications achieved the highest circulations among weekly penny magazines, they by no means had that market all to themselves. Other similar miscellanies—all providing illustrated serial fiction, short stories, sundry anecdotes, poems, and informational items— proliferated from the mid-1840s especially. One such publication, the *Welcome Guest*, 'an illustrated journal of recreative literature', had an 1858 circulation of 120,000; meanwhile other comparable magazines like *Lloyd's Weekly Miscellany* and the *Home Magazine* did well enough to enjoy runs of several years. Their recipe for commercial success was the same as their three largest competitors: a sprinkling of mildly instructive nonfiction, and a generous measure of highly spiced stories and pictures of wronged serving-girls, beautiful and beset heiresses, evil poisoners, corpses, spectres, and chambers of death. Apart from this sort of miscellany, there were also a number of other roughly contemporary weekly magazines that confined themselves to a more restricted range of subject-matter. There were, for example, illustrated magazines of fiction such as the *Weekly Novelist*, as well as several, often short-lived journals and gazettes of humour, horror, or crime with titles like the *Penny Satirist*, *Annals of Crime*, and *Calendar of Horrors*.

Inexpensive novels, many of which had at least one illustration, became widely available from the 1840s. Because they were commonly sold in penny parts, such works were now within the means of a large number of working people. One of the most popular of these was [American Harriet Beecher] Stowe's *Uncle Tom's Cabin*, published in England in the early 1850s by two dozen or so different publishers. Three working-class autobiographers fondly recalled the story, and one of this group, the son of a Northumberland coal-miner, recorded that in 1852 *Uncle Tom's Cabin* 'was read aloud in our little family circle'. . . .

Charles Dickens was another successful author of this period and many of his works, such as *The Pickwick Papers* and *Nicholas Nickleby*, appeared in illustrated editions. It is uncertain, though, whether or not many working people read these or other stories by Dickens: he is not mentioned in any of the working-class autobiographies in our sampling; in addition, one-time editor for the house of Cassell, Thomas Frost, believed that Dickens did not become popular among working people until the 1870s. Before then more than a few might well have purchased the cheaply produced and crudely engraved imitations that were about in the 1830s and 1840s: *The Penny Pickwick*, *The Sketchbook by 'Bos'*, *Oliver Twiss*, and *Nickelas Nickelbery*.

The Penny Dreadfuls

If pirated versions of Dickens and the romantic outpourings of [George W.M.] Reynolds lacked the uplifting tone and moral purpose of Mrs Stowe's tale of slavery, they none the less demonstrated a modicum of restraint in style and content when compared to another form of saleable fiction: the so-called 'penny dreadful'. The stories contained in exam-

An Illustration from *The Newgate Calendar*, 1845

The Newgate Calendar *was an anthology recounting the murders, crimes, and escapes of notorious felons. This illustration of the murderer Greenacre and his victim is graphic and gruesome.*

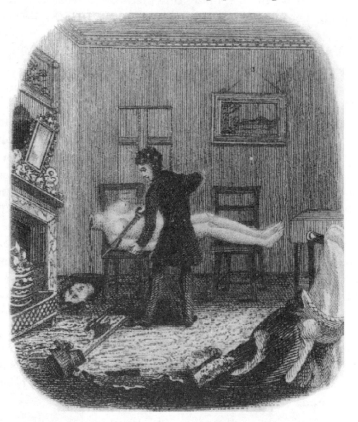

Patricia Anderson, *The Printed Image and the Transformation of Popular Culture: 1790–1860*. New York: Oxford University Press, 1991. "The Murderer Greenacre and his Victim" was first published in *The Newgate Calendar* (London, 1845), title page. British Library.

ples of this type of small, inexpensive, paper-bound book invariably tended to dwell lovingly on crime, horror, and the seamier side of relations between the sexes. So, naturally, they attracted a substantial following of people in search of pleasurable terror, revulsion, titillation, and general escapism. After all, who but the most dedicatedly serious-minded reader could fail to respond to the lure of titles such as *Ada, the Betrayed, or, The Murder at the Old Smithy*, *The Apparition*, *Crimes of the Aristocracy*, *The Secret of the Grey Turret*, *The Death Ship, or, The Pirate's Bride*, and *Varney, the Vampyre*, also published as *The Feast of Blood*?

An illustration from an 1847 edition of this last work provides as good an example as any of the kind of imagery that attracted readers with a penny to spend and a taste for the dreadful. Prominent in the centre of the composition is a horrifically bony and toothy vampire (Varney without doubt) whose lips are fastened on to the neck of a young female victim who flails her arms in agony. As she tormentedly arches her back, she thrusts her breasts upwards, thus providing Varney with a convenient place to rest a loving hand while he takes his nourishment. Here indeed was what our expert on 'cheap literature' called a *'pièce de résistance*[1] for the strong stomach of the million.' Astute publishers of such illustrated fiction were well aware of the popular appetite for graphic images of violence and horror. Edward Lloyd, one of the most prominent and successful of the penny dreadful publishers, was purported to have directed his chief artist to put an extra dollop of saleable 'vigour' into illustrations destined for the dreadfuls. 'There must be more blood—', Lloyd ordered, 'much more blood!'

Blood was not only a staple of tales of supernatural horror, but . . . it was also a basic ingredient in fictional and fact-based tales of crime, . . . [like] that popular anthology of notorious felons and their crimes, the *Newgate Calendar*. Like so many examples of the depiction of crime and horror, one [of them] presented the viewer with a gratifyingly lurid scene of gruesome violence, spiced with the sexual sugges-

1. an outstanding accomplishment

tiveness of the murderer's saw and the victim's naked body, which somehow manages to look both nubile and in a state of incipient rigor mortis.

Of all the *Calendar*'s murderers and miscreants, there were no two more renowned than Dick Turpin, the legendary highwayman, and his contemporary, Jack Sheppard, the one-time carpenter's apprentice turned 'housebreaker', who was especially famous for his daring escapes from various places of incarceration—until Newgate and the gibbet[2] finally claimed him. . . .

Religion and Self-Improvement

With their high popular appeal, Jack Sheppard, Dick Turpin, Varney, and, indeed, all of the villains, heroes, heroines, incidents, events, and imagery associated with entertainment together predominated in the cultural life of the English worker at mid-century. But the transformed popular culture of this period also took in other categories of imagery and experience. As it had in the earlier period, religion and its cultural expressions figured large in many working people's lives. This was reflected in the success of publications such as Charles Knight's *Pictorial Bible* (1835–7, with numerous subsequent editions) and several illustrated religious magazines such as the *Sunday School Penny Magazine* and the *Leisure Hour*, both published in the 1850s. The *Leisure Hour* was a periodical of the Religious Tract Society, which was among those Evangelicals who recognized that religious literature must find a way to match the popular appeal of secular competition like the *London Journal*. The *Leisure Hour* offered its readers fiction, but of a moralistic sort, mildly titillating accounts of idolatry and other heathenish practices in uncivilized corners of the world, pietistic aphorisms, and a generous amount of improving general information. . . .

For those workers whose creed was self-improvement— both intellectual and moral—a transformed popular culture included a greater number of affordable educational publi-

2. a device for hanging a person until dead; a gallows

cations. As we have come to expect, many of these had pictures. Cassell was a leader in the field of illustrated educational publishing with his *Working Man's Friend* (1850-51) and the *Popular Educator* (begun in 1852). Both of these penny weekly periodicals were serious-minded publications for the dedicated autodidact:[3] the latter featured series of lessons in science, foreign languages, history, literature, and so forth; the former offered weighty discussions and occasional tiny illustrations of such general-knowledge subjects as the solar system, the wonders of vegetation, Cromwell[4] and his times, [poet William] Wordsworth, gravity, and the properties of water. Neither publication included fiction, and the *Working Man's Friend* even went so far as to run an essay which, with some force, argued that novels and the reading of them contributed to shallow thinking, immoral tendencies, and the wasting of time and money. . . .

The new educational publications that found their way into working men's associations and into individual hands for private study were replete with articles and anecdotes extolling that set of civilized and civilizing virtues with which we are now well acquainted: self-improvement, thriftiness, hard work, emotional restraint, perseverance, and temperance. The encouragement of the last virtue was of such widespread concern that by the 1850s temperance publications constituted a major sub-genre of the literature of improvement. In addition to the myriad pamphlets and tracts in support of the cause, a number of magazines made their appearance in the 1840s and 1850s: among others were Cassell's *Teetotal Times*, the *Weekly Record, British Temperance Advocate*, and *Band of Hope Review*. . . . Cassell, who was throughout his adult life an active and unwavering advocate of temperance, was understandably more ambitious in his pictorial support of the cause. In 1858, as his biographer recounts it,

> He issued a pair of engravings, 16 inches by 24, entitled GIN and WATER, the artist being Kenny Meadows, and it was

3. self-taught person   4. Oliver Cromwell, the English military, political, and religious leader who led the Parliamentarian victory in the English civil war (1642–1649); served as lord protector (1653–1658)

hoped that these would be hung on the walls of schools, workshops, and cottage houses. 'In the first—GIN—we have the interior of the drunkard's home with a glimpse of the horrors which belong peculiarly to such homes; in the second—WATER—we see how comfort, cleanliness, and peace attend the steps of the temperate man.'

We have no evidence of who actually purchased these engravings, although they appear to have been aimed primarily at working people, and some presumably must have purchased them. Many more must have seen the new temperance magazines, for according to Cassell their 'joint issue' in 1858 was 200,000 to 300,000. He did not specify the precise period of time to which this figure applied, but it is still suggestive that a substantial number of people, workers among them, must have practiced, aspired to, or at the very least taken a mild interest in temperance. . . .

The Printed Imagery of Advertising

By about 1840 that world abounded in a pictorial type which had been comparatively scarce before 1832: the printed imagery of advertising. Advertisers who used the medium of print (rather than painted signboards, for instance, or moving displays on horse-drawn vehicles) now increasingly appreciated the value of imagery for enhancing their messages. The majority of printed advertisements were in the form of posted bills and handbills or insertions in magazines and newspapers. In either case, illustration figured often. In the 1830s the firm of Warren's, the Strand, for example, used a range of images from black cats to portraits of Shakespearian characters, all to advertise their superior brand of bootblacking. Other advertisers similarly used imagery to promote a variety of household goods, food, patent medicines, and cosmetics. Illustrated theatrical playbills also became common by the late 1830s and, in addition to engravings of dramatic scenes, they often used two or three colours of print to advertise such entertainments as the Dramatic Spectacle of MAZEPPA! and THE WILD HORSE!, the BAZAAR OF WONDERS!!, and a host of other spectacles, romances, comedies, and melodramas—many of the latter taking as their subject the dashing, if not wholly civilized, deeds of Dick Turpin and Jack Sheppard.

Advertising in the press became perhaps even more prevalent than bills from the 1840s. In its later years, even the *Penny Magazine* succumbed to the lure of advertising revenue, and while much of its contents might still have dealt in high culture, its wrappers now presented a contrasting study in the mundane, with imagery used to advertise Parr's Life Pills and the like. Similarly the *Journal, Miscellany*, and *Paper*, as well as their many imitative competitors, all carried numerous pictorial advertisements, usually grouped together on one or two pages of endpapers. . . .

Illustrated News and Pictures for Walls

The press was also the medium through which working people began to acquaint themselves with yet another comparatively new pictorial type: the illustration of the news. But even as late as the 1850s this was necessarily a nodding acquaintance, for periodicals such as the *Illustrated London News* and daily newspapers were all well beyond the budgets of working people and, indeed, those of many members of the middle class. The 1840s and 1850s saw the beginnings of a change in this situation with the emergence of penny weekly papers; and such papers further proliferated after the repeal of the newspaper tax in 1855. Of the three most popular mid-century weeklies two—*Reynolds's News* and *News of the World*—were not illustrated. The third, however, *Lloyd's Weekly Newspaper*, offered readers of limited means relatively serious news reporting and illustrations of some of the most important events. . . .

When they were not taking in the news through pictures, or wistfully studying some expensive product in an illustrated advertisement, or losing themselves in the flamboyant world of Jack Sheppard, some working people might well have paused for a few seconds' glance at a picture on the wall of their own small room or cottage. After 1832 this would have been more and more likely a possibility, as inexpensive printed imagery of all kinds and from several sources became widely affordable and available. For example, a working person who wished to relieve a little of the cheerlessness of his or her surroundings might paste a pictorial broadside on the wall, or do the same with an engraving cut from the *Penny Magazine* or any of its illustrated successors. Alternatively, there were also cheap prints of popular actors, society beauties, children, and cats to be had from street sellers. In addition, for only a penny apiece, Cassell offered the *Paper*'s readership 'splendid engravings' of subjects of 'national and historic interest'—all executed 'in the first style of art, with the view of contributing to the adornment of the dwellings of the people'. . . .

By 1860 a Mass Culture Had Evolved

In structuring our understanding of that world as a whole, there are two crucial points to bear in mind. First of all, rapid though it was, the expansion of popular culture and pictorial experience between 1832 and 1860 was not only a matter of change—of the new emerging and the old disappearing. Rather, side by side with all the artefacts of a transformed popular culture—weekly newspapers, pictorial advertisements, mass-circulation magazines, and penny dreadfuls—there remained pictorial survivals with their origins in an earlier popular cultural experience. . . .

The new culture was not simply the non-élitist lived experience of working people, although it was partly that. More significantly, through the primary agency of wide-circulation magazines like the *Penny Magazine* and its three main successors, a transformed popular culture was increasingly a mass experience. Several magazines and newspapers now regularly reached hundreds of thousands of people; and some successful books, *Uncle Tom's Cabin*, for instance, had initially traded in the tens of thousands, and might in exceptional cases top 1 million in total sales over the course of a year and several editions.

A mass experience entailed more, however, than just high sales and circulation figures, and more even than the great number of people that these figures represented. It is most crucial to remember that the most widely sold artefacts of the new culture reached a social cross-section of people, not just a single definitive group or class of them. We have seen this in our consideration of the readership of the *Penny Magazine* and its three successors, and might reasonably assume that imitative magazines like *Lloyd's Miscellany* drew a similarly diverse market. Additionally, the *Saturday Magazine* reached both the middle and working classes, and this was perhaps true of later religious magazines. . . .

Of course not all cultural expressions of the time engaged a social cross-section. It is, for example, difficult to believe that a publication like Cassell's *Working Man's Friend* could attract anyone other than a fairly select segment of the working class in search of intellectual improvement. Even so, from 1832 popular experience was dominated by the magazines, books, advertisements, and imagery that spoke to, pictured, and reflected the interests of a range of people of different ages, sexes, occupations, and classes—that cultural formation which is best characterized by the term 'mass'.

Double Standards in Middle-Class Sexual Morality

J.B. Priestley

J.B. Priestley speculates that middle-class Victorian men determined the public sexual roles both for delicate ladies and for gentlemanly men. According to Priestley, only middle-class men—not upper- or lower-class men—insisted on sexual taboos, perhaps because sexual activity did not suit their efficiency and work ethic. Priestley also speculates about the popularity of prostitution and pornography and those who patronized these businesses. J.B. Priestley is the author of the novel *The Good Companions*; the collection of essays *Delight*; and a play *Dangerous Corner*. He is also the author of the literary history *Literature and Western Man*.

Probably the terms 'gentleman' and 'gentlemanly' were never more freely used than by this middle class. (It is only fair to add that in Dinah Mulock's *John Halifax, Gentleman*, one of the most popular novels of the later 1850s, the hero is first seen as a poor, hard-working orphan.) And all these 'gentlemen' were the husbands and fathers of 'ladies'. It was not the hard-riding tough aristocracy but this middle class that produced so many vaguely invalidish 'ladies' lying half the day on sofas. With them went those other favourite terms—'delicate' and 'delicacy'. Many a middle-class 'lady' and the women who waited on her seemed hardly to belong to the same species. The mistress of the house might seem almost too delicate for this world. The women who kept that house clean and warm or worked sixty hours a week in the husband's factory were assumed to be as strong as horses. This mid-Victorian middle class raised itself as high as possible above the common people, by one sex being determinedly 'gentle-manly' and the other sex being so refined and 'delicate'.

Middle-Class Masculine Values

At one end then we have this deliberately heightened social status, and at the other end the traces that remained of Puritanism and the Evangelical style of life. Between them was the solid core of commercialism, the triumphant trading of mid-Victorian England that earned the money. After all, these were the world's workshop men, who in the 1850s, with their narrow dark clothes and black elongated 'stove-pipe' hats, dressed almost to look like steam engines. No matter what fancywork their wives and daughters might be engaged in, these men could not help being deeply influenced by their engineering, their manufacturing, their careful profit-and-loss accounts. Not for them the careless extravagance of the aristocratic types. They had a strongly conscious dislike and fear, almost amounting to horror, of whatever seemed to them ruinously wasteful, distracting businesslike attention, recklessly consuming energy. It was this, rather than the old puritanical hatred of pleasure, that made them so prudish, so suspicious of sex, so determined that this notorious spendthrift of energy should be kept within narrow bounds. (It is significant that all contemporary warnings, applied to everything from voluptuous heterosexual activities to onanism,[1] emphasize the wasteful effects, the appalling debility following indulgence.) Because the all-important money came not from land but from commerce, from manufacturing, from factories roaring with great steam engines, from a mysterious realm governed by the male, this was a society dominated by the masculine principle, entirely patriarchal. Most women are fairly clear-sighted and realistic and tend to deceive themselves only about some close relationship in which they have heavily invested their emotions—'I know my son loves me and depends upon me.' On the other hand, most men insist upon deceiving themselves, refusing to be clear-sighted and realistic.

---

1. withdrawal in sexual intercourse so that ejaculation takes place outside the vagina; masturbation

They are all the more at the mercy of irrational unconscious drives just because they are so proud of their conscious rationality. We cannot be surprised, therefore, if this mid-Victorian middle-class society, dominated as it was by the masculine principle, with Papa so great a figure of authority and wisdom, should remain a monument of self-deception.

It was this society—certainly neither the upper class nor the common people—that put the Angel in the House. (For a superbly well-documented, if rather too Freudian, study of this whole trend, see Gordon Rattray Taylor's *The Angel-Makers*.) Now while most women could enjoy a few angelic endearments, their experience did not encourage them to believe they were sexless beings, especially at a time when pregnancies were all too frequent. But this was also the time when they were economically dependent on the dominant male, so many of them accepted the angel-role, delicate, tender, comforting and sexually undemanding, that he offered them. The accepted authority on sex in mid-Victorian England was Dr. William Acton, whose study of *The Functions and Disorders of the Re-productive Organs* was published in 1857. He was chiefly concerned with male sexuality, which from boyhood onwards, he believed, was a menace to health and sanity unless severely checked. Marriage offered the safest refuge. He wrote:

> The best mothers, wives, and managers of households, know little or nothing of sexual indulgences. Love of home, children, and domestic duties, are the only passions they feel.
>
> As a general rule, a modest woman seldom desires any sexual gratification for herself. She submits to her husband, but only to please him; and, but for the desire of maternity, would far rather be relieved from his attentions. No nervous or feeble young man need, therefore, be deterred from marriage by any exaggerated notion of the duties required from him. The married woman has no wish to be treated on the footing of a mistress. . . .

But here, we feel, Dr. Acton wrote one sentence too many—the last. In this he gives the game away. Woman herself has now been divided into two. There are modest women, the wives of middle-class citizens in good standing, who submit to their husbands while still thinking about those domestic duties: all the household angels. There are also those sexual demons, the mistresses, delighted to waste a man's money, time and energy. So clearly—and here he was right, as we shall see—a man might have two very different relationships with the fair sex, one delicate and the other wildly indelicate. Indeed, though he does not mention this horror, there might be a woman so lost to decency she could play both roles, submitting in her own house and enjoying herself under another roof. But it is a safe guess that if Dr. Acton had contemplated such a creature he would have seen her as a maenad[2] from the raffish upper class or one of the common people caring nothing for middle-class virtue, refinement, delicacy.

No doubt the 'ladies' in this society were ready to be severe with their erring sisters. Even so, I think the harsh demands for absolute 'purity' came from the men. Though they always announced that they were protecting their wives and daughters from shock or pollution, I also think the rigid taboo of sex came from them. It was Papa himself, not the family, who prohibited in popular fiction any account of specifically sexual feelings, motives, activities. It was he who wanted the wretched seduced girl, no longer 'pure', to be buried in shame, a stranger now to decent society. (Though even Dr. Acton made the startling disclosure that downright prostitutes often made good marriages instead of sinking into the gutter.) It was Papa and not Mama and the girls who compelled men of genius like [Charles] Dickens and [William Makepeace] Thackeray to ignore so much, to write too often with one eye closed. Had the feminine principle been in the ascendant (leading eventually to a 'permissive society') the mid-Victorian novel might have been very different. But the masculine principle was firmly in control of this middle class.

Repressed Feelings and Hypocrisy

However, what is severely repressed by the conscious mind may return in greater force from the unconscious. So determinedly rational and hard-headed men can be overcome by

2. a woman member of the orgiastic cult of Dionysis; a frenzied woman

feeling that is almost hysterical. Employers in this commercial society had to be hard, working as they did within an economic theory that was like a steel mantrap. But either they were frequently overcome by repressed emotion or they deliberately wanted to show how much they could feel. For while their women and girls, as the representatives of sensibility, delicacy and responsive feelings, easily gave way to tears, so too, when the occasion arose, did their masterful men. Expansive pathos, now so distasteful to us, unmanned them at once. Hanging judges would sob over the deaths of [Dickens's characters] Little Nell and Paul Dombey. Dickens in his public readings would have whole audiences in tears, just as when he read aloud his Christmas stories he would be surrounded by weeping friends. A male mid-Victorian quarrel might be ended at the club, not only with a hearty handshake but also with some quick shedding of tears. [Essayist Thomas] Macaulay, a Whig stalwart and no softy in public life, could not revive any happy memory without his eyes filling. Reading biographies and memoirs of this age, we begin to feel that all those side-whiskers and beards must have been damp with tears.

It cannot be said that this middle-class society had inherited that curious strain of melancholy, with all its churchyard brooding, which was characteristic of the eighteenth century. It still lost too many of its young children, but its death rate was better, not worse. Yet mid-Victorian fiction is filled with wasting diseases, slow-motion dying, funerals and cemeteries. (Even school stories, like [F.W.] Farrar's, could not do without them.) Where we have sex at every turn, they had death. Where we linger with lovers, after watching them strip, they lingered round the deathbed, aware of each ebbing pulse. We would find this—if any young novelist or playwright risked it—as shaming and shocking as they would have found the removal of a petticoat, a glimpse of a girl's thigh. They were afraid of sex: we are afraid of death. It seems there must be *something* that frightens us. No society can be on easy terms with everything. It is possible—and it has been generally supposed—that the sexual taboo was imposed because popular mid-Victorian fiction was intended for family reading. Dickens, for one, certainly assumed this. We all have a picture of this family, with the older children listening to Papa or Mama reading aloud one of the safer novels, or Macaulay's *History*, or a popular account of astronomy or geology. We feel that this middle-class society was above all *domestic*. The family and the hearth were at its centre. This was probably true of those members of it who lived in the country or one of the new semi-rural suburbs. But it cannot have been altogether true of the middle-class men who lived in London or in one of the growing provincial cities. To begin with, there were more and more clubs, entirely male creations, and there is plenty of evidence that the more prosperous mid-Victorian husband and father was very much a clubman. He cannot have been reading aloud at home or playing Halma or Happy Families if he was also dining and wining his cronies. There was something else that cannot be ignored, something representing the reverse of that shining medal of purity, delicacy, sexual innocence— all that notorious mid-Victorian night life.

Active London Nightlife

The workshop of the world gave way every night in central London to the whoreshop of the world. An hour spent in or around the Haymarket after midnight would have left any member of our own 'permissive society' speechless from shock. Foreign visitors were staggered by it. Once respectability was left behind, they were in a Venusberg. Even [Russian writer Feodor] Dostoyevsky, no wandering innocent, cried in astonishment at the prostitutes gathering in their thousands. (This was only 1862.) There were mothers, as well as bawds, offering young children. The streets round the Haymarket were crowded with brothels and 'accommodation houses'. Notorious *madames* held nightly festival, to the accompaniment of popping champagne corks, in their own large drawing-rooms of harlotry. The famous courtesans drove down from their villas in St. John's Wood for caviare and oysters and more champagne with the nobility and gentry. The taverns and supper rooms might be wide open until 3 or 4 in the morning. Various notorious night haunts mixed chops and baked potatoes with entertainment, often very obscene. In the humbler streets and alleys to the north and east half-naked whores displayed themselves at their windows or even came running out to catch a customer. Not only were hundreds and hundreds of prostitutes and men meeting in the parks every night, there were women waiting to be picked up as far out as the building sites in the new London suburbs, around recently-built surburban railway stations, indeed almost anywhere if there was sufficient light for a pick-up and darkness nearby for some hasty copulation. So long as a man could pay for it, there was no perversion, no sado-masochistic experiment, no degradation of

The Fashionable Middle Class

In the magazine Punch, *Richard Doyle illustrates the newly rich middle class showing their superiority by parading in Hyde Park, London. The poor outsiders sit on the sidelines.*

John W. Dodds. *The Age of Paradox: A Biography of England 1841–1851.* New York: Rinehart, 1952.

sexuality, that would be denied him. It was as if Aphrodite herself was taking a savage revenge for all that talk of purity, that insistence upon female delicacy, that taboo of sex. Where the modest and merely submissive wives left off, brazen and rapacious whores took over. Eros, as the symbol of natural loving sexuality, was defeated both day and night.

It would be absurd to suggest that most men belonging to this solid middle class spent late nights in or around the Haymarket looking for bawds who would provide them with girls in their 'teens. But, to my mind, it would be equally absurd to believe that this extravagant night life could be maintained without any contribution from the middle class. We read a lot about 'wild young noblemen', on the one hand, and, on the other, about the drunken workmen, sailors and soldiers, ready to spend a shilling or two on a whore. But after all there were not so many young noblemen, and the flash supper rooms, brothels and 'accommodation houses' were well outside the shilling range. This night life must have largely depended upon the patronage of the middle class, which was sufficiently numerous and had the money. However, a fairly large number of its men must have been too timid, perhaps physically too fastidious, probably going in fear of gonorrhea and syphilis (a great scourge during most of the nineteenth century, when so many notable men were among its victims), to risk adventures with loose women. The result of this was an enormous increase in the publication of pornography, that vast—and very tedious—dreamland of the huge unwearied phallus and its endless procession of delighted sexual objects. There is a useful note on this by Gordon Rattray Taylor:

> By making normal sexual activity more difficult, they increased the amount of auto-erotic, perverted and fantasied sexual behaviour; but since these kinds of behaviour are obsessive in character, individuals who exhibit them have recourse to it more frequently than normal individuals have recourse to normal sexual behaviour.

It cannot be denied that it was this middle class, sitting solidly in the centre and controlling most of the money and the votes, that was responsible for this appalling division in sexual behaviour, as bad for women as it was for men. It was these men, so complacently sure they were right, who created the legend of social hypocrisy so notoriously attached to mid-Victorian England, making other peoples distrust all its opinions and activities.

In the main the upper class—as represented, for example, by Lord Palmerston and his circle—did not share this middle-class view of sex. Nor did most of the lower orders, the working class, the common people, though there were among them some groups that were puritanical or strongly evangelical. By and large mid-Victorian working people still took sex naturally. Their girls were modest until aroused by the appeal of a personal relationship. Some country girls were of course seduced by promise of marriage, and then, after bearing an illegitimate child or having an abortion, fled from their homes and made for London or the nearest city to become prostitutes. But this situation, so familiar in fiction, was not at all the commonest. What drove most girls and women into prostitution or semi-prostitution was poverty, the hard conditions of female labour, and starvation wages. Two points are worth making here. The first is, most of the very people who denounced prostitution and tried to 'rescue fallen women' made no attempt to end poverty, hard conditions, very low wages. The second point is that it was not until much later, in our own time, that the more comfortable members of the working class began to acquire the excessive prudishness of the old Victorian middle class.

Mid-Victorian Pornography

The pornography of the mid-Victorian period tells us little or nothing because it is so much fantasy. The best evidence we have so far comes from an extraordinary saga of sexuality, undoubtedly quite genuine, called *My Secret Life*. At this time of writing the full text is not generally available, but longish typical extracts, about as much as most of us want, can be found in 'Walter', *My Secret Life*, recently edited by Drs. Eberhard and Phyllis Kronhausen, and *The Other Victorians* by Professor Steven Marcus. Though it is completely frank in its account of a wide range of sexuality, *My Secret Life* is not pornography, no long trip through a priapic[3] dream world, but a completely realistic description of all his sexual adventures by a man unusually obsessed by eroticism. He did not seek out prostitutes, as many men have done, because he hated women and wanted to degrade them. A sexual athlete, he loved having them, all kinds and at all times, and about 1,200 altogether, he calculated. He has left us a loving epic of the English vulva, and no man, English or alien, can ever have doted on it more. With middle age and satiety creeping in, he tries perverse or silly antics, even disgusting himself at times, but throughout most of his chronicle he is genuinely interested in and concerned about his very wide range of sexual partners, and his complete frankness and his attention to details make him a very good witness indeed. Revealing his own Secret Life, he takes the lid off a great many other people's secret lives, male and female, and gives us not merely a transformation scene but a whole hidden panorama of Victorian England with its clothes off. He made use of his money but he was not wholly dependent upon prostitution. His relations with women were far from being completely commercial—more often than not, they enjoyed him because it was so obvious he enjoyed them— and both his sexual and his social evidence are very valuable.

Two Kinds of Dinner Parties

When we leave sex we can find in the letters, memoirs, novels of these 1850s many accounts, hardly enticing, of this dominant middle class amusing itself. Here a notable part is played by its solemn and pretentious dinner parties, with the tables weighed down by massive silver plate and overloaded with food and often graced, snobbery being so rampant, by some titled guest of honour. Ultra-respectability, complacency, stiffness and stuffiness do not help to create a lively or even easy social life. But one section of this society had broken away almost completely from its general style, manners,

3. of, relating to, or resembling a phallus; phallic; relating to or overly concerned with masculinity

prejudices. It was 'Bohemian' (their term, not mine) and largely made up of authors (Dickens prominent among them), journalists, painters, actors, and versatile odd fellows like Albert Smith, the provider of one-man entertainments. Most of them worked hard and were far from being seedy spongers, but when work was done they liked parties, late suppers, planning amateur theatricals, games and singing, and jaunts out of town on Sundays. In the chapter on his early married life, during the 1850s, Edmund Yates in his *Recollections* describes the more respectable Bohemians enjoying themselves:

> As may be readily imagined, I had not very much leisure in the midst of all this employment, but such as I had was always pleasantly passed. Sundays with us were always 'Sundays out'—at Skindles, at that time a delightfully quiet place, with no lawn, no river-rooms, no neighbouring Guards' Club; at Thames Ditton; at Richmond; at the Swan at Staines; at Laker's Hotel at Redhill—sometimes my wife and I alone, oftener with the Keeleys and Albert [Smith] and a party. On Friday nights, there was always a gathering in Gower Street, at the house of Abraham Solomon, who had just made a hit with his picture 'Waiting for the Verdict', where would be Millais with his 'Huguenot' success upon him, young and handsome, as in the medallion which Alexander Munro had just completed of him; and Frith, putting the finishing touches to his 'Derby Day'. Frank Stone, Augustus Egg, and Sant; Dutton Cook, undecided whether to take to pen or pencil as his means of living; Ernest Hart, whose sister Solomon afterwards married, and William Fenn. A quietly Bohemian evening: a little dancing, a few games of 'tonneau', a capital supper with a speciality of cold fish, then cigars, and singing by Frank Topham or Desanges, and imitations by Dillon Croker, 'and so home'.

Appendix of Documents

Document 1: Liberty and Individualism

In this excerpt from On Liberty, *John Stuart Mill argues that humans should have the liberty to form opinions and to act on them. He also argues, however, that liberty is limited to insure that an individual's opinions and actions do not harm or unnecessarily bother others. Without liberty to choose, Mill asserts, humans are little more than apelike imitators.*

Such being the reasons which make it imperative that human beings should be free to form opinions, and to express their opinions without reserve; and such the baneful consequences to the intellectual, and through that to the moral nature of man, unless this liberty is either conceded, or asserted in spite of prohibition; let us next examine whether the same reasons do not require that men should be free to act upon their opinions—to carry these out in their lives, without hindrance, either physical or moral, from their fellow men, so long as it is at their own risk and peril. This last proviso is of course indispensable. No one pretends that actions should be as free as opinions. On the contrary, even opinions lose their immunity, when the circumstances in which they are expressed are such as to constitute their expression a positive instigation to some mischievous act. An opinion that corn-dealers are starvers of the poor, or that private property is robbery, ought to be unmolested when simply circulated through the press, but may justly incur punishment when delivered orally to an excited mob assembled before the house of a corn-dealer, or when handed about among the same mob in the form of a placard. Acts, of whatever kind, which, without justifiable cause, do harm to others, may be, and in the more important cases absolutely require to be, controlled by the unfavourable sentiments, and, when needful, by the active interference of mankind. The liberty of the individual must be thus far limited; he must not make himself a nuisance to other people. But if he refrains from molesting others in what concerns them, and merely acts according to his own inclination and judgement in things which concern himself, the same reasons which show that opinion should be free, prove also that he should be allowed, without molestation, to carry his opinions into practice at his own cost. . . .

It is desirable, in short, that in things which do not primarily concern others, individuality should assert itself. Where, not the person's own character, but the traditions or customs of other people are the rule of conduct, there is wanting one of the principal ingredients of human happiness, and quite the chief ingredient of individual and social progress. . . .

He who lets the world, or his own portion of it, choose his plan of life for him, has no need of any other faculty than the ape-like one of imitation. He who chooses his plan for himself, employs all his faculties. He must use observation to see, reasoning and judgement to foresee, activity to gather materials for decision, discrimination to decide, and when he has decided, firmness and self-control to hold to his deliberate decision.

John Stuart Mill, *On Liberty*, 1859. In *The World of the Victorians: An Anthology of Poetry and Prose*, ed. E.D.H. Johnson. New York: Charles Scribner's Sons, 1964.

Document 2: The Necessity of Government Interference

Thomas Hill Green argues in Liberal Legislation and Freedom of Contract *that laissez-faire, the economic doctrine that opposes government regulation of or interference in commerce, is an inadequate economic system so long as society includes poor, downtrodden, overworked masses. By their own self-reliance those poor cannot lift themselves to independence; nor can employers, left to their own profit taking, provide for the welfare of the poor without government regulation and help in providing health, education, and housing.*

Now, we shall probably all agree that a society in which the public health was duly protected, and necessary education duly provided for, by the spontaneous action of individuals, was in a higher condition than one in which the compulsion of law was needed to secure these ends. But we must take men as we find them. Until such a condition of society is reached, it is the business of the state to take the best security it can for the young citizens' growing up in such health and with so much knowledge as is necessary for their real freedom. In so doing it need not at all interfere with the independence and self-reliance of those whom it requires to do what they would otherwise do for themselves. . . . But it was not their case [that of the self-sufficient man] that the laws we are considering were especially meant to meet. It was the overworked women, the ill-housed and untaught families, for whose benefit they were intended. And the question is whether without these laws the suffering classes could have been delivered quickly or slowly from the condition they were in. Could the enlightened self-interest of benevolence of individuals, working under a system of unlimited freedom of contract, have ever brought them into a state compatible with the free development of the human faculties? No one considering the facts can have any doubt as to the answer to this question. Left to itself, or to the operation of casual benevolence, a degraded population perpetuates and increases itself. Read any of the authorised accounts, given before royal or parliamentary commissions, of the state of the labourers, especially of the women and children, as they were in our great industries before the law was first brought to bear on them, and before freedom of contract was first interfered with in them. Ask yourself what chance there was of a generation, born and bred under such conditions, ever contracting itself out of them. Given a certain standard of moral and material well-being, people may be trusted not to sell their labour, or the labour of their children, on terms which would not allow that standard to be maintained. But with large masses of our population, until the laws we have been considering took effect, there was no such standard. There was nothing on their part, in the way either of self-respect or established demand for comforts, to prevent them from working and living, or from putting their children to work and live, in a way in which no one who is to be a healthy and free citizen can work and live. No doubt there were many high-minded employers who did their best for their workpeople before the days of state-interference, but they could not prevent less scrupulous hirers of labour from hiring it on the cheapest terms. It is true that cheap labour is in the long run dear labour, but it is so only in the long run, and eager traders do not think of the long run. If labour is to be had under conditions incompatible with the health or decent housing or education of the labourer, there will always be plenty of people to buy it under those conditions, careless of the burden in the shape of rates and taxes which they may be laying up for posterity. Either the standard of well-being on the part of the sellers of labour must prevent them from selling their labour under those conditions, or the law must prevent it. With a population such as ours was forty years ago, and still largely is, the law must prevent it and continue the prevention for some generations, before the sellers will be in a state to prevent it for themselves.

Thomas Hill Green, *Liberal Legislation and Freedom of Contract*, 1885–1888. In *The Victorian Mind*, ed. Gerald B. Kauvar and Gerald C. Sorensen. New York: G.P. Putnam's Sons, 1969.

Document 3: Antagonism Toward the Coming Railways

Scottish author and biographer Samuel Smiles enumerates public objections to the coming railways, which, he maintains, stem from ignorance and prejudice. The public, according to this excerpt from The Life of George Stephenson, Railway Engineer, *predicted ruin and disaster for the promoters.*

Railways had thus, like most other great social improvements, to force their way against the fierce antagonism of united ignorance and prejudice. Public-spirited obstructives were ready to choke the invention at its birth, on the ground of the general good. The forcible invasion of property—the intrusion of public roads into private domains—the noise and nuisance caused by locomotives, and the danger of fire to the adjoining property, were dwelt upon *ad nauseam*. The lawlessness of navies was a source of great terror to quiet villages. Then the breed of horses would be destroyed; country innkeepers would be ruined; posting towns would become depopulated; the turnpike roads would be deserted; and the institution of the English Stagecoach, with its rosy gilled coachman and guard, known to every buxom landlady at roadside country inns, would be destroyed for ever. Fox-covers and game-preserves would be interfered with; agricultural communication destroyed; land thrown out of cultivation; landowners and farmers alike reduced to beggary; the poor rates increased in consequence of the numbers of labourers thrown out of employment by the railways; and all this in order that Liverpool, Manchester, and Birmingham manufacturers, merchants, and cotton-spinners, might establish a monstrous monopoly in railroads! However, there was always this consolation to wind up with,—that the canals would beat the railroads, and that, even when the latter were made, the public would not use them, nor trust either their persons or their goods to the risks of railway accidents and explosions. They would thus prove only monuments of the folly of their projectors, whom they must inevitably involve in ruin and disaster.

Samuel Smiles, *The Life of George Stephenson, Railway Engineer,* 1857. In *The Victorian Mind,* ed. Gerald B. Kauvar and Gerald C. Sorensen. New York: G.P. Putnam's Sons, 1969.

Document 4: The Opening of the Manchester and Liverpool Railway

On September 19, 1830, the newspaper Observer *reported the celebration opening the railway between Manchester and Liverpool. Amazed by the prediction of a speed of sixteen to eighteen miles per hour, the reporter describes the locomotive's grace and power, comparing it to a pony.*

This great national work [the Manchester and Liverpool Railway] was opened to the public on Wednesday last, with all the ceremonies befitting such an important occasion. The Duke of Wellington, Mr. Huskisson, Sir R. Peel, Prince Esterhazy, and Mr. Holmes were guests of the Committee, together with almost every person of consideration in the neighbouring counties. . . .

The rate of travelling is spoken of as being likely to average about sixteen or eighteen miles an hour, so that it will bring the two great towns, Manchester and Liverpool, within half the present distance from each other. . . .

As early as seven o'clock, the people of Liverpool were seen flocking in crowds to the Tunnel, in order to secure good places for a view of the procession. . . . Eight of the Company's beautiful loco-motive engines were brought down to the mouth of the Tunnel. . . . While these masterly productions of human intellect were being paraded up and down on the road with the same ease and under as much command as a small pony, we could hardly persuade ourselves that we were not looking on animal life. The steam flowed from them with a curiously sharp noise, and considerably heightened the delusion. A person who has not seen it can have no idea of the graceful and easy movement of one of these machines, and the power with which they perform their work is really surprising even in these days of mechanical improvement.

Marion Miliband, ed., *The Observer of the Nineteenth Century: 1791–1901*. London: Longmans, 1966.

Document 5: The Mechanical Age

In an essay published anonymously in the Edinburgh Review *in June 1829, Thomas Carlyle criticizes his age for its lack of heroism, spiritualism, and morality. Instead, he says, it is a mechanical age with all manner of handmade efforts replaced by machinery.*

Were we required to characterise this age of ours by any single epithet, we should be tempted to call it, not an Heroical, Devotional, Philosophical, or Moral Age, but, above all others, the Mechanical Age. It is the Age of Machinery, in every outward and inward sense of that word; the age which, with its whole undivided might, forwards, teaches and practises the great art of adapting means to ends. Nothing is now done directly, or by hand; all is by rule and calculated contrivance. For the simplest operation, some helps and accompaniments, some cunning abbreviating process is in readiness. Our old modes of exertion are all discredited, and thrown aside. On every hand, the living artisan is driven from his workshop, to make room for a speedier, inanimate one. The shuttle drops from the fingers of the weaver, and falls into iron fingers that ply it faster. The sailor furls his sail, and lays down his oar; and bids a strong, unwearied servant, on vaporous wings, bear him through the waters. Men have crossed oceans by steam; the Birmingham Fireking has visited the fabulous East; and the genius of the Cape, were there any Camoens[1] now to sing it, has again been alarmed, and with far stranger thunders than Gama's.[2] There is no end to machinery. Even the horse is stripped of his harness, and finds a fleet fire-horse yoked in his stead. Nay, we have an artist that hatches chickens by steam; the very brood-hen is to be superseded! For all earthly, and for some unearthly purposes, we have machines and mechanic furtherances; for mincing our cabbages; for casting us into magnetic sleep. We remove mountains, and make seas our smooth highways; nothing can resist us. We war with rude Nature; and, by our resistless engines, come off always victorious, and loaded with spoils.

Thomas Carlyle, essay in *The Edinburgh Review*, June 1829. In E.D.H. Johnson, ed., *The World of the Victorians: An Anthology of Poetry and Prose*. New York: Charles Scribner's Sons, 1964.

Document 6: "God's Grandeur"

Written in 1877, Gerard Manley Hopkins's sonnet is a nature poem in which the speaker regrets what humans have done to the grand handiwork of God. Even the language plods: "ooze of oil," "smeared," "smudge," "smell." But the sestet—the last six lines—counters the speaker's despair by remembering that the world is still hovered over by a warm and bright spirit.

The world is charged with the grandeur of God.
It will flame out, like shining from shook foil;
It gathers to a greatness, like the ooze of oil
Crushed. Why do men then now not reck his rod?
Generations have trod, have trod, have trod;
And all is seared with trade; bleared, smeared with toil;
And wears man's smudge and shares man's smell—the soil
Is bare now, nor can foot feel, being shod.
And for all this, nature is never spent;
There lives the dearest freshness deep down things;
And though the last lights off the black West went

1. Luiz Vaz de Camoen was a Portuguese writer whose epic poem *Os Lusíadas* is one of Portugal's greatest literary works.   2. Vasco da Gama, the hero of Camoen's *Lusíadas*, was the first to sail around the Cape of Good Hope.

Oh, morning, at the brown brink eastward, springs—
Because the Holy Ghost over the bent
World broods with warm breast and with ah! bright wings.

Gerald B. Kauvar and Gerald C. Sorensen, eds., *The Victorian Mind.* New York: G.P. Putnam's Sons, 1969.

Document 7: The Chartists Adopt the People's Charter

The Chartist movement evolved from the London Working Men's Association founded in 1836; by 1838 members had drafted a charter demanding universal suffrage. On September 23, 1838, the newspaper Observer *published a story covering the meeting at which the people's charter was adopted.*

The Meeting of the Working Classes took place on Monday, in New Palace-yard. The announcement of the Meeting assumed the title of 'The Great Metropolitan Demonstration of the Working Classes'. . . . For the last fortnight the whole of the metropolis and the surrounding hamlets and villages have been placarded with posters and hand-bills, announcing the demonstration, and inviting attendance from the ranks of the democracy. . . . All lovers of the people's charter, with its six principles, had been implored to attend and give force to the Meeting. . . .

Mr. Robert Hartwell moved the resolution:

'That the principles of representation, as defined by the "people's charter," are just and reasonable, embracing, as it does, universal suffrage, no property qualification, annual parliaments, equal representation, payment of members, and vote by ballot; which, in their practical operation, would, in the opinion of this meeting, be the means of returning just representatives to the Commons' House of Parliament—persons who, being responsible to and being paid by the people, would be more likely to promote the just interests of the nation than those who now constitute that assembly. This meeting, therefore, solemnly adopts the "people's charter", as a measure of justice they are resolved by all legal means to endeavour to obtain. . . .'

Mr. Leader followed. He said he looked upon the present meeting, and the agitation out of which it sprung, as the first step in a great struggle. . . . The barons had got Magna Carta, the middle classes had obtained the Reform Bill, and it was now for the working men to rally round the 'people's charter'.

Marion Miliband, ed., *The Observer of the Nineteenth Century: 1791–1901.* London: Longmans, 1966.

Document 8: Chartist Petitions Presented to Parliament

Three times—in 1839,1841, and 1848—the Chartists, a working-class movement demanding universal suffrage, presented petitions to Parliament, and three times Parliament rejected them. Thomas Atwood, a Birmingham banker, member of Parliament, and friend of Chartists, presented their petitions in 1839. An excerpt from these petitions follows. Though the Chartists' petitions were formally rejected, all of their demands but one (annual elections) were adopted by the end of the nineteenth century.

That the only authority on which any body of men can make laws and govern society, is delegation from the people.

That as Government was designed for the benefit and protection of, and must be obeyed and supported by all, therefore all should be equally represented.

That any form of Government which fails to effect the purposes for which it was designed, and does not fully and completely represent the whole people, who are compelled to pay taxes to its support and obey the laws resolved upon by it, is unconstitutional, tyrannical, and ought to be amended or resisted.

That your honourable House, as at present constituted, has not been elected by, and acts irresponsibly of, the people; and hitherto has only represented parties, and benefitted the few, regardless of the miseries, grievances, and petitions of the many. Your honourable House has enacted laws contrary to the expressed wishes of the people, and by unconstitutional means enforced obedience to them, thereby creating an unbearable despotism on the one, and degrading slavery on the other.

That if your honourable House is of opinion that the people of Great Britain and Ireland ought not to be fully represented, your petitioners pray that such opinion may be unequivocally made known, that the people may fully understand what they can or cannot expect from your honourable House: because if such be the decision of your honourable House, your petitioners are of opinion that where representation is denied, taxation ought to be resisted.

That your petitioners instance, in proof of their assertion, that your honourable House has not been elected by the people; that the population of Great Britain and Ireland is at the present time about twenty-six millions of persons; and that yet, out of this number, little more than nine hundred thousand have been permitted to vote in the recent election of representatives to make laws to govern the whole.

That the existing state of representation is not only extremely limited and unjust, but unequally divided, and gives preponderating influence to the landed and monied interests to the utter ruin of the small-trading and labouring classes.

Sydney W. Jackman, ed., *The English Reform Tradition: 1700–1910*. Englewood Cliffs, NJ: Prentice-Hall, 1965.

Document 9: Peasants Protest the Corn Laws

The Corn Laws were passed to keep grain prices (in Great Britain all grains are called corn, and what Americans call corn is called maize) high enough to ensure good profits for landowners. The Anti-Corn League was established to abolish price setting and to allow free trade, thus lowering prices so that grain and bread would be affordable for poor workers. On February 15, 1846, the newspaper Observer *covered a protest rally where peasants explained their poverty and expressed their objections to the Corn Laws and the "bread-taxing oligarchy."*

On Tuesday night last a moonlight meeting of the . . . hewers of wood and drawers of water in the agricultural county of Wilts, was held at Bremhill. . . . It was no ordinary public meeting. Women spoke at it as well as men. It was a meeting of the local peasantry, held to interchange the sad history of their slow starvation. It had originated entirely with the working men. . . .

It was an intensely cold, but beautifully clear and serene night. . . . It was curious to see the groups—the men with their smock frocks showing like white moving patches in the moonlight—making their way from all sides—appearing from the narrow streets—gliding across the churchyard—to the place of meeting. . . .

The proceedings commenced soon after seven, when there were probably about 1,500 persons present—clustered in a dense mass round the stone cross of the market place, and the canvas tent. A labourer, Job Gingel, took the chair, that is, seated himself upon one of the stone steps, forming the basement of the cross. . . .

Mr. Edwards of Marlborough, helped the rustic chairman in the official part of his duties—of which of course the poor man had no more notion than a Hindoo of icebergs.

'My friends—I be a labouring man, I have a wife and seven children in family. My wages at the present time is 8s. a week (cries of 'you can't live on that—you can't'). In the beginning of December last I only got 7s. . . . I do ask what the Wiltshire labourer has done, or what crimes he has committed, that he be so deprived of necessaries—that he be worse off than the convicts on board the hulks (loud cheers)? . . . Oh, friends . . . the hunger and distress which we have been lying under so long be owing to the Corn-laws (cheers). They protect us, do they (a voice: 'Bean't you one of the Wiltshire protected labourers')? I be protected, but I be starving (hear, hear). And now let any other labouring man come forward and speak (cheers)'. . . .

Mr. Gale, a Chartist, understood to be from London, here made an attempt to create a disturbance. He claimed, as a working man, to be heard, and commenced a tirade against machinery, full of the usual thinking. His exhortations, however, to charge, not the Corn-laws, or any laws, but the thrashing and dressing machines with their misery, was groaned down by the multitude with a promptness which did them very great credit, and the *Gale* got down as suddenly as it had arisen.

One of the speakers afterwards charged this man with being the agent of the monopolists sent down to disturb the meeting. . . . His interference was met by a general chorus of groaning, and cries of 'We come here to speak of the Corn-laws, not of machinery,' in the midst of which Mr. Gale disappeared.

John Batchelor, of Pewsey, a labourer, was the next speaker. For the last fortnight he had only received 6s. a week. He knew many men with four children who had only 6s. and 5s. (shame). For himself he did not know what to do. He expected to be discharged when he got home for having come to the meeting. . . . 'It be them Corn-laws, them cursed Corn-laws, which made bread dear. The poor man must labour, and the farmer could not afford to pay, all through the Corn-laws (hear, hear). The repeal, and small farms for large ones—that was what they wanted (hear, hear). He had been employed like a horse in drawing a cart (shame). Yes, but he had: he had pulled it more than twelve miles a day, and it was fully a ton weight (shame, shame). He was one of five men yoked to the cart. That was the way protection used them.' . . .

A female then stood forward to speak. She was a middle-aged woman, dressed in a long grey cloak, and old bonnet, and she partly read what she had to say by the light which the chairman held—partly spoke it fluently enough.

'My name (she began) is Lucy Simpkins. I am from Preston. I am the wife of a labouring man. I have had seven children all born in lawful wedlock. There are five living—two I buried. I have a boy seven years of age. He works for 3d. a day; . . . Yes, and when I was confined last, I had nothing to eat from one o'clock one day until four o'clock the next day (shame, shame). I wished I had a good jug of gruel; but a poor labouring woman like myself came in, and said, "I have brought you something to eat; bread with sugar on it. I had no cheese, or I would have brought that" (shame). And recollect, neighbours, this is under a protecting law (a voice, "I am a witness to the truth of what she says"). My husband is not a drunkard, nor anything of the kind, but a good husband to me, and a good father to his children, but he can't make his money go farther than it will (hear, hear). Many a Monday morning I say to him, "Well, how be we to get through this week, we have no food and no fire." Well, but Saturday comes, and we have got through, but how I don't rightly know. We manage it somehow. But that ain't living ("no more it be") . . . if free trade will make bread cheap, then I want free trade (loud cheers).'

Marion Miliband, ed., *The Observer of the Nineteenth Century: 1791–1901*. London: Longmans, 1966.

Document 10: The Corn Law Rhymes

The Corn Laws, tariffs on grain established to ensure landowners a profit for their corn, were opposed by the Anti-Corn League. Poet Ebenezer Elliott supported the anti–Corn Law movement and wrote poems in protest, one of which follows.

> Avenge the plunder'd poor, oh Lord!
> But not with fire, but not with sword,
> Not as at Peterloo[1] they died,
> Beneath the hoofs of coward pride.
> Avenge our rags, our chains, our sighs,
> The famine in our children's eyes!
> But not with sword—no, not with fire
> Chastise thou Britain's locustry!
> Lord, let them feel thy heavier ire;
> Whip them, oh Lord! with poverty!
> Then, cold in soul as coffined dust,
> Their hearts as tearless, dead and dry,
> Let them in outraged mercy trust,
> And find that mercy they deny!
>
> Bread-tax eating absentee,
> What hath bread-tax done for thee?—
> Crammed thee from our children's plates,

1. In 1819 at Peter's Field, Manchester, troops panicked and charged a peaceable crowd of sixty thousand people. Protesting their lack of Parliamentary representation, eleven were killed and at least four hundred injured.

Made thee all that nature hates,
Filled thy skin with untaxed wine,
Filled thy purse with cash of mine,
Filled thy breast with hellish schemes,
Filled thy head with fatal dreams
Of potatoes basely sold
At the price of wheat in gold,
And of Britons styed to eat
Wheat-priced roots instead of wheat.

England! what for mine and me,
What hath bread-tax done for thee?
It hath shown what kinglings are,
Stripp'd the hideous idols bare,
Sold thy greatness, stain'd thy name,
Struck thee from the rolls of fame.

Make haste, slow rogues! prohibit trade,
Prohibit honest gain;
Turn all the good that God hath made
To fear, and hate, and pain;
Till beggars all, assassins all,
All cannibals we be,
And death shall have no funeral,
From shipless sea to sea.

Child, what hast thou with sleep to do?
Awake, and dry thine eyes!
Thy tiny hands must labor too;
Our bread is taxed. Arise!
Arise, and toil long hours twice seven,
For pennies two or three;
Thy woes make angels weep in heaven,—
But England still is free.

Up, weary man of eighty-five,
And toil in hopeless woe!
Our bread is tax'd, our rivals thrive,
Our gods will have it so.
Yet God is undethroned on high,
And undethron'd be:
Father of all! hear thou our cry,
And England shall be free!

Ebenezer Elliott, *Corn Law Rhymes and Other Poems*, 1844. In *The English Reform Tradition: 1790–1910*, ed. Sydney W. Jackman. Englewood Cliffs, NJ: Prentice-Hall, 1965.

Document 11: The Great Exhibition, 1851

Prince Albert instigated an international exhibition of industry, science, and commerce held in Hyde Park, London, in the Crystal Palace, designed by Joseph Paxton especially for the exhibition. The event attracted over 6 million foreign and British visitors. On May 4, 1851, the news-paper Observer *reported on the opening ceremonies.*

On Thursday, May 1st, at twelve o'clock, the Great Exhibition of the Industry of all Nations was inaugurated with the ceremonial observances of a solemn act of State, by her Majesty the Queen of Great Britain and Ireland. The 1st of May 1851, will, therefore, be a memorable day in the history of England, marking thus as it does, through all time, a great epoch in the annals of human industry. The whole world, invited to a vast competition in the power of conceiving and perfecting works of art and industry; examples of such works forwarded from every clime, and collected in a structure itself so novel, so ingenious and so graceful as only not to sur-pass in interest the congregated wonders of its contents; this dis-play of marvels inaugurated by the most powerful Monarch of the earth, greeted in the solemn act by the most affectionate homage and the most devoted loyalty that has ever acknowledged at once, and supported the majesty and the might of human government, presented a scene not often recorded in the annals of the world.
. . . The first impression is that of a great and brilliant specta-cle. The eye, whether of intelligent science or of untaught taste, dwells gladly on the long lines of architectural symmetry—is charmed with the striking and graceful contrasts of bright waters, gorgeous fittings, and green feathery foliage in the transept. . . .[2]
As the first conception of the scheme now so happily completed came forth from Buckingham Palace . . . so it was in harmony with the whole idea and the whole execution of it, that the last finishing touch should be given to it by royalty—that Queen Victoria, in short, should have opened in person the Great Parliament of Labour. . . .
The Great Exhibition of all Nations will form an era at once in the national and in the industrial annals of the world; for as it will attract, probably, the greatest human assemblage ever collected to-gether upon one small spot of the earth's surface, so will it likewise determine the exact degree up to which, in the middle of the 19th century, the skill and ingenuity of man have arrived. . . . To judge from the aspect of the building between twelve and three o'clock, the country visitors, by whom it is now inundated, divide their

2. the Crystal Palace designed by Joseph Paxton

time pretty fairly between the sight-seeing and the eating and drinking. . . . Now that a bountiful supply of bread and cold meat can be had for 7d., the working classes are rather disposed to rely upon the resources of the establishment than to burden themselves with baskets and bundles. . . .

Marion Miliband, ed., *The Observer of the Nineteenth Century: 1791–1901*. London: Longmans, 1966.

Document 12: What They Ate at the Great Exhibition

The First Report of the Commissioners of the Exhibition of 1851 itemized the following list of food and drink consumed at the exhibition.

Bread, quarterns	52,094	Savoury Patties	23,040 lbs
" cottage loaves	60,698	Italian cakes	11,797
" French rolls	7,617	Biscuits	37,300 lbs
Pound cakes	68,428	Bath buns	934,691
do at 3d	36,950	Plain buns	870,027
Savoury cakes	20,415	Banbury cakes	34,070
" Pies	33,456 lbs	Sausage rolls	28,046
Victoria biscuits	73,280	Mustard	1,120 lbs
Macaroons	1,500 lbs	Jellies	2,400 quarts
Rich cakes	2,280 lbs	Coffee	14,299 lbs
Pastry at 2d	36,000	Tea	1,015 lbs
Schoolcakes	4,800	Chocolate	4,836 lbs
Preserved cherries, etc.	4,840 lbs	Milk	33,432 quarts
Pine apples	2,000	Cream	32,049 quarts
Pickles	1,046 gallons	Schweppe's Soda	
Meat	113 tons	Water, Lemonade,	
Potted meat,		& Ginger beer	1,092,337 bottles
tongues, etc.	36,130 lbs	Masters' Pear Syrup	5,350 bottles
Hams	33 tons	Rough ice	363 tons
Potatoes	36 tons	Salt	37 tons

E. Royston Pike, *"Golden Times": Human Documents of the Victorian Age*. New York: Frederick A. Praeger, 1967.

Document 13: The Death of Prince Albert

Prince Albert, husband of Queen Victoria, became ill with typhoid and died on December 14, 1861. The newspaper Observer *reported his death and a tribute on December 15 and a further reflection on December 22.*

Prince Albert is dead! It was only yesterday that he was, as it were, full of 'lusty life'—today he lies in 'cold obstruction'. Alas for the Queen! who has lost the partner of her life—the first and dearest object of her affections. Alas for pomp and vanity! that this erstwhile mighty prince should now be insensible to praise or blame, food for the worm. . . .

Placed in a difficult position, Prince Albert knew how to deport himself so discreetly and so well, that he has died without leaving a single enemy, while his friends were a host. . . . He was a man of elegant mind, of cultivated tastes, of a clear understanding, and of high and lofty aspirations for the public good. The Great Exhibition of 1851 will be a lasting monument to his memory; and the Great Exhibition of 1862 will be not less so. It was entirely owing to his perseverance and patronage that these international monuments of peace and progress were erected, and to him is honestly owing their perfection as well as their inception.

Peace to his ashes! A good husband, a good father, a wise prince, and a safe counsellor, England will not soon 'look upon his like again.'

• • • • •

. . . The Prince's sufferings during the last day or two of his life are said to have been agonising. When an attempt was made to lift him, or move his position, his groans were distressing to hear. During the latter part of the week his weakness was so great that he could not raise his head from his pillow. On Saturday evening, shortly after eight o'clock, when no hope remained, Her Majesty and her children were admitted into the chamber of death to take a last earthly farewell of the Prince. All were present save the Crown Princess of Prussia, Prince Alfred, and Prince Leopold. The scene was intensely painful and affecting. . . .

After death the features of His Royal Highness had more than the usual pallor. The face, always composed and statuesque in expression, was wonderfully calm, placid, and peaceful in death, as if the figure had been suddenly transmuted into the whitest alabaster.

Marion Miliband, ed., *The Observer of the Nineteenth Century: 1791–1901*. London: Longmans, 1966.

Document 14: A University's Practical Purpose

In this excerpt from The Idea of a University, *John Henry Newman lays out his ideas of what a university should accomplish: Rather than trying to produce heroes and great artists and leaders, a university should train ordinary citizens to be good members of society, to think clearly, to make realistic judgments, to articulate ideas eloquently, and to live comfortably with fellow human beings.*

If then a practical end must be assigned to a University course, I say it is that of training good members of society. Its art is the art of social life, and its end is fitness for the world. It neither confines its views to particular professions on the one hand, nor creates heroes or inspires genius on the other. Works indeed of genius fall under no art; heroic minds come under no rule; a University is not a birthplace of poets or of immortal authors, of founders of schools, leaders of colonies, or conquerors of nations. It does not promise a generation of Aristotles or Newtons, of Napoleons or Washingtons, of Raphaels or Shakespeares, though such miracles of nature it has before now contained within its precincts. Nor is it content on the other hand with forming the critic or the experimentalist, the economist or the engineer, though such too it includes within its scope. But a University training is the great ordinary means to a great but ordinary end; it aims at raising the intellectual tone of society, at cultivating the public mind, at purifying the national taste, at supplying true principles to popular enthusiasm and fixed aims to popular aspiration, at giving enlargement and sobriety to the ideas of the age, at facilitating the exercise of political power, and refining the intercourse of private life. It is the education which gives a man a clear conscious view of his own opinions and judgments, a truth in developing them, an eloquence in expressing them, and a force in urging them. It teaches him to see things as they are, to go right to the point, to disentangle a skein of thought, to detect what is sophistical, and to discard what is irrelevant. It prepares him to fill any post with credit, and to master any subject with facility. It shows him how to accommodate himself to others, how to throw himself into their state of mind, how to bring before them his own, how to influence them, how to come to an understanding with them, how to bear with them. He is at home in any society, he has common ground with every class; he knows when to speak and when to be silent; he is able to converse, he is able to listen; he can ask a question pertinently, and gain a lesson seasonably, when he has nothing to impart himself; he is ever ready, yet never in the way; he is a pleasant companion, and a comrade you can depend upon; he knows when to be serious and when to trifle, and he has a sure tact which enables him to trifle with gracefulness and to be serious with effect. He has the repose of a mind which lives in itself, while it lives in the world, and which has resources for its happiness at home when it cannot go abroad. He has a gift which serves him in public, and supports him in retirement, without which good fortune is but vulgar, and with which failure and disappointment have a charm. The art which tends to make a man all this, is in the object which it pursues as useful as the art of wealth or the art of health, though it is less susceptible of method, and less tangible, less certain, less complete in its result.

John Henry Newman, *The Idea of a University*, 1873. In *British Literature: 1800 to the Present*, ed. Hazelton Spencer, Walter E. Houghton, Herbert Barrows, and David Ferry. Vol. 2, 3rd ed. Lexington, MA: D.C. Heath, 1974.

Document 15: In Defense of Literature

In this excerpt from "Literature and Science," a lecture delivered during an American tour in 1883, Matthew Arnold argues that literature, or humane letters, offers the most people the best education because its study teaches individuals to understand themselves and their world. By literature, Arnold means literary works and all the other writing that informs a culture, ancient or modern. He sees no danger that the study of science and nature will replace the study of humane letters, as many Victorians advocated.

Some of you may possibly remember a phrase of mine which has been the object of a good deal of comment; an observation to the effect that in our culture, the aim being *to know ourselves and the world*, we have, as the means to this end, *to know the best which has been thought and said in the world.* . . . I assert *literature* to contain the materials which suffice for thus making us know ourselves and the world. . . .

When I speak of knowing Greek and Roman antiquity, therefore, as a help to knowing ourselves and the world, I mean more than a knowledge of so much vocabulary, so much grammar, so many portions of authors in the Greek and Latin languages. I mean knowing the Greeks and Romans, and their life and genius, and what they were and did in the world; what we get from them, and what is its value. That, at least, is the ideal; and when we talk of endeavouring to know Greek and Roman antiquity, as a help to knowing ourselves and the world, we mean endeavouring so to know them as to satisfy this ideal, however much we may still fall short of it.

The same also as to knowing our own and other modern nations, with the like aim of getting to understand ourselves and the world. . . . By knowing modern nations, I mean not merely knowing their *belles lettres* [literature regarded for its aesthetic value], but knowing also what has been done by such men as [scientists] Copernicus, Galileo, Newton, Darwin. . . .

Let us therefore, all of us, avoid indeed as much as possible any invidious comparison between the merits of humane letters, as means of education, and the merits of the natural sciences. But when some President of a Section for Mechanical Science insists on making the comparison, and tells us that "he who in his training has substituted literature and history for natural science has chosen the less useful alternative," let us make answer to him that the student of humane letters only, will, at least, know also the great general conceptions brought in by modern physical science. . . .

If then there is to be separation and option between humane letters on the one hand, and the natural sciences on the other, the great majority of mankind, all who have not exceptional and over-powering aptitudes for the study of nature, would do well, I cannot but think, to choose to be educated in humane letters rather than in the natural sciences. Letters will call out their being at more points, will make them live more. . . .

And therefore, to say the truth, I cannot really think that humane letters are in much actual danger of being thrust out from their leading place in education, in spite of the array of authorities against them at this moment. So long as human nature is what it is, their attractions will remain irresistible. As with Greek, so with letters generally: they will some day come, we may hope, to be studied more rationally, but they will not lose their place. What will happen will rather be that there will be crowded into education other matters besides, far too many; there will be, perhaps, a period of unsettlement and confusion and false tendency; but letters will not in the end lose their leading place. If they lose it for a time, they will get it back again. We shall be brought back to them by our wants and aspirations. And a poor humanist may possess his soul in patience, neither strive nor cry, admit the energy and brilliancy of the partisans of physical science, and their present favour with the public, to be far greater than his own, and still have a happy faith that the nature of things works silently on behalf of the studies which he loves, and that, while we shall all have to acquaint ourselves with the great results reached by modern science, and to give ourselves as much training in its disciplines as we can conveniently carry, yet the majority of men will always require humane letters; and so much the more, as they have the more and the greater results of science to relate to the need in man for conduct, and to the need in him for beauty.

Matthew Arnold, "Literature and Science." In *The Victorian Mind*, ed. Gerald B. Kauvar and Gerald C. Sorensen. New York: G.P. Putnam's Sons, 1969.

Document 16: Educating Workers for the Middle Class

Education was supposed to transform the son of a worker into a middle-class citizen set to make his way in the new Victorian society. In this excerpt from The Mill on the Floss *by George Eliot—Mary Ann Evans's pseudonym—the author illustrates how the Reverend Walter Stelling uses his position as tutor to humiliate rather than help Miller Tulliver's son Tom.*

The immediate step to future success was to bring on Tom Tulliver during this first half-year; for, by a singular coincidence, there had been some negotiation concerning another pupil from the same neighbourhood, and it might further a decision in Mr. Stelling's favour if it were understood that young Tulliver, who, Mr. Stelling observed in conjugal privacy, was rather a rough cub, had made prodigious progress in a short time. It was on this ground that he was severe with Tom about his lessons: he was clearly a boy whose powers would never be developed through the medium of the Latin grammar, without the application of some sternness. Not that Mr. Stelling was a harsh-tempered or unkind man—quite the contrary: he was jocose with Tom at table, and corrected his provincialisms and his deportment in the most playful manner; but poor Tom was only the more cowed and confused by this double novelty, for he had never been used to jokes at all like Mr. Stelling's; and for the first time in his life he had a painful sense that he was all wrong somehow. When Mr. Stelling said, as the roast-beef was being uncovered, "Now, Tulliver! which would you rather decline, roast-beef or the Latin for it?"—Tom, to whom in his coolest moments a pun would have been a hard nut, was thrown into a state of embarrassed alarm that made everything dim to him except the feeling that he would rather not have anything to do with Latin: of course he answered, "Roast-beef," whereupon there followed much laughter and some practical joking with the plates, from which Tom gathered that he had in some mysterious way refused beef, and, in fact, made himself appear "a silly." If he could have seen a fellow-pupil undergo these painful operations and survive them in good spirits, he might sooner have taken them as a matter of course. But there are two expensive forms of education, either of which a parent may procure for his son by sending him as solitary pupil to a clergyman: one is, the enjoyment of the reverend gentleman's undivided neglect; the other is, the endurance of the reverend gentleman's undivided attention. It was the latter privilege for which Mr. Tulliver paid a high price in Tom's initiatory months at King's Lorton.

George Eliot, *The Mill on the Floss.* In *The Victorian Mind*, ed. Gerald B. Kauvar and Gerald C. Sorensen. New York: G.P. Putnam's Sons, 1969.

Document 17: The Artist's Choice of Subject

In Modern Painters, *essayist John Ruskin explains that a good artist chooses a noble subject or makes an ordinary subject noble. He ranks three categories of noble subjects and three ordinary subjects.*

Greatness of style consists, then: first, in the habitual choice of subjects of thought which involve wide interests and profound passions, as opposed to those which involve narrow interests and slight passions. The style is greater or less in exact proportion to the nobleness of the interests and passions involved in the subject. The habitual choice of sacred subjects, such as the Nativity, Transfiguration, Crucifixion (if the choice be sincere), implies that the painter has a natural disposition to dwell on the highest thoughts of which humanity is capable; it constitutes him so far forth a painter of the highest order, as, for instance, Leonardo [da Vinci], in his painting of the Last Supper: he who delights in representing the acts or meditations of great men, as, for instance, Raphael painting the School of Athens, is, so far forth, a painter of the second order: he who represents the passions and events of ordinary life, of the third. And in this ordinary life, he who represents deep thoughts and sorrows, as, for instance, [Pre-Raphaelite painter William Holman] Hunt, in his Claudio and Isabella, and such other works, is of the highest rank in his sphere: and he who represents the slight malignities and passions of the drawing-room, as, for instance, [Charles Robert] Leslie, of the second rank; he who represents the sports of boys, or simplicities of clowns, as [Thomas] Webster or [David] Teniers, of the third rank; and he who represents brutalities and vices (for delight in them, and not for rebuke of them), of no rank at all, or rather of a negative rank, holding a certain order in the abyss. . . .

The artist who sincerely chooses the noblest subject will also choose chiefly to represent what makes that subject noble, namely, the various heroism or other noble emotions of the persons represented. If, instead of this, the artist seeks only to make his picture agreeable by the composition of its masses and colours, or by any other merely pictorial merit, as fine drawing of limbs, it is evident, not only that any other subject would have answered his purpose as well, but that he is unfit to approach the subject he has chosen, because he cannot enter into its deepest meaning, and therefore cannot in reality have chosen it for that meaning.

John Ruskin, *Modern Painters*, 1856. In *The World of the Victorians: An Anthology of Poetry and Prose*, ed. E.D.H. Johnson. New York: Charles Scribner's Sons, 1964.

Document 18: The Revolt of the Pre-Raphaelites

In his "Address on the Collection of Paintings of the English Pre-Raphaelite School in the City of Birmingham Museum and Gallery on Friday, October 24, 1891," poet William Morris identifies the leaders of the pre-Raphaelite Brotherhood and explains their revolt against the academic art of their day; that is, they broke the tradition that art is the handmaiden of religion. Pre-Raphaelites painted nature, but in each painting, they told their own story. Their revolt began a new movement, art for art's sake.

Let us consider what these pre-Raphaelites were. They were certainly a very small body of men. The three original leaders, the chief members of the pre-Raphaelite Brotherhood, as you probably know, were Dante Gabriel Rossetti. Everett Millais, and Holman Hunt. . . . There were several others, but those named were not only the greatest, but also the most characteristic.

However, these few young men, wholly unknown till they *forced* the public to recognize them, began what must be called a really audacious attempt; a definite revolt against the Academical Art which brooded over all the Schools of civilized Europe at the time. . . .

It seems to me that somewhere about the year 1848 will cover the date for the first general appearance of the pre-Raphaelites before the public.

Well, let us consider, first of all, what their first and underlying doctrine was. What was the special and particular standpoint they took up? . . . I think that the special and particular doctrine of the pre-Raphaelites is not very far to seek. It is, in one word, Naturalism.

That is to say the pre-Raphaelites started by saying, "You have Nature before you, what you have to do is to copy Nature and you will produce something which at all events is worth people's attention.". . .

Besides the mere presentment of natural facts, they aimed at another kind of thing which was far more important. The painters aimed, some of them no doubt much more than others, at the conscientious presentment of incident. In other words they certainly had entirely come to the conclusion that not only was it necessary that they should paint well, but that this painting, this good painting, the excellent execution, the keen eyesight, the care, the skill, and so on, should be the instrument for telling some kind of story to the beholder. That you see completes the Naturalism. Granted that you have something to say, and that you say it well by means of the Art of Painting, you are then, and then only, a Naturalistic Painter.

William Morris, "Address on the Collection of Paintings of the English Pre-Raphaelite School in the City of Birmingham Museum and Gallery on Friday, October 24, 1891." In *British Literature: 1800 to the Present*, ed. Hazelton Spencer, Walter E. Houghton, Herbert Barrows, and David Ferry. Vol. 2, 3rd ed. Lexington, MA: D.C. Heath, 1974.

Document 19: Employment of Children

On August 4, 1840, Anthony Ashley Cooper, earl of Shaftesbury, reported to the House of Commons on the employment of children, using firsthand reports from observers in several industries. He called for a commission of inquiry, which led to several acts of legislation protecting workers.

Few persons, perhaps, have an idea of the number and variety of the employments which demand and exhaust the physical energies of young children, or of the extent of suffering to which they are exposed. It is right, Sir, that the country should know at what cost its pre-eminence is purchased,

> Petty rogues submit to fate,
> That great ones may enjoy their state.

. . . The first I shall take is the manufacture of tobacco, a business of which, perhaps, but little is generally known; in this I find that—

> Children are employed twelve hours a-day. They go as early as seven years of age. The smell in the room is very strong and offensive. They are employed in spinning the twist tobacco; in the country, the children work more hours in the day, being frequently until nine and ten o'clock at night. Their opportunities for education are almost none, and their appearance altogether sickly.

. . . As to the frame-work-knitters, a department of the lace trade, nothing can be worse or more distressing. Mr. Power, a factory commissioner, wrote from Nottingham, 1833:—

> A great proportion of the population of the county of Leicester is employed in the frame-work, knitting; of this number more than one-half, probably two-thirds, are young persons between the ages of six and eighteen; that they work an inordinate number of hours daily; that the hours of work of the young persons are, for the most part, commensurate with those of the older class; that the occupation is pursued in very low and confined shops and rooms, and that the hours of labour are sixteen in the day. . . .

. . . I put to a gentleman resident in the neighbourhood of some card-setting establishments, he says:—

> Children are employed from five years old and upwards; their length of labour extends from five or six o'clock in the morning to eight at night.

I will now, Sir, exhibit the state of the collieries, and I cannot well imagine any thing worse than these painful disclosures. In reference to this, I will read an abstract of evidence collected from three witnesses by Mr. Tuffnell, in 1833:—

> Labour very hard, nine hours a day regularly, sometimes twelve,

sometimes above thirteen hours; stop two or three minutes to eat; some days nothing at all to eat, sometimes work and eat together; have worked a whole day together without stopping to eat; a good many children in the mines, some under six years of age; sometimes can't eat, owing to the dust, and damp, and badness of the air; sometimes it is as hot as an oven, sometimes so hot as to melt a candle. A vast many girls in the pits go down just the same as the boys, by ladders or baskets; the girls wear breeches; beaten the same as the boys; many bastards produced in the pits; a good deal of fighting amongst them; much crookedness caused by the labour; work by candlelight; exposed to terrible accidents; work in very contracted spaces; children are plagued with sore feet and gatherings. "I cannot but think, (says one witness), that many nights they do not sleep with a whole skin, for their backs get cut and bruised with knocking against the mine, it is so low. It is wet under foot; the water oftentimes runs down from the roof; many lives lost in various ways. . . .

. . . I speak of the business of pinmaking. Several witnesses in 1833 stated that:—

It is very unwholesome work; we do it near the wire-works, and the smell of the aquafortis, through which the wire passes is a very great nuisance. Children go at a very early age, at five years old, and work from six in the morning till eight at night. There are as many girls as boys.

One witness, a pin-header, aged twelve, said:—

I have seen the children much beaten ten times a-day, so that with some the blood comes, many a time; none of the children where I work can read or write.

Another witness said:—

It is a sedentary employment, requiring great stress upon the eyes, and a constant motion of the foot, finger, and eyes.

. . . Now, Sir, may I ask, is this not a system of legalized slavery? Is not this a state of things which demands the interposition of Parliament, or at least an investigation, that we may know to what an extent these horrid practices have been carried?

Lord Ashley, "Employment of Children," August 4, 1840. In *The English Reform Tradition: 1790–1910*, ed. Sydney W. Jackman. Englewood Cliffs, NJ: Prentice-Hall, 1965.

Document 20: Good Fortune for a London Girl of the Streets

On May 15, 1853, the newspaper Observer *reported the story of Member of Parliament William Gladstone's ongoing benevolence toward a poor girl from the London streets.*

The scene opens in May of last year. Two young women are passing by the top of the Haymarket about eleven o'clock in the
evening. They are annoyed by an elderly man, who persists in following them. They desire him to leave them, but without effect.
The slight altercation that arises attracts the attention of a gentleman passing. He asks the cause, and is told. He threatens to call
the police, and the man then takes himself off. This incident leads
to a conversation with one of the girls. He is attracted by her respectable appearance and manners, and asks her some questions.
The answers she gives excite his curiosity, and increase the interest he at first felt for her. Upon his wishing her to leave the Haymarket and go home, she says she durst not unless she takes some
money with her. He gives her the sum she names, puts her into a
cab, and sends her home. He next day makes inquiries respecting
her, and finds that everything she told him was true, and which
further inquiries only served to confirm. From that time he has
been a kind, and, moreover, a disinterested friend to that girl, and
has left no means untried for the purpose of reclaiming her. As will
be anticipated, the gentleman of whom I am now speaking was Mr.
Gladstone. The discovery of his name was made by mere chance,
for all this was done without the least parade or ostentation on his
part. To account for the interest he took in her I must refer to the
girl's story. It is a very simple though a cruel one, and no wonder
that the discovery of its truth should have favourably influenced
Mr. Gladstone towards her.

Her father keeps an inn on the seacoast in the county of Sussex.
A . . . lady took her into her service as maid and companion to herself, at the same time paying considerable attention to her education.

She remained with this lady about four years. Towards the close
of this time the nephew of a clergyman, at whose house she was
visiting in the suburbs of London, a lieutenant in the navy, came
home from sea and remained in his uncle's house for some time;
while there he gained the affections of the lady's companion, then
under 18 years of age, and seduced her. He returned to sea, where
he still remains. As for the poor girl, she proved pregnant, had to
leave her situation, and became the mother of a child, for whose
support she has to pay 7s. per week.

After this, what was left for her to do? She could not return to
her former situation, and she had no chance of obtaining another.
Her own mother was dead, and her father had married again—
therefore that door was closed.

Marion Miliband, ed., *The Observer of the Nineteenth Century: 1791–1901*. London: Longmans,
1966.

Document 21: Saving Fallen Women

On December 2, 1860, the newspaper Observer *reported on a meeting of prostitutes called by clergymen. During the meeting, held at a restaurant after midnight, the women were offered refreshments and sermons chastising their sins and fallen lives. If they repented of their ways, the clergy offered them a safe place at a public house.*

A most interesting meeting took place on Wednesday morning (having commenced at midnight on Tuesday), at the St. James's Restaurant, St. James's Hall, in connection with the Great Social Evil. The meeting was one of fallen women, invited for the purpose of hearing prayer and admonitions. It was originated by gentlemen connected with the Country Towns Missions, the Monthly Tract Society, Female Aid Society, London Female Preventive and Reformative Associations, and other societies who—anxious for the spiritual welfare of the fallen women who congregate nightly in the Haymarket and the casinos in the neighbourhood—had determined to convene them to some suitable place in the neighbourhood, where judicious addresses might be given, followed by prayer.

. . . Shortly before midnight a large number of these unfortunate creatures arrived at the entrance of St. James's Restaurant, the majority of them most fashionably attired, and displaying large quantities of jewellery, etc. Here they were shown into the large dining-room of the hall, capable of holding some hundreds of persons.

There was an abundant supply of tea and coffee, with bread and butter, toast and cake, to which the strange assembly did good justice, at the various tables about the room, and round which they clustered in small parties of six or eight, chatting over the peculiarity of the meeting, and wondering what was to be the course of proceeding. The number gradually increased, till at least 250 persons were present, solely composed of the females of the class described, excepting nearly forty clergymen and gentlemen who had convened the assembly, no other male visitors being admitted. . . .

The Hon. and Rev. Baptist Noel then addressed the assembled in an eloquent, pathetic, and affectionate discourse, styling his hearers his 'dear young friends.' He then drew a contrast between the history of a virtuous woman from her childhood, and the position of those who have strayed from the paths of virtue. He then assured his hearers that some of them might yet be happy, for they had a friend who was more tender than a mother and stronger in his love than a father, and who would never desert them—that friend was Jesus, their Saviour.

. . . Several of the fallen sisterhood buried their faces in their handkerchiefs and sobbed aloud, and more than one had to be removed in an almost unconscious condition from the room. It was announced that any present who repented their sins would be received into the London Reformatory or the Trinity House, and arrangements would be made and funds provided for their reception elsewhere. The meeting broke up at three o'clock a.m. The conduct of the females present was highly creditable and quite void of levity.

Marion Miliband, ed., *The Observer of the Nineteenth Century: 1791–1901.* London: Longmans, 1966.

Document 22: Middle-Class Arrogance

In Our Mutual Friend, *Charles Dickens creates an exaggerated and shocking portrait of pompous middle-class attitudes in John Podsnap, a rich insurance broker.*

Mr. Podsnap was well to do, and stood very high in Mr. Podsnap's opinion. Beginning with a good inheritance, he had married a good inheritance, and had thriven exceedingly in the Marine Insurance way, and was quite satisfied. He never could make out why everybody was not quite satisfied, and he felt conscious that he set a brilliant social example in being particularly well satisfied with most things, and, above all other things, with himself.

Thus happily acquainted with his own merit and importance, Mr. Podsnap settled that whatever he put behind him he put out of existence. There was a dignified conclusiveness—not to add a grand convenience—in this way of getting rid of disagreeables, which had done much towards establishing Mr. Podsnap in his lofty place in Mr. Podsnap's satisfaction. "I don't want to know about it; I don't choose to discuss it; I don't admit it!" Mr. Podsnap had even acquired a peculiar flourish of his right arm in often clearing the world of its most difficult problems, by sweeping them behind him (and consequently sheer away) with those words and a flushed face. For they affronted him.

Mr. Podsnap's world was not a very large world, morally; no, nor even geographically: seeing that although his business was sustained upon commerce with other countries, he considered other countries, with that important reservation, a mistake, and of their manners and customs would conclusively observe, "Not English!" when, PRESTO! with a flourish of the arm, and a flush of the face, they were swept away. Elsewise, the world got up at eight, shaved close at a quarter-past, breakfasted at nine, went to the City at ten, came home at half-past five, and dined at seven. Mr. Podsnap's notions of the Arts in their integrity might have been stated thus. Literature; large print, respectively descriptive of getting up at eight, shaving close at a quarter-past, breakfasting at nine, going to the City at ten, coming home at half-past five, and dining at seven. Painting and Sculpture; models and portraits representing Professors of getting up at eight, shaving close at a quarter-past, breakfasting at nine, going to the City at ten, coming home at half-past five, and dining at seven. Music; a respectable performance (without variations) on stringed and wind instruments, sedately expressive of getting up at eight, shaving close at a quarter-past, breakfasting at nine, going to the City at ten, coming home at half-past five, and dining at seven. Nothing else to be permitted to those same vagrants the Arts, on pain of excommunication. Nothing else To Be—anywhere!

As a so eminently respectable man, Mr. Podsnap was sensible of its being required of him to take Providence under his protection. Consequently he always knew exactly what Providence meant. Inferior and less respectable men might fall short of that mark, but Mr. Podsnap was always up to it. And it was very remarkable (and must have been very comfortable) that what Providence meant, was invariably what Mr. Podsnap meant.

Charles Dickens, *Our Mutual Friend*, 1864–1865. In *The World of the Victorians: An Anthology of Poetry and Prose*, ed. E.D.H. Johnson. New York: Charles Scribner's Sons, 1964.

Chronology

1815
End of the Napoleonic wars; passage of the Corn Laws, a tariff on grain

1830
William IV ascends throne; Charles Lyell publishes *Principles of Geology;* rioting by workers; election of reformer Earl Gray, a Whig

1832
First Reform Bill gives middle class men the right to vote as national law

1833
Abolition of slavery in colonies; Factory Act passes that protects children from being overworked

1834
New Poor Law sends the poor to workhouses; establishment of London University

1837
King William IV dies; Victoria ascends the throne

1838
First railroad train enters London

1839
Chartist riots rage over social and economic conditions

1840
Annexation of New Zealand; Queen Victoria marries Prince Albert

1842
Mine Act keeps women and young children from underground mines; anesthesia first used in surgery; railway from Manchester to London opens

1843
First telegraph line

1844
Children's Factory Act restricts work hours for women and children

1845
Irish potato famine

1846
Repeal of the Corn Laws

1848
Public Health Act

1850
Tennyson becomes Poet Laureate

1851
The Great Exhibition begins at Crystal Palace

1854
Crimean War begins; construction of London subway begins

1855
Florence Nightingale nurses wounded in Crimea

1856
Treaty of Paris ends Crimean War

1858
Jews admitted to Parliament; removal of property qualification for House of Commons

1859
Charles Darwin publishes *The Origin of Species*

1861
Prince Albert dies of typhoid

1867
Second Reform Bill allows more individuals the right to vote

1869
Imprisonment for debt abolished; Suez Canal opened

1870
Forster's Education Act makes elementary education available to all children

1871
Abolition of religious test at universities

1872
Ballot Act ensures secrecy in voting; first women admitted unofficially to Cambridge University examinations

1875
England purchases control of Suez Canal

1876
Greater control of India

1878
Electric lights installed on some London streets

1879
First telephone exchange opens in London

1884
Third Reform Bill equalizes electoral districts and enfranchises almost all adult males

1888
County Councils Act; "Jack the Ripper" murders five women in London

1889
London dock strike

1890
First moving picture shows appear

1891
Free Elementary Education Act

1893
Independent Labor Party organized

1899
Boer War in South Africa (ends in 1902); first motor bus in service

1901
Queen Victoria dies; Edward VII becomes king

For Further Research

About Queen Victoria

E.F. Benson, *Queen Victoria*. London: Longmans, Green, 1935.

Hector Bolitho, *The Reign of Queen Victoria*. New York: Macmillan, 1948.

Elizabeth Longford, *Victoria R.I.* New York: Harper & Row, 1973.

Lytton Strachey, *Queen Victoria*. New York: Harcourt, Brace, 1921.

Stanley Weintraub, *Victoria: An Intimate Biography*. New York: Truman Talley Books, 1987.

Cecil Woodham-Smith, *Queen Victoria: From Her Birth to the Death of the Prince Consort*. New York: Alfred A. Knopf, 1972.

About Victorian England

James Truslow Adams, *Empire on the Seven Seas: The British Empire 1784–1939*. New York: Charles Scribner's Sons, 1940.

Francois Basch, *Relative Creatures: Victorian Women in Society and the Novel*. New York: Schocken Books, 1974.

Alan Bott, ed., *Our Mothers: A Cavalcade in Pictures, Quotations and Description of Late Victorian Women, 1870–1900*. New York: Benjamin Blom, 1932.

Arthur Bryant, *Pageant of England 1840–1940*. New York: Harper and Brothers, 1941.

C.E. Carrington and J. Hampden Jackson, *A History of England*. Cambridge, England: Cambridge University Press, 1945.

Winston S. Churchill, *The Great Democracies*. New York: Dodd, Mead, 1958.

John W. Deery, *A Short History of Nineteenth-Century England*. London: Blandford Press, 1963.

Joan Evans, ed., *The Victorians*. Cambridge, England: The University Press, 1966.

Carlton J.H. Hayes and Margareta Faissler, *Modern Times: The French Revolution to the Present*. New York: Macmillan, 1966.

W.D. Hussey, *British History 1815–1939*. Cambridge, England: University Press, 1971.

J.N. Larnod, *A History of England*. Boston: Houghton Mifflin, 1900.

W.E. Lunt, *History of England*. New York: Harper, 1956.

Kenneth O. Morgan, *The Oxford Illustrated History of Britain*. Oxford: Oxford University Press, 1984.

Jo Murtry, *Victorian Life and Victorian Fiction: A Companion for the American Reader*. Hamden, CT: Archon Books, 1979.

Daniel Pool, *What Jane Austen Ate and Charles Dickens Knew: From Fox Hunting to Whist—The Facts of Daily Life in Nineteenth-Century England*. New York: Simon and Schuster, 1993.

Marjorie Quennell and C.H.B. Quennell, *A History of Everyday Things in England: The Rise of Industrialism 1733–1851*. London: B.T. Batsford, 1933.

———, *A History of Everyday Things in England 1851–1914*. London: B.T. Batsford, 1934.

Stephen W. Sears, ed., *The Horizon History of the British Empire*. New York: American Heritage, 1975.

Lytton Strachey, *Eminent Victorians*. New York: G.P. Putnam's Sons, 1926.

Philip A.M. Taylor, ed., *The Industrial Revolution in Britain: Triumph or Disaster?* Lexington, MA: D.C. Heath, 1970.

G.M. Trevelyan, *History of England*. Vol. 3. Garden City, NY: Doubleday, Anchor Books, 1926.

Works Consulted

Richard D. Altick, *Victorian People and Ideas*. New York: W.W. Norton, 1973.

Elizabeth Burton, *The Pageant of Early Victorian England, 1837–1861*. New York: Charles Scribner's Sons, 1972.

Charles Dickens, *Hard Times*. 1854. Reprint, New York: New American Library, 1961.

Hilary and Mary Evans, *The Victorians: At Home and at Work*. New York: Arco, 1973.

Bernard D. Grebanier et al., *English Literature and Its Backgrounds*. Vol. 2. *From the Forerunners of Romanticism to the Present*. Rev. ed. New York: Dryden, 1949.

Sally Mitchell, ed., *Victorian Britain: An Encyclopedia*. New York: Garland, 1998.

W.J. Reader, *Victorian England*. New York: G.P. Putnam's Sons, 1973.

Hazelton Spencer et al., *British Literature: 1800 to the Present*. Vol. 2. 3rd ed. Lexington, MA: D.C. Heath, 1974.

T. Walter Wallbank and Alastair M. Taylor, *Civilization Past and Present*. Vol. 2. *From the Beginnings of the Modern Era to the Present Time*. Rev. ed. Chicago: Scott, Foresman, 1949.

Anthony Wood, *Nineteenth Century Britain: 1815–1915*. New York: David McKay, 1960.

Index